THE CROWN IN CRISIS

Countdown to the Abdication

ALEXANDER LARMAN

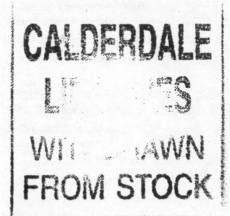

WEIDENFELD & NICOLSON

First published in Great Britain in 2020 by Weidenfeld & Nicolson
This paperback edition published in 2021 by Weidenfeld & Nicolson
an imprint of The Orion Publishing Group Ltd
Carmelite House, 50 Victoria Embankment
London EC4Y 0DZ

An Hachette UK Company

1 3 5 7 9 10 8 6 4 2

A CIP catalogue record for this book is
available from the British Library.

ISBN (Mass Market Paperback) 978 1 4746 1258 6
ISBN (eBook) 978 1 4746 1259 3

Typeset by Input Data Services Ltd, Somerset

Printed and bound in Great Britain by Clays Ltd, Elcograf S.p.A.

www.weidenfeldandnicolson.co.uk
www.orionbooks.co.uk

81 160 88 7

For my grandmothers, Barbara Stephenson (1926–2018) and Terese Larman (1922–2019), who saw it all first-hand.

Alexander Larman is a historian and journalist. He is the author of three previous acclaimed books of historical and literary biography. He writes for *The Times*, *Observer* and *Telegraph*, as well as *The Spectator* and *The Critic*. He lives in Oxford.

Contents

Dramatis personae

Royalty & their circle

Edward Albert Christian George Andrew Patrick David, later
  Edward VIII, later Duke of Windsor, Prince-turned-King-
  turned-Duke
Prince Albert 'Bertie' George, Duke of York, later George VI,
  Edward's younger brother
George V, the late King; Edward's father
Queen Mary, Edward's mother
Prince George, Duke of Kent, Edward's younger brother
Prince Henry, Duke of Gloucester, Edward's younger brother
Mary, Princess Royal, Countess of Harewood, Edward's younger
  sister
Charles Edward, Duke of Saxe-Coburg, Edward's cousin
Louis Mountbatten, Edward's cousin
Elizabeth, Duchess of York, Bertie's wife
Princesses Elizabeth and Margaret, Bertie's children and Edward's
  nieces

Wallis Simpson, Edward's own Helen of Troy
Earl Winfield Spencer Jr, Wallis's first husband
Ernest Simpson, Wallis's second husband
Bessie Merryman, Wallis's aunt
Freda Dudley Ward, Edward's former mistress
Thelma Furness, Edward's mistress prior to Wallis

Alec Hardinge, private secretary to Edward VIII
Helen Hardinge, wife to Alec
Sir Godfrey Thomas, assistant private secretary to Edward VIII

Alan 'Tommy' Lascelles, assistant private secretary to Edward VIII
John Aird, royal equerry
Admiral Sir Lionel Halsey, royal equerry
Mabell Ogilvy, Countess of Airlie, Queen Mary's lady-in-waiting
Ulick Alexander, royal courtier
Peregrine 'Perry' Brownlow, Edward's lord-in-waiting
Sir Eric Miéville, Bertie's private secretary
Edward Peacock, receiver-general of the Duchy of Cornwall
Clive Wigram, Baron Wigram, former royal private secretary
Sir William Fisher, Admiral and Commander-in-Chief of the Navy

The lawyers

Walter Monckton, lawyer and counsellor to Edward VIII
St John 'Jack' Hutchinson, George McMahon's barrister
Alfred Kerstein, George McMahon's solicitor
Sir Donald Somervell, the Attorney-General
Theodore Goddard, Wallis's divorce solicitor
Robert Egerton, Goddard's clerk
Norman Birkett, Wallis's divorce barrister
Sir Anthony Hawke, High Court judge
George Allen, Edward's solicitor
Sir Thomas Barnes, The King's Proctor

The press

Lord Beaverbrook, newspaper magnate
Lord Camrose, owner of the *Daily Sketch*
Lord Rothermere, owner of the *Daily Mail*
Esmond Harmsworth, his son and Chairman of the Newspaper
    Proprietors' Association
Bernard Rickatson-Hatt, Reuters editor-in-chief
Geoffrey Dawson, Times editor
John Reith, director-general of the BBC
HL Mencken, *Baltimore Sun* columnist

Politicians

Stanley Baldwin, Prime Minister of Great Britain
Clement Attlee, leader of the Labour Party
David Lloyd-George, former Prime Minister of Britain
Ramsay MacDonald, former Prime Minister
Neville Chamberlain, Chancellor of the Exchequer
Anthony Eden, Foreign Secretary
JCC Davidson, Chancellor of the Duchy of Lancashire
Sir John Simon, Home Secretary
Duff Cooper, Secretary of State for War
Sir Robert Vansittart, Permanent Under-secretary of state for
    foreign affairs
David Lindsay, Earl of Crawford, former Conservative chief whip
Winston Churchill, Conservative politician
Sir Samuel Hoare, First Lord of the Admiralty
Sir Horace Wilson, senior civil servant and aide to Baldwin
Robert 'Bob' Boothby, Conservative politician
Edward Spears, Conservative politician
Thomas 'Tommy' Dugdale, Baldwin's private secretary
Leo Amery, Conservative politician
Henry Margesson, Conservative chief whip
Oswald Mosley, leader of the British Union of Fascists
Adolf Hitler, Führer of Germany
Joachim von Ribbentrop, German ambassador to Britain
Konstantin von Neurath, German foreign minister
Fritz Hesse, press attaché to the German embassy
Sir Eric Phipps, British ambassador to Germany
Kemal Atatürk, President of Turkey
Sir Ronald Lindsay, British ambassador to the United States

Religion

Cosmo Lang, Archbishop of Canterbury
Alfred Blunt, Bishop of Bradford

Society – high

Lady Maud 'Emerald' Cunard, society hostess and German
    sympathiser
Henry 'Chips' Channon, Conservative politician and diarist
Diana Cooper, wife to Duff, 'the most desirable woman in
    England'
Cecil Beaton, society photographer and diarist
Sir Maurice Jenks, Lord Mayor of London
'Buttercup' Kennedy, aka Mary Kirk, friend of Wallis and Ernest
    Simpson
Harold Nicolson, Conservative politician and diarist
Lucy Baldwin, wife of the Prime Minister
Vernon Kell, founder and first director of MI5
John Ottaway, head of the Detective Branch at MI5
Thomas Argyll 'Tar' Robinson, MI5 operative
Carew Robinson, Home Office employee
Herman & Katherine Rogers, friends of Wallis
Osbert Sitwell, writer and wit
Margaret 'Aunt Maggie' Greville, society hostess
Sibyl Colefax, socialite

Society – low

Guy Trundle, car salesman and friend of Wallis
George McMahon, would-be royal assassin
May McMahon, his wife
Alice Lawrence, royal well-wisher and patriot
Anthony Dick, Special Constable

For God's sake, let us sit upon the ground
And tell sad stories of the death of kings;
How some have been deposed; some slain in war;
Some haunted by the ghosts they have deposed;
Some poison'd by their wives: some sleeping kill'd;
All murder'd; for within the hollow crown
That rounds the mortal temples of a king
Keeps Death his court and there the antic sits,
Scoffing his state and grinning at his pomp,
Allowing him a breath, a little scene,
To monarchize, be fear'd and kill with looks,
Infusing him with self and vain conceit,
As if this flesh which walls about our life,
Were brass impregnable, and humour'd thus
Comes at the last and with a little pin
Bores through his castle wall, and farewell king!
Cover your heads and mock not flesh and blood
With solemn reverence; throw away respect,
Tradition, form and ceremonious duty,
For you have but mistook me all this while:
I live with bread like you, feel want,
Taste grief, need friends: subjected thus,
How can you say to me, I am a king?

William Shakespeare, *Richard II,* Act III Scene II

Introduction

On 8 December 1936, Evelyn Waugh wrote his impressions of the abdication saga in his diary. 'The Simpson crisis has been a great delight to everyone', he remarked gleefully. 'At Maidie's nursing home they report a pronounced turn for the better in all adult patients. There can seldom have been an event that has caused so much general delight and so little pain.' Waugh's witty and flippant observation was accurate in one respect. But though the delight was indeed unsurpassed for some, the pain that counterbalanced it for others was equally so.

The year's events were unparalleled in English history. There had been monarchs before Edward VIII who had been variously wicked, heroic, incompetent, vain and saintly. There had never been a king who had abdicated his throne so that he could marry. If previous rulers had wished to take a wife and found the status quo against them, they acted with brutal force.

Social change on this level was not an option for Edward, who lacked a brilliant - and pliant - advisor to bring about his desired reforms. Instead, he was pitted against the most powerful figures in British society, many of whom tried to frustrate his wishes. Some acted out of principle; others from personal animosity. It should have been an unequal contest, but Edward was both king and in possession of considerable charisma and charm. Accordingly, the battle of wits and influence that ensued was more balanced than has often been assumed. Victory was far from assured for either side until the conclusion of the crisis, and if the half-compromise, half-defeat that Edward was presented with was a triumph for the forces of establishment conservatism, it was not without significant damage to its proponents along the way.

Nor had they taken full account of the woman who nearly brought down the monarchy: Wallis Simpson. One of the most photographed and discussed women of the age, right up to until her death in 1986, she was nevertheless largely condemned as an ambitious gold-digger. Today, those who consider her a feminist pioneer have made a convincing case for her rehabilitation, arguing that she was a woman in a man's world who achieved her eventual position through her own auspices and intelligence. Others contend that she was a Machiavellian figure who manipulated an emotionally and intellectually weak figure into a position that benefitted her, rather than his country. I am sympathetic to aspects of both perspectives, and to the nuances of those in between. Yet the relationship between Edward and Wallis, crucial though it is to this narrative, was not the sole basis of the abdication.

This book originally began as a biography of one of the leading figures in the abdication saga, Walter Monckton. As I researched Monckton and his role during the crisis, I began to see that not only had the abdication been the dominant event of his life, but that of many of the people involved in it. It is unlikely that we would remember the king's private secretary Alec Hardinge if it had not been for his extraordinary, even treacherous, actions towards his monarch. And it is certain that Jerome Brannigan, aka George McMahon, would have been long forgotten had it not been for his still-mysterious attempt to assassinate Edward in July 1936.

As I continued looking into the memoirs (published and otherwise) of those involved in the crisis and contemporary journalistic accounts, an increasingly complex picture emerged. Why was Edward not able to take the unilateral decision to abdicate as soon as it was clear that he would not be able to take Wallis as his queen? What was the hold that she had over him? What was the relationship like between the king and his inner circle? Who were his allies, and enemies? And these questions led to yet more. Why did Wallis's husband Ernest sit back and do nothing? What were

Wallis's true feelings about her situation? What was 'the King's party', and did it come close to ousting the government? Why did Stanley Baldwin and Lord Beaverbrook hate one another so much? Did Edward really have Nazi sympathies? And why would an occasional informer for MI5 have tried to murder him?

It has been a privilege to use a mixture of rare archival sources, many of which have only been made public recently and some that are published here for the first time, new interviews with those who knew Edward and Wallis, a comprehensive selection of the diaries, letters and records written by those with first-hand experience of the abdication crisis and my own informed conjecture. It has been a revelatory and rewarding opportunity to explore one of the most dramatic periods in English history. I hope that the book is a fitting distillation of my research, and that its conclusions and discoveries are as surprising to the reader as they were to its author.

Some of these are less equivocal than others. I found myself with little sympathy for Edward VIII, even if, to my surprise, I was reduced to tears one day in Windsor Castle while reading the heartbreakingly sad letters his friends and admirers wrote to him as he prepared to abdicate. While I would not go so far as the Prime Minister and the courtier Tommy Lascelles, who openly pined for his untimely death before he acceded the throne, Edward was one of the least distinguished figures ever to have reigned in Britain, and the country was fortunate to have the considerably more dutiful George VI as its king when WWII broke out a few years later.

Thanks to the superb performances of Alex Jennings and Derek Jacobi as the older Duke of Windsor in the first three series of Peter Morgan's *The Crown*, many will feel that they have a good sense of who he became later in life. Actors of their intelligence and versatility can lend the most unappealing of figures dignity, and Edward skilfully reinvented himself as an elder statesman after the abdication, synonymous with sharp tailoring and an even sharper interest in royal protocol, insofar as it reflected his own interests. His less distinguished career as monarch was seldom publicly discussed, unless there was a large cheque involved. Yet it was the events of 1936 that dominated the rest of his life, and his reputation.

While taking care to offer a fair case for the defence, not least by acknowledging his charm, charisma and the undeniable affection and loyalty that he inspired in considerably greater people, I cannot feel admiration for someone who even his friend Monckton regarded as believing in a deity 'who dealt him trumps all the time and put no inhibitions upon his main desires.' He lived ultimately for his own desires and pleasure, and expected others to fulfil his wishes without question or delay. As his private secretary Alec Hardinge wrote, 'One can hardly be surprised that during ten months of unremitting work and heavy responsibilities no word of gratitude or appreciation to anyone in his employment was ever heard to pass his lips.' Others may find themselves better inclined towards him; his ghost-written memoir, *A King's Story*, offers his own, unavoidably partial, account of his involvement in the crisis.

Yet this book is not simply Edward's tale, or Wallis's. Instead, it depicts a time in British history when conventional ideas of regal behaviour and duty were cast aside, and where the resulting moral and social vacuum could have led to disaster far beyond the worst nightmares of many of those involved in the crisis. Its eventual resolution was a testament to both traditional strengths of the British character – stoicism, resourcefulness and courage – and to less-trumpeted but equally integral aspects of the national psyche, including dissimulation and betrayal. Such was the price for saving the throne. And, as a far worse international situation dawned, few would have argued in retrospect that it was a price, unprecedented though it was, well worth paying.

Oxford, February 2020

Prologue

'Bring Me the English Alliance'

As an opportunity to create a new world order, it was unprecedented.

The two men who faced each other in the private room at Bayreuth on 21 July 1936 both knew something of society's murkier workings. The first was a former wine salesman who had risen to his current impressive eminence as Reich Minister Ambassador-Plenipotentiary at Large thanks to a willingness to flatter anyone he needed to impress. His enemies hated him, dismissing him as a parvenu and a sycophant, but he knew that their scorn mattered little compared to the approval of the man opposite him: the Führer of Germany. Joachim von Ribbentrop and Adolf Hitler had met to decide which diplomatic role in the latter's gift might befit the ambitious would-be ambassador.

Ribbentrop had long coveted the post of State Secretary at the Foreign Ministry, but Hitler paused before granting his acolyte this distinction. Although he deferred to Ribbentrop in many regards, he also knew that there were those - not least Germany's foreign minister Konstantin von Neurath - who would not tolerate such an appointment. He decided instead to offer him another post, which would subsequently prove equally important: ambassador to London. Vacant since the death of its previous incumbent, Leopold von Hoesch, a few months before, it was a considerable opportunity for an ambitious and influential man.

For an Anglophile such as Ribbentrop, who collected English books and who could speak the language fluently, it was an honour. Although he was initially disappointed not to be offered the more

prestigious role, he quickly acclimatised himself to the idea. Hitler
had made it clear to the power-hungry Ribbentrop that public support in London for his regime would be an unparalleled coup, and
suggested that, should he succeed, he would be made Minister for
Foreign Affairs, replacing von Neurath.

As they parted, Hitler reputedly said, 'Ribbentrop, bring me the
English alliance.'[1]

A decade later, Ribbentrop lurked miserably in a cell in Nuremberg, awaiting his inevitable fate, which duly came on 16 October
1946. It was a long way from the lavish household he had kept at
Dahlem, outside Berlin. As he composed his self-serving and often
inaccurate memoirs, he had enough time to reflect on his notable
failures, not least his embassy to England. Had he been a less vain
and arrogant man, he could have taken his cue from a meeting in
Berlin in August 1936 with Sir Robert Vansittart, the Permanent
Under-secretary of State for Foreign Affairs. Vansittart had read
Mein Kampf and been appalled by it, believing that 'Nothing but
a change of German heart can avert another catastrophe and that
was unlikely to come from within, for the true German nature has
never changed'.[2]

Even as Ribbentrop bleated that 'Hitler offered a unique opportunity for a really enduring association between Germany
and Britain . . . the Führer was ready for a sincere understanding
based on equality',[3] he failed to recognise the contempt and deep
suspicion implicit in the other man's silence. Perhaps he never understood it until Nuremberg, when Vansittart's affidavit stated that
'I have never advocated an agreement with Germany, since Germans rarely keep their word.'[4] Only then did Ribbentrop respond
by scoffing that 'I believe . . . Hitler's policy was a consequence of
Vansittart's policy in 1936.'[5]

When Ribbentrop arrived in London on 26 October 1936, the
city had a charged and febrile atmosphere to it, although this had
little to do with Germany. Indeed, the newspaper magnate Lord
Beaverbrook, always attuned to his readership, believed the man in

the street was largely impervious to Hitler, viewing him as merely 'a political phenomenon who would soon pass into oblivion'.[6] Ribbentrop's embassy was not a success, as had been predicted by Sir Eric Phipps, the British ambassador to Germany, in a letter to Vansittart two weeks before his arrival. Phipps suggested that von Neurath was 'rather worried ... [they] view his London mission with foreboding, as he has no respect for established custom and no sense of time'.[7]

Ribbentrop duly lived down to expectations. As the new ambassador committed faux pas after faux pas, such as trying to give a Nazi salute at Durham Cathedral when the hymn 'Glorious Things of Thee Are Spoken' began – it is sung to the same tune as 'Deutschland über Alles' – he became known by the sobriquet 'Ambassador Brickendrop', threatening to shame his office and embarrass his Führer. The former prime minister David Lloyd George said of him that 'That man could never hold his own in a political conversation, and as for representing his country at an international conference, he would be quite out of his element and at the mercy of any intelligent opponent'.[8] In order to make a success of his embassy, he needed to achieve a conspicuous diplomatic innovation. There was one man, he believed, who might be interested in much closer Anglo-German relations, 'a kind of English National Socialist'.[9] Fortunately for Ribbentrop, this man was also the King of England.

The nation's new monarch, Edward VIII, had inherited the throne on 20 January 1936, after the death of his father, George V. Good-looking, possessed of considerable charm and relatively youthful, Edward was a popular ruler, and one who brought a dash of glamour to the throne. Gossip suggested that he was partial to a cocktail or three in nightclubs, to say nothing of the company of beautiful women. It was his dedication to *cherchez la femme* that had contributed to the uncertain mood in London in late 1936, although Ribbentrop had, for the moment, little inkling of the enormity of the coming crisis.

The king was also a committed nationalist and occasional xeno-
phobe. He had decried indigenous Australians in a 1921 letter to his
mistress Freda Dudley Ward as 'the most revolting form of living
creatures I'd ever seen . . . the nearest thing to monkeys'. He consorted with Oswald Mosley, charismatic leader of the British Union
of Fascists, and a police report of March 1935 attested to Edward
admiringly asking Mosley about the 'strength and policy'[10] of the
BUF. He was also reputed to hold Hitler in high esteem, seeing
him as a vigorous reformer; his own German heritage engendered
a residual affection for the country. Ribbentrop sighed admiringly
that 'He desired good Anglo-German relations . . . King Edward
VIII had shown his sympathy for Germany on several occasions
[and] had warmly supported a meeting of German and British leaders of ex-servicemen's organisations.'[11] None other than the king's
private secretary, Alec Hardinge, later complained that 'The possibilities [of his associations] were serious enough to create alarm
among those who were aware of the pro-German leanings of this
clique, and who were watching with apprehension the trend of
German policy.'[12]

When the then Prince of Wales attended the German embassy
as guest of honour in July 1935, he was the first member of the royal
family to have visited since 1914. With the gift for empathy – some
called it attention-seeking – that had defined his public life since
he came of age, he declared his belief that 'the hand of friendship'
should be outstretched to the Germans by former soldiers 'who
fought them and have now forgotten all about it and the Great
War'.[13] Although this caused considerable controversy in England,
the Nazis greeted it with delight. It was a propaganda triumph
for them, and Edward seemed like a man with whom Germany
could partner. This was strengthened by the prince's cousin, the
Duke of Saxe-Coburg, reporting that the prince believed an Anglo-
German alliance to be 'an urgent necessity and a guiding principle
for British foreign policy'. The undeniably partisan Saxe-Coburg
claimed that, once Edward had ascended the throne, he said, when
challenged about the prime minister's fears that he was acting in

too political a fashion, 'Who is King here? Baldwin or I? I myself wish to talk to Hitler, and will do so here or in Germany. Tell him that, please.'[14]

The ambitious Ribbentrop made it his personal business to ingratiate himself with this apparently open-minded prince. He had prepared for this since their first encounter in June 1935, at a lunch given by the society hostess and German sympathiser Lady Maud 'Emerald' Cunard, who was thrilled by the presence of a man she delightedly described as 'a real, live Nazi'.[15] The event proved an embarrassing one.* Lord Wigram, George V's private secretary, wrote to the king to inform him that 'Ribbentrop poured out all the German propaganda, which I expect bored HRH. However I am told that Ribbentrop telegraphed to Germany that the Prince entirely agreed with his views, and that HRH added that after all he was half a German.' He qualified this by writing that 'I cannot believe there is any truth in this', but also complained that 'This is the result of accepting invitations from people like Lady Cunard to meet such men as German propagandists.'[16]

In fact, the consequences of the meeting were unfortunate. Wigram subsequently informed a no doubt unimpressed king that 'The French ambassador had said to [Sir Samuel Hoare, the First Lord of the Admiralty] that he presumed this reconstruction of the Government and change in Foreign Secretaries meant a change of policy as regards Germany, and that we were now going to become pro-German. Evidently Ribbentrop had telegraphed to Germany the most favourable account of the Prince of Wales' speech and also, I gather, of a conversation which he had had with His Royal Highness . . . there is no doubt that this indiscretion has been most embarrassing to the Foreign Office.'

---

* Ribbentrop also met Wallis Simpson at the same lunch, and rumours of an affair between the two developed subsequently, fanned by Ribbentrop's penchant for sending her seventeen roses at regular intervals: allegedly the number of times the two had slept together. Yet the rumour seems implausible, as the notably uxorious Ribbentrop was unlikely to jeopardise his career, marriage and the chance of the English alliance for such a liaison.

Edward was at least partly to blame. Not only did Wigram have to tell George that his son 'last night had a long conversation with the German Ambassador in full view of the Diplomatic Corps, who appeared to be straining their ears to hear what was going on . . . doubtless many rumours are flying around',[17] but Cabinet minutes of 19 June 1935 reported that, after Edward had made a favourable reference to Germany at the Annual Conference of the British Legion on the 11th, 'The Cabinet were informed that the friendly reference to Germany had proved somewhat embarrassing, and had complicated relations both with France and Germany, especially during the week when the Anglo-German Naval Conversations were taking place.'[18]

An Anglo-German naval agreement was signed on 18 June, and Ribbentrop, who had seen Edward again on the 20th, presented himself as a diplomatic genius capable of uniting two European nations less than twenty years after the end of World War I. While there was considerable self-promotion involved within this, with the real credit instead lying with von Hoesch, the much-desired grand alliance between England and Germany seemed in reach. A not-so-delicate debutante could not have wished to seduce Edward more than Ribbentrop and Hitler did, knowing that the prince's tacit support – or at least open neutrality –would have a significant impact, both on his own people and internationally.

Thus the Ribbentrop influence and charm were pressed into service. Thanks to his assuming the credit for the naval agreement, it was widely expected that, during his appointment to London, he would achieve similar success, despite Lloyd George belittling his achievements by remarking, 'Any fool can give cream to a cat.'[19] Even his enemy Goering praised him for his 'extraordinary influence in England and special skill as a negotiator'.*[20] Edward VIII's authorised biographer Philip Ziegler describes him as 'quite capable

---

* Notably, this statement was made over a decade later to Allied interrogators, implying that Ribbentrop's mastery of smoke and mirrors enraptured his audience at home.

in his way, and he gained his position through considerable skills and ability', although he also acknowledges that 'I don't think I'd have liked him.'[21]

It was unfortunate for Ribbentrop that the smarm and sycophancy that had so impressed the German high command did not carry much conviction in London, where its higher-born denizens treated him and his family with the particularly English contempt that the aristocracy reserve for arrivistes.*

The politician and diarist Henry 'Chips' Channon wrote scathingly of Ribbentrop's 'dentist's smile',[22] and Phipps described him as 'a tremendous snob, [who] is convinced that what counts in England is equally snobbish . . . He made [his daughter] take intensive golf lessons at the golf club here, which is much frequented by Jews. He thereby incurred the wrath of the Nazi extremists, who complained to Hitler.' Ribbentrop, however, was able to explain away his actions by stating, with a touch of P. G. Wodehouse's Oldest Member, that 'to conquer England, it was indispensable for the younger members of his family to play golf'. Phipps, who believed the German to be 'a lightweight . . . irritating, ignorant and boundlessly conceited',[23] concluded that 'I cannot help thinking that before his own game has gone very far he himself will get rather badly bunkered.'[24]

Herr Brickendrop's fervent adherence to fascism, combined with his stiffness and aggression of manner, meant that his first ambassadorial meeting with Edward carried a weight of expectation that would have frustrated virtually any encounter. Ribbentrop considered his formal reception, which took place on 30 October 1936, a success. They had met earlier that year, in March, but little was exchanged other than conventional pleasantries. Now, he had a responsibility, as he saw it, to press home his situational advantage and recruit the king unequivocally to the cause. While

---

* This went well beyond simple snobbery, into the realms of a principled anti-Nazi stance. For instance, Duff Cooper, the Secretary of War at the time, commented at one dinner, 'I only hope he dies in pain.'

his memoirs punctiliously noted that he did not offer Edward a Nazi salute,* he also found the king, whom he met in the company of his foreign secretary Anthony Eden, 'most affable'. Edward enquired after Hitler's well-being and Ribbentrop was pleased that he 'repeated clearly that he desired good Anglo-German relations'.[25]

Ribbentrop hoped that the next step would be to meet Edward on a confidential basis, aided by various shadowy 'friends', and see what new understanding might be brought about. He was to be disappointed. Edward, for his part, subsequently called Hitler a 'somewhat ridiculous figure, with his theatrical posturings and his bombastic pretensions',[26] and later wrote that his first encounter with the unctuous ambassador, whom he described as a 'polished but bombastic opportunist', was 'not without strain', not least because 'This intimate of the Führer had been . . . a champagne salesman, a circumstance that had offended the sensibilities of those who had been accustomed to a long sequence of distinguished German ambassadors.'[27] Class as much as competence informed Edward's judgements. The 'tall, rigid figure' (attired, naturally, in 'faultless tail coat and white tie') talked of 'his Führer's desire for peace', and the king, preoccupied by his mistress Wallis Simpson's decree nisi having been granted three days before, dealt with him politely but formally, wishing him 'a successful mission to my country'.[28] Diplomatic triumphs have emerged from inauspicious meetings before, but this hardly repaid the hopes that Hitler had invested in his lieutenant.

Over the following weeks, Edward and Ribbentrop saw each other about London, but purely on a social basis. The ambassador bemoaned their 'brief talks', and that he had failed to 'establish any special contact with Edward VIII . . . something unforeseen always intervened'.[29] It also did not help that Ribbentrop, ignorant of the balance of influence in England between sovereign and Parliament

---

* He did not make the same omission when he met George VI at a Buckingham Palace garden party the following year: acting, naturally, under instructions from the Führer.

and the lack of autonomous power that the monarch enjoyed, came to believe that innocuous, even facile, utterances of Edward's were imbued with revolutionary yearning. He perceived a tension between 'influential circles' who would have preferred the king to remain silent, and a vast and adoring populace who loved this new, outspoken style of monarchy.

The irony was that he was closer to the truth than he could have imagined.

The 'influential circles' that stood against Edward contained many of the most powerful men in the country. They included the prime minister, Stanley Baldwin, and virtually all of his Cabinet, his private secretary, the Archbishop of Canterbury, newspaper editors, businessmen and many of the best-informed salon hostesses and members-club habitués, many of whom saw the imminent likelihood of conflict with Germany. Most of them knew that England's ruler could not be relied upon to act within the national interest. Subsequent events confirmed their instincts as prescient. Ribbentrop remained at a distance from the truly influential, lurking on the periphery of relevance even as his Führer plotted the beginnings of his Thousand-Year Reich.

The embassy's press attaché Fritz Hesse, who was considerably more attuned to the slow, steady drumbeat of confidential developments than his superior, dared to suggest to the ambassador that Edward's likely abdication and consequent departure from Britain would render association with him irrelevant in any practical sense. Ribbentrop responded with a mixture of horror and disbelief, telling Hesse, 'Don't you know what expectations the Führer has placed on the king's support in the coming negotiations? He's our greatest hope! Don't you think that the whole affair is an intrigue of our enemies to rob us of one of the last two big positions we hold in this country?'[30]

While Brickendrop, despite his tainted reputation, was not a stupid man, his devotion to Hitler and his grand schemes meant that he was unable to accept that events that took place within

another country – even one within which he now had an ambassadorial role – existed outside of his own realm's jurisdiction. Even as
he blustered, 'You'll see, the King will marry Wally and the two will
tell Baldwin and his whole gang to go to the devil',[31] the likelihood
of Hitler being robbed of his much-desired prize increased inexorably. This could not – would not – be allowed to happen.

Hesse's warnings that the royal affair would transform from
a matter conducted in whispers behind closed doors and into
the country's defining news story were soon vindicated. By 3
December 1936, a semi-open secret had become the major cause
of conversation and discussion in every echelon of society, and
Ribbentrop, who had promised Hitler that he would be instrumental in bringing about the Anglo-German entente that was so
desperately wished for in Berlin, was left looking both amateurish
and incompetent: simultaneously Brickendrop and Blowhard.
Yet he still had his leader's confidence, and during the course of a
conversation with Hitler, he managed to persuade the Führer that
much of the press coverage in England was malicious falsehood
designed to destabilise German hopes of an alliance, dictated by 'a
clique of reactionaries and Jews'.[32]

Such was his ability to present the outlandish and fanciful as
common sense that he ended the telephone call triumphant rather
than cowed. He proudly informed Hesse that 'The Führer will be
proved right, the whole affair will go up in smoke, and the King
will be grateful to us for having treated the crisis with such tactful
reticence.'[33] Hitler, incongruously given to greetings-card-level sen-
timentality on occasion, reiterated his belief that 'these plutocrats
and Marxists' were attempting to frustrate Edward's desire to marry
'a girl of the people'[34] – itself a tendentious way of describing the
worldly-wise Wallis – and ensured that the German papers were
gagged from reporting any of the details of the crisis. After all, his
ambassador had assured him it was all nonsense.

Ribbentrop talked convincingly, but his pig-headed blindness to
British society and politics ('his ignorance is limitless',[35] one senior
official moaned) meant that his blithe protestations that all would

be well took him into Panglossian levels of delusion. He was notoriously difficult to work with, either demanding that his staff achieve
endless tasks in impossibly short amounts of time, or taking to his
bed beset by often imagined ailments. These periods were known
as 'tango nocturno', and were welcomed by his officials, as it afforded them a chance to accomplish the work that his preening
and prevaricating usually frustrated. Yet when he was horizontal
once more, the not-so-merry-go-round of self-delusion dominated
the workings of his embassy. Even as the abdication saga wore on,
he refused to believe that it was possible that Edward VIII would
no longer be king. Baldwin's friend J. C. C. Davidson, the Chancellor of the Duchy of Lancaster, reported with astonishment that
Ribbentrop was cheerfully convinced that before the sovereign
would voluntarily give up his throne, 'there would be shooting in
the streets . . . this [is] the end of Baldwin',[36] and that the so-called
'King's Party' would bring down the government rather than see
their monarch deposed.

Davidson, like his peers, was unimpressed by Ribbentrop ('he
talked more nonsense than I have ever heard from anybody in a
responsible position of the level of Ambassador'),[37] but there was a
kernel of accuracy in some of the ambassador's wilder statements.
For a man who was never allowed into the best houses, and was
sneered at by those who 'belonged' there, he understood that
public opinion was not simply an amorphous mass but a shift-
ing, complex entity, one that could be manipulated by the media
and politicians but was equally susceptible to the entreaties of a
charismatic and apparently sincere monarch in love. Had Edward
been able to make a public statement directly to the people – 'his'
people – that overturned every existing constitutional precedent
imaginable but inspired a surge of empathy in the hearts of every
Englishman, anything might have happened. Including, perhaps,
the fulfilment of Ribbentrop's predictions.

The events before, during and after the abdication crisis of 1936
represent a social and political upheaval like England has seldom

known. The only suitable analogy is the years 1642–1660, which included the Civil War, the trial and execution of Charles I, and the Commonwealth government of Oliver Cromwell; a period that established that the king could only govern with the consent of Parliament, a constitutional issue that became crucial in 1936. It was a time in which the country was similarly torn apart, and in which royal arrogance and heedlessness found an equally cold reception.

The so-called 'Year of the Three Kings' was a time of high passion and low cunning, of noble ideals and ignoble treachery on all sides. It was a period in which the carefully cultivated certainties of centuries of *noblesse oblige* looked as if they could be set aside and swept away – or even reinforced. And for all his ridiculousness, social solecisms and ignorance, Ribbentrop was the official representative of a rapacious state that exploited others' weakness, just as those involved in the abdication crisis detected opportunity, whether for themselves or their country.

Yet ultimate responsibility lies with one person. She was a slight, immaculately dressed American divorcee of unexceptional appearance, childless and in early middle age, who was in the right place at the wrong time. This woman swiftly established herself as the most significant royal mistress since Maria Fitzherbert, 'the wife of my heart and soul' of George IV. There have been countless rumours and misattributions over the subsequent decades regarding her involvement in Edward's life and in the abdication crisis. Yet the most remarkable fact about her is the simplest. Wallis Simpson was the woman who brought Britain to a state of crisis that threatened its very stability as a nation. It was ultimately resolved, but at great cost that could have been even greater. As the Duke of Wellington said of the Battle of Waterloo, it was 'the nearest-run thing you ever saw'.

This is its story.

Chapter One
The Royal Concubine

When the courtier Alan 'Tommy' Lascelles was asked whether Edward and Wallis had a platonic relationship before their marriage, he replied scornfully that it was as likely 'as a herd of unicorns grazing in Hyde Park and a shoal of mermaids swimming in the Serpentine'.[1] While Lascelles, who served as Edward's assistant private secretary while he was Prince of Wales, cannot be regarded as an impartial chronicler of the events leading to the abdication, his thoughts on Wallis Simpson were broadly representative of contemporary court and political opinion about her.

Lascelles starkly described the events of 1936 as 'the nightmare', and placed the responsibility firmly with Wallis. He wrote that 'The philosophers of the Prince Hal school were wishful thinkers . . . . The leopard, so far from having changed his spots, was daily acquiring more sinister ones from the leopardess.'[2] Acknowledging that Wallis's second husband Ernest was 'nothing worse than a nincompoop', Lascelles believed that one of the primary reasons for the abdication was finance. George V's will had left Edward nothing, save the lucrative Duchy of Cornwall, while his brothers inherited three-quarters of a million pounds apiece.

Lascelles noted that 'Money, and the things that money buys, were the principal desiderata in Mrs Simpson's philosophy, if not in his, and when they found that they had, so to speak, been left the Crown without the cash, I am convinced that they agreed, in that interminable telephone conversation, to renounce their plans for a joint existence as private individuals, and to see what they could make out of the Kingship, with the subsidiary prospect of the Queenship for her later on.'[3]

There has been endless speculation, during and after her lifetime, as to what motivated Wallis. Romantics assert that she and Edward were deeply in love, and that it was mere ill fortune that he happened to become King of England during their liaison. Her well-intentioned and selfless generosity even led her to attempt to leave both her adopted country and her lover in an attempt to stop him from abandoning the crown. This interpretation was – and remains – an especially powerful view of the saga in America, where the magazine *Liberty* printed two and a half million copies with the headline 'The Most Envied Woman in the British Empire'. This enduring affection explains the way in which the musician-turned-film-director Madonna was able to represent the story as one of the great historical love affairs in her 2011 film *W.E.*, starring Andrea Riseborough as Wallis and James D'Arcy as Edward.*

Given Edward's previously utilitarian, rather than romantic, nature, this is not wholly accurate. Lascelles wrote scathingly of a myth in which 'a lonely bachelor "fell deeply in love" for the first time in his life with the soul-mate for whom he had long been waiting'. With a warning to 'sentimental biographers' who might wish to present this version of events as accurate, he dismissed it simply as 'moonshine', declaring that Edward 'was never out of the thrall of one female after another . . . There was always a *grande affaire*, and, as I know to my cost, an unbroken series of *petites affaires*.'[4] A typical example of this was Edward's successful seduction of a Mrs Barnes, wife of a local commissioner in Dodoma, Tanzania, in 1928. What led a disgusted Lascelles to call it 'incredibly callous behaviour' was that he had been informed of his father's grave illness immediately before. Edward dismissed the news as

---

* Neither the critical nor the commercial reception was kind. The world will never be wholly ready for the film's depiction of Wallis dancing to the Sex Pistols' 'Pretty Vacant' while gyrating libidinously with a young man dressed as an African tribesman as a Benzedrine-popping Edward looks on delightedly.

'some election-dodge of Baldwin's',[5] before pursuing his libertine entertainments.

Wallis offered something out of the ordinary. Cynics have long claimed that she was vain, mercenary and wilful, able to manipulate Edward through a mixture of exotic sexual wiles and simple force of character. That she had two husbands still alive, and was married to the second when she became Edward's consort, was enough on its own to outrage public opinion. She was, by her own frank admission, no great beauty – 'I'm nothing to look at, so the only thing I can do is to try and dress better than anyone else'[6] – and had no especial intellectual interest, despite a certain dry wit. Even her best-known saying, 'You can neither be too rich nor too thin', has a trite glibness to it. And yet she was the much-photographed woman who captured the heart of a prince, nearly brought down the monarchy and inspired countless articles, biographies and discussions. Who, then, was the real Wallis Simpson?

Somewhere in the bowels of an anonymous archive is said to lurk a document that, although it hardly ranks with the secrets of the Kennedy assassination or the whereabouts of the passengers of the *Mary Celeste*, has attained its own curiously mythic status. This is the so-called China dossier, reportedly compiled, on Stanley Baldwin's instructions, to detail Wallis's 'lotus year' in Shanghai between 1924 and 1925. Although no previous biographer or historian has seen the dossier – and Philip Ziegler has cast doubt on its very existence, although he concedes that 'There must have been *something*, but it has been built up in people's imaginations into something else'[7] – the nature of what Wallis did during her time in China has led to rumours of her precise hold over Edward, discussed with varying degrees of authority and salaciousness. While she may indeed have been a sexual adventuress, inducting her lover into hitherto unknown pleasures, this is only part – albeit an extremely revealing part – of her history.

Wallis Warfield was born on 19 June 1896 in Blue Ridge Summit, Pennsylvania. Her origins were mysterious. It has been suggested both that she was conceived out of wedlock and that she was born intersexual, with both male and female sexual organs. Many of her recent biographers, most notably Michael Bloch and Anne Sebba, have suggested that this explained a great deal about attitudes towards both her appearance and her sexuality, although Ziegler argues that 'I came across nothing that made me think she was [intersexual] and there is no convincing evidence.'[8] Her square-jawed, somewhat androgynous mien often led to speculation about her attributes even during her lifetime, as in the writer James Pope-Hennessy's 1958 comment that 'She is one of the very oddest women I have ever seen . . . I should be tempted to classify her as an American woman *par excellence* . . . were it not for the suspicion that she is not a woman at all.'[9]

Whatever the truth behind Wallis's femininity, her early life was uneasy. Her mother Alice was widowed when her daughter was only a few months old, and the pair embarked upon a financially uncertain and troubled odyssey, which probably included them being subjected to the unwelcome attentions of 'Uncle Sol', Wallis's uncle Solomon Warfield. Money was lacking throughout her early years, and her intense relationship with Alice led her to understand that if she were to succeed in making her way in the world, it would be through her wits and skills rather than beauty or privilege. She was sent to the best schools that her mother could afford, where she developed her poise and sophistication, as well as a romantic attachment to ideas of beauty and glamour.

After she came out as a debutante in the autumn of 1914, she met and was romanced by the naval pilot Earl Winfield Spencer Jr. The son of a stockbroker, he was handsome and chivalrous, the square-jawed embodiment of her youthful fantasies. The two married on 8 November 1916, but the union was doomed. Wallis, who had been raised to be all but teetotal, asserted that 'The bottle was seldom far from my husband's thoughts or his hand.'[10] Her dashing husband proved to be a boor, and a bore. His drinking might have been fuelled by frustration at an unconsummated union. Wallis was said, albeit by an unreliable source,* to have commented that, before she knew Edward, 'She never had sexual intercourse with either of her first two husbands, nor had she ever allowed anyone else to touch her below what she called her personal Mason-Dixon line.'[11] It might have irritated Spencer that she was, in her own words, 'naturally gay and flirtatious'.[12] For her part, after enduring his 'running barrage of subtle innuendoes and veiled insults', as well as physical violence, she finally separated from him and obtained a divorce in 1927, although not before heading to China in search of a very specific kind of experience.

Even if the China dossier were never to surface, some of the contents are already public knowledge. Friends of Wallis such as Cynthia Jebb, Lady Gladwyn, described her Oriental skills as nothing more outré than oral sex – 'nothing Chinese about it'[13] – and argued that she was essentially conservative. Duff and Diana Cooper's son John Julius Norwich described her as '[not] particularly sexually motivated . . . not in the least bit depraved'.[14] Others have taken a less wholesome view of her activities. During her time in China, she flitted between Hong Kong, Shanghai and Peking, making the acquaintance of architects, diplomats and the Italian naval attaché Alberto Da Zara, 'an excellent horseman with a keen and practised eye for charming women [who] fell under her spell'.[15] It was later suggested that one of these friendships resulted in 'an obscure internal ailment', with which she fell ill while en route home in September 1925, although whether this was the legacy of a botched abortion, the result of a sexually transmitted disease or simple ill health was not clarified by Wallis herself referring to it, coyly, as 'a very puzzling case'.[16]

She confessed to visiting the 'sing-song houses' of Hong Kong, but suggested that she did this because she was compelled to by Spencer, who 'ostentatiously [made] a fuss over the girls'.[17] At both these and the later ones that she visited in Shanghai – 'a narrow

---

* The American biographer Donald Spoto.

level of heaven on a thick slice of hell'[18] – she was in a milieu that had no obvious berth for a well-brought-up American girl. It was only relatively recently that concubinage had been made illegal in China, and so Wallis encountered a wide variety of former concubines and courtesans who had made the iniquitous decline from being an accepted member of a well-to-do Chinese family to either plying their trade publicly, if they still had their looks, or acting as an instructress for younger women.

The role of the sing-song girls was to attract wealthy male company by being beautiful, immaculately presented, discreet and, in the case of the *changsan* class, the most discerning and exquisite of paid companions. Unlike the cheaper *yao'er*, who were only a step or two above streetwalkers, and the *shuyu*, who found it demeaning to be associated with the commercial transaction of sex, the *changsan* had the particular skill of enticing high-status men to fall in love with them, but to deny them the release they craved until they had shown themselves worthy of such a gift.

Whether Wallis spent time in these sing-song houses as anything other than a tourist cannot be known. Dozens of scurrilous rumours have arisen from this interlude, vying with one another in both outrageousness and doubtful veracity. All that can be known is that she posed for suggestive photos, which have not survived, wearing only a lifebuoy, and may well have learned specific sexual arts in the brothels, possibly revolving around the tantalising techniques of the *changsan*. She was said to have 'the ability to make a matchstick feel like a cigar',[19] and one biographer stated that she learned a specific Chinese technique of a 'prolonged and carefully modulated hot oil massage of the nipples, stomach, thighs and, after a deliberately, almost cruelly protracted delay, the genitals'.[20]

Of course, the significance of her 'lotus year' might be overstated by the salacious. After all, learning how to pleasure royalty, or the ordinary man, does not require a sojourn in China. Nonetheless, regardless of how depraved or innocent her time in the East was, the experiences she amassed there added to the growing mystery as to who this woman was.

After her divorce, she met the shipping broker Ernest Simpson, who seemed as unadventurous and unchallenging as Spencer had been demanding and vigorous. She summed him up in a letter to her mother: 'I am very fond of him and he is *kind* which will be a contrast.'[21] She married him in July 1928, a few months after her divorce, and they made their home in London, where Wallis found herself out of place and adrift. She had never known any real happiness in her life to this point, merely different forms of neglect, fleeting comfort and abuse, all of which she absorbed with the same clenched control that she would later exhibit in all of her public appearances. The issue of children with Ernest was not raised. Instead, Wallis amused herself by decorating their flat in Bryanston Court in Marylebone, and eventually came to make herself the centre of a small social circle with a reputation for holding elaborate entertainments. 'Wallis' parties have so much pep no one ever wants to leave',[22] one satisfied guest reported. Yet she did not dispense the champagne and brandy – a surprising display of largesse, given her loathing of Spencer's drinking – out of altruism, or even a desire to befriend the society ladies of London. Her aim was a more specific one.

In 1931, Prince Edward, known as 'David' to his family and intimates, was living in a privileged state of torpor. He was in his late thirties, and everything he had done so far in his life had been largely unsuccessful. His relationship with his parents was cold and distant, as they openly favoured his younger brother George, or 'Bertie', the Duke of York. Edward had attended Magdalen College, Oxford (left without a degree), joined the Grenadier Guards (forbidden to join the fighting in World War I on the grounds of his safety) and embarked on a masochistic series of diets and health regimes designed to punish his slim, boyish figure as much as to maintain his health. He was almost certainly suffering from what we now know as anorexia nervosa.

The affairs that Lascelles condemned him for, whether *grande* or *petite*, can be seen as a desperate attempt for stimulation and attention. Yet even these were undercut by a desire on his part to be sexually subservient to his mistresses in order to achieve a satisfactory result. As Ziegler says, 'Sex meant an awful lot to Edward, but a rather specialised form of sex. He craved to be dominated, and Mrs Simpson provided that service.'[23] This was a consistent feature in his dealings with women. As far back as 1918, he had written to Freda Dudley Ward ('a good influence, but not good enough'),[24] 'my very own darling beloved little mummie', to tell her, 'You ought to be really foul to me sometimes . . . I'm the kind of man who needs a certain amount of cruelty without which he gets abominably spoilt and soft.'[25]

Publicly, though, he maintained a cheery and breezy attitude towards his future subjects as he glided from one well-laid table to another. His current mistress, Thelma Furness, was half-American, and knew of the prince's fascination with the modernity and glamour that her country appeared to connote. It was therefore her pleasure, on 10 January 1931, to introduce him to her friend Wallis and her husband Ernest at her country house in Melton Mowbray. The conversation was unexceptional, mainly revolving around the differences between their cultures, but it was enough for Wallis, who had spent the previous day obsessing over 'hair and nails etc.',[26] to write excitedly to her Aunt Bessie to boast, 'You can imagine what a treat it was to meet the Prince in such an informal way . . . As I've made up my mind to meet him ever since I've been here, I feel relieved.'[27]

Wallis and Edward met again on 15 May, again at Thelma Furness's, where he remarked how much he had enjoyed their first encounter. A more impressive honour came on 10 June, when she was formally presented at court. Although rather old* to be most people's idea of a debutante, she charmed Edward enough to be complimented on her appearance. Having overheard him mutter about how the bright lighting did not flatter the assembled women, she responded, 'But sir, I understood that you thought we all looked

---

* Although, by her own account, possibly still virginal.

ghastly!'[28] The prince, unused to such studied displays of American brashness, was enchanted. Their intercourse continued early the following year, when he came for dinner at Bryanston Court and enjoyed Wallis's cooking, ending with a raspberry soufflé that he appreciated sufficiently to ask for its recipe. Whether Mrs Simpson merely wished to inveigle herself into the grandest social circles or already had other designs, she was rewarded for her tenacity by an invitation to stay at Edward's much-beloved Surrey residence, Fort Belvedere, along with Ernest.

One of Edward's few tangible achievements at this time was to have turned a decrepit and slightly odd-looking miniature castle into a grand retreat fit for a prince – if not a king. While the worldly socialite Diana Cooper might have sneered at some of the more flamboyant decorative touches ('I am in a pink bedroom, pink Venetian-blinded, pink-sheeted, white-telephoned and pink and white-maided'),[29] Wallis was entranced, pronouncing it 'astonishingly warm and attractive'.[30] It seemed to be a retreat that would not have disgraced a fairy tale by the Brothers Grimm, and the prince who strode its corridors in plus fours, whistling and followed by his Cairn terriers Cora and Jaggs, struck her as an isolated and rather sad figure in need of rescuing. John Simon, the Home Secretary, acknowledged this when he noted that 'It is almost impossible to conceive the loneliness of a monarch who . . . does not enjoy the blessing of a happy home with wife and children.'[31] As Wallis later wrote, with the considerable benefit of experience, 'I had been one of the first to penetrate the heart of his inner loneliness.'[32]

The weekend, which consisted of gardening by day and drinking by night, was a success. At one point, Wallis noted that Edward, fresh from a steam bath, was 'radiating utter contentment'.[33] When she and Ernest returned home, they sent a piece of doggerel to thank him. Typical lines included 'Our weekend at "Fort Belvedere"/Has left us both with memories dear/Of what in every sense must be/Princely hospitality.'[34] Anyone with a poetic spirit might have blanched; as it was, Wallis barely saw Edward for the remainder of 1932. It was a miserable year for her. Ernest's business ventures failed, her health suffered and her position at the highest levels of society seemed precarious. All she could do was to maintain her friendship with Thelma Furness, who, concerned that Edward was tiring of her, took care to present herself as one who consorted with the fun and frivolous: Wallis, in other words.

The plan worked. Wallis was able to reminisce that, from the beginning of 1933, 'we found ourselves becoming permanent fixtures at the Fort weekends', and, triumphantly, 'the association imperceptibly but swiftly passed from an acquaintanceship to a friendship'.[35] The 'we' was used in its most regal sense; as Ernest trudged between the City, Europe and America, Wallis was at leisure to 'chaperone' Thelma Furness on a weekly basis. She had become so indispensable to Edward that, by his birthday on 23 June – four days after hers – she could 'make whoopee' at his house until 4.30 in the morning. The first letter she wrote to the prince, a formal note enclosing a present for him, ends with the sign-off 'your obedient servant'. The questions of obedience, and who was whose servant, would remain tantalisingly ambiguous.

It is impossible to know the precise date that Edward and Wallis became lovers. However, educated supposition places it around January 1934, when Thelma left for the United States to visit her family. Both women recall some conversation in which it was acknowledged that 'the little man' would be lonely without his mistress present; Wallis wrote to her Aunt Bessie that 'I tried my best to cheer him up.'[36] She succeeded admirably in this particular act of transatlantic union: rather too admirably. While she later wrote of responding to his 'deep loneliness, an overtone of spiritual isolation',[37] it was inevitable that, in another letter of 18 February to her no doubt intrigued aunt, she felt she had to explain that 'It's all gossip about the Prince . . . I'm not in the habit of taking my girlfriends' beaux.'[38] This was, at best, disingenuous. Others might call it a lie. When Thelma returned, she realised that the dynamic between her friend and her lover had changed. On 1 April 1934, she watched, aghast, as the two indulged in over-affectionate private jokes together in front of her. 'I knew then that she had looked after him exceedingly well.'[39]

Thelma was soon dismissed from the regal sphere, and the 'light friendship' grew and strengthened as Ernest took increasingly convenient business trips. Edward later claimed that he decided to marry Wallis as early as 1934, and never wavered from that decision. On one holiday, the royal equerry John Aird noted with surprise that the Prince 'has lost all confidence in himself and follows W around like a dog'.[40] He gave Wallis the first of many expensive gifts, a Cartier diamond and emerald charm, and, perhaps as a result of this conspicuous largesse, she later acknowledged that 'We crossed the line that marks the indefinable boundary between friendship and love.'*[41]

By November, the boundary had been so transgressed that Edward, forgetting or simply dismissing any concept of propriety or protocol, presented Wallis to King George and Queen Mary at Buckingham Palace for what she called 'a few words of perfunctory greeting',[42] with Ernest loitering awkwardly in the background. The king was so appalled at his son's effrontery that he howled, 'That woman in my own house!'[43] He refused to meet her again for the remainder of his life. The courtier Godfrey Thomas mournfully complained to Wigram early the next year, while Edward was on a trip to Austria with Wallis, that 'HRH is apparently a law unto himself, and devoid of any commonsense in such matters. He simply and honestly cannot understand why anyone should question his actions ... I am in despair about the whole situation and really don't know how long I can hang on at my job.'[44]

If she could not have royal approval, then at least Wallis could bear herself with regal composure. As Ernest 'seemed less and less

---

* On the basis of this and countless other regrettably florid inclusions in her memoirs, it is an enormous pity for posterity that Wallis did not invest in a better ghostwriter.

interested in what I had to say about the Prince's latest news and interests',[45] she wore expensive clothes and jewellery with 'awfully nice stones'[46] that was said to have cost over a hundred thousand pounds: a truly stupendous amount when the average annual income was about £200. Lionel Halsey, the Prince of Wales's treasurer, subsequently confirmed the king's suspicions that Wallis was a gold-digger, informing Wigram that 'She was at present receiving a very handsome income. [This] was really a bad breach of confidence on my part as HRH's Treasurer but HM has promised to hold the information as a dead secret . . . I also told HM that in my opinion both Mrs S and her husband were just hand in glove in getting all they could out of HRH.'[47]

Edward and Wallis's letters began to use the abbreviation 'WE' to denote their unbreakable bond, and a typical communication from him in spring 1935 declared, 'I love you more & more & more each & every minute and miss you so terribly here', before he ended, with typical understatement, 'God bless WE.'[48] Nonetheless, she hesitated before committing herself, alarmed by the intensity and fervour of his attraction to her. Remembering what had happened to Thelma, who had been discarded more or less overnight, she knew that she had to either extricate herself from the situation altogether or temper his obsession.

One letter, from the early summer of 1935, referred to him by his family's intimate name of David, and made the perceptive observation that 'Your life has been such that . . . quite naturally you only think of what you want and take it too without the slightest thought of others.' Appealing to a possibly non-existent better nature – 'Doesn't your love for me reach to the heights of wanting to make things a little easier for me?' – Wallis denigrated Edward's 'boyish passion', bemoaned 'how very alone I shall be one day', and ended by writing, not without dignity, that 'I have lost something noble for a boy who may always remain Peter Pan.'[49] She asked that he tear up the 'very inadequate' letter; he did not.

Perhaps in response to this, she pursued a friendship with a car salesman and motor engineer, Guy Trundle. At the time, detectives from Special Branch followed her, and took great interest in her movements. A police document from 25 June 1935 noted that 'Mrs Simpson is very jealous of a woman whom POW [the Prince of Wales] met on his recent visit to Austria. This woman has since been to London and spent time with POW. Mrs Simpson is, in consequence, apprehensive of losing the affection of POW which she is very anxious to avoid for financial reasons. She is therefore extremely careful and is spending as much time as possible with POW and keeping her secret lover in the background.'[50] Her insecurity was sufficiently widely known to be noted – 'She has said that she does not want to be treated like Lady Furness' – and Ernest Simpson was said to expect, after a drink, 'to be created a Baron, at least'.[51]

It was soon revealed that Trundle, a married man, was 'a charming adventurer, good looking, "well bred" and an excellent dancer . . . He is said to boast that every woman falls for him.'[52] Wallis was rumoured to shower him with money and expensive presents – royal cast-offs, perhaps – but feared the exposure of her association with him, although more for the tensions that it would cause with the prince than out of any concern for her husband. Whether or not she engaged in a full-blown affair with him – and it is doubtful that she did – it was proof to those watching that not only was she not to be trusted, but that she did not return Edward's devotion. The Reuters editor Bernard Rickatson-Hatt believed that 'but for the King's obstinacy and jealousy, the affair would have run its course without breaking up the Simpson marriage'.[53] As Ziegler says, 'Wallis did have a great capacity for inspiring dislike. She laid herself wide open to malevolent gossip; if one had been Mrs Simpson, it is hard to see how one would have behaved differently. There was no wickedness involved, but there was ambition and unscrupulousness. But she wasn't a bad woman.'[54]

Although there was nothing written in the newspapers about Edward's new 'friendship', there was nobody in society who did not know of Wallis's status. Her American background made her exotic and a figure of interest, but also someone not to be trusted. Alec Hardinge, then assistant private secretary to George V, and his wife Helen civilly disliked her, as did most of the rest of the royal family, but other, less elevated types had more sympathy for her. Cecil Beaton 'liked her immensely' for being 'bright and witty and chic',[55] and just as Wallis had set her cap at the likes of Thelma Furness to be introduced into the right circles, so the so-called 'Ritz Bar set' saw her as a 'heaven-sent opportunity to enter Royal society'.[56] The major difference was that this time there was little chance of anyone else making so seismic an impact upon the prince.

Wallis continued to be a ubiquitous figure at society functions, with or without Ernest. She appeared at the Silver Jubilee in May 1935, once Edward had falsely assured his father that she was not his mistress. She remained ironically detached about the way in which she was lionised by some of the greatest society matrons on both sides of the Atlantic, telling her aunt that 'It is very amusing what one is invited to in hopes of [Edward coming as well] . . . All the best titles come across whereas no-one noticed Mrs Simpson before.'[57] She holidayed with the prince and friends of his including Louis Mountbatten at Cannes that summer, briskly took charge of household matters (a note exists in which she suggests the kinds of cocktail and wine that should be on offer to the guests) and received letters from Edward written in cloying sub-Mills & Boon romanticism. One stated: 'A boy is holding a girl so very tight in his arms tonight . . . A girl knows that not anybody or anything can separate WE – not even the stars – and that WE belong to each other for ever.'[58] The chances of the relationship being platonic seem as slender as the prince.

By the end of 1935, Wallis considered her options. She still felt a tender affection for Ernest, but it is unlikely that their relationship had any physical content. He pursued his own affairs, to her disinterest, and she continued to revel in her status as 'the Prince of Wales's girl'. Edward's fixation on her was both intoxicating and overwhelming. In a letter of 1 January 1936, he wrote,

'Oh! my Wallis I know we'll have until Viel Glück* to make us *one* this year.'[59] She began the year as queen of her surroundings, in the rare position of having her regal cake and being able to eat it as well.

And then everything changed.

---

* German for 'good luck'.

Chapter Two

'The Most Modernistic Man in England'

In ancient Rome, it was traditional for conquering generals entering the city in triumph to be accompanied by an *auriga*, a high-status slave who would hold a laurel crown over his victorious master's head. As the commander basked in the adulation of his people, the *auriga* would repeat two words in his ear, over and over again: '*Memento homo*' – remember that you are human.

It would have been useful for the newly crowned Edward VIII to have his own *auriga* by his side on 22 January 1936, as he watched the proclamation of his accession to the throne at St James's Palace. Instead, inevitably, it was Wallis who was there, as they realised that their life together had changed irrevocably. He believed that 'my relations with Wallis had suddenly entered a more significant stage', even as she remarked that 'It was all very moving, but it has also made me realise how different your life is going to be.'[1] As they stood talking, a photographer took their picture, so the next day, for the first time, the king and his anonymous friend appeared in the papers together. It would not be the last.

Edward's elevation to the throne came about suddenly. His father's health had been poor, but there was no obvious indication that he was about to die. The relationship between George V and the Prince of Wales was not warm, occasioned in part by the king's belief that his son was set to bring shame and disgrace upon the royal family. His younger son Bertie, the future George VI, later commented that '[He] had always treated the brothers as if they were all the same, whereas in fact they were totally different in character ... It was very difficult for David. He found fault with him over unimportant things – like what he wore.' Edward responded in kind – 'he did the things which he knew would annoy my father' – and so, as a result, 'they did not discuss the important things quietly'.[2]

This difficulty was illustrated by an 'on the whole amicable' interview in March 1932, which Wigram recorded. George pointed out to Edward that 'at the moment the Public worshipped him, and that he was at the zenith of his popularity – but would this last, when the Public began to realise at last the more or less double life the Prince was leading; that the great nonconformist conscience of England would begin to take effect'. Edward demurred, suggesting that times had moved on, but the king pressed him, 'saying that the days when royal Princes had well-known mistresses (and families by them) were gone for ever, and that the people of England looked for a decent home life in their Royal House. All young men sowed their wild oats; but wasn't the Prince at 38 rather beyond that age?'

Edward, as ever, would have none of it, as he displayed what Wigram called a 'frowning attitude', admitting under questioning that he wasn't particularly happy. As the king suggested that 'England had never had an unmarried King, and wouldn't the position be invidious?', Edward argued that 'There was only one lady that he had ever wished to marry, and that was Mrs Dudley Ward, and he would still like to marry her – but the King said he didn't think that would do.'[3] Thus the interview, like many others before and since, broke up inconclusively, with father and son unable to understand each other.

George V had no illusions as to his son's fitness to be king. Hardinge believed that '[Edward's] own conduct was to a large extent responsible for [his father's death], and there is little doubt that, if it had not occurred until a few months later, he would never have succeeded to the Throne at all.'[4] George confided to Stanley Baldwin that 'after I am dead, the boy will ruin himself in twelve months',[5] and, before he died, even exclaimed, 'I pray to God that my eldest son will never marry and have children, and that nothing will come between Bertie and Lilibet and the throne.'[6]

The last months of the king's life were racked with concern about Edward's actions. Wigram recorded a meeting on 10 May 1935 in which the two spoke candidly about Wallis. 'The King was very frank and referred to Mrs S as his mistress. The Prince was very annoyed and gave the King his word of honour that he had never had any immoral relations with Mrs S. HRH admitted that he had done so with Lady Furness, whom he now described as a filthy beast. He had got rid of her as the King had asked him to do so; but Mrs S was quite different – a charming cultivated woman, who made him supremely happy. The King said that naturally everyone regarded her as his mistress as people did not go abroad with other people's wives.'

Edward was asked for, and gave, his word of honour that the relationship was platonic; Wigram's memorandum noted that 'The Prince's staff were horrified at the audacity of the statements of HRH. Apart from actually seeing HRH and Mrs S in bed together, they had positive proof that HRH lived with her.'[7] An equally appalled Godfrey Thomas wrote to Wigram that 'It's hopeless stressing the moral aspects of the affair, because he simply doesn't understand dignity – letting down the monarchy; he just doesn't believe it'; and, noting that 'almost the whole of London is laughing at the way he is making himself ridiculous, being so patently under this woman's thumb and at her beck and call', complained that 'I do most intensely resent having my health affected and my hair turned grey simply and solely by this woman.'[8]

It was not only Thomas's health that was unduly affected by the Wallis affair. On 16 January 1936, as he was shooting in Windsor Great Park, Edward was informed that his father was ebbing. He flew to Sandringham to see George V once more, before, on 20 January, the bulletin was issued that 'The King's life is moving peacefully to its close.' What was unknown until decades later was that the royal physician, Bertrand Dawson, had injected the king with a mixture of morphine and cocaine, with the intention of speeding up his death. This was done partly in order to ease his end, but also with a view to posterity. This way, the news of his passing would appear in the following day's morning papers, rather than the less prestigious evening news.

As the king faded, his wife and children gathered around him. Wigram noted tartly that 'Just before the end the Prince of Wales became hysterical, cried loudly and kept on embracing the Queen . . . [who] was most plucky and courageous.'[9] Almost immediately after her husband died, Queen Mary kissed her son's hand and spoke the words that, had anyone present known, would be the first foretaste of the national crisis: 'The king is dead. Long live the king.'

Edward VIII's friend and adviser Walter Monckton later wrote a candid, unpublished* memoir of his impressions of the King during 1936. He described how Edward 'had the highest standards that he set himself of right and wrong. They were irritatingly unconventional. One sometimes felt that the God in whom he believed was a God who dealt him trumps all the time and put no inhibitions upon his main desires.'[10]

From the outset of his reign, this manifested itself in petty and even spiteful manners. It had been a tradition of George V to keep the clocks running half an hour fast at Sandringham. Edward, frustrated by what he saw as a pointless adherence to 'the old ways', announced angrily, 'I'll fix those bloody clocks',[11] and insisted on having them all put back to the right time. This was accompanied by what Helen Hardinge called 'frantic and unreasonable'[12] grief.

His behaviour seemed to have no rational cause, other than panic at having at last arrived at a reckoning with destiny that he had no idea how to manage.

There was no reason, as far as his public were concerned, why Edward VIII should not be a great monarch. Unlike his

---

* Late in life, Monckton called this material 'too full and too intimate for publication, even after the lapse of years'.

predecessors, he was young, handsome and possessed of what *The Times* described as 'his winning smile . . . his laughter-loving boyishness . . . his attractive habit of identifying himself with the different nationalities of the United Kingdom and the Empire'. Reading the leader with hindsight, much of it comes across as a wry dig at Edward's contemporary activities – 'his thoughtful tact . . . his delightful sense of humour . . . his freedom . . . he has won the hearts of unnumbered men, women and children'. The irony was that it was initially written as far back as 1928, though updated whenever necessary, like an obituary. Geoffrey Dawson, the paper's editor, was no especial admirer of the new king, but for the time being he was more interested in selling newspapers. Describing 20 January in his diary as 'a long and difficult day', he complained that they had already printed 30,000 copies of the paper by the time George V died, but after making the necessary changes, he proudly noted that a memoir of the late king and a picture supplement was eventually included in a sold-out edition of 300,000 copies.[13]

Baldwin publicly hailed Edward as possessing 'a personality richly endowed with the experience of public affairs, with the fruits of travel and universal goodwill', and, perhaps with some shade, suggested that 'He has a wider and more intimate knowledge of all classes of his subjects than his predecessors.'[14] The new king undeniably had his strengths. He was charming, energetic and seemed genuinely engaged with the idea of being a new ruler for a new era. He was not Victorian in his outlook, but was a contemporary, forward-looking figure. John Simon even described him as 'the most universally popular personality in the world',[15] which did not seem hyperbolic.

Yet from the outset, his reign had the taint of unease to it. Simon also noted that 'if he had any serious intellectual interests, they were concealed even from his intimates', he had 'no sense of royalty' and his attempts to introduce more informality into occasions that were essentially ceremonial were not always 'crowned with success'.[16] Sometimes these efforts were unintentional. There was an unfortunate incident when, in the midst of the pageantry of his father's coffin being borne through the streets of Westminster, the Maltese cross atop the crown fell into the road, leading Edward to exclaim, nearly hysterically, 'Christ! What will happen next?' As one observer sardonically remarked, 'A fitting motto for the coming reign.'[17]

Once the funeral rites had been observed, Edward had to choose his staff, the most important of whom was his private secretary, or 'the king's prime minister'. It was the private secretary's responsibility to be the ruler's *consigliere*, keeping him abreast of all political and social movements within the country and offering as impartial and informed a judgement as possible. Alec Hardinge, a veteran of Buckingham Palace and George V's assistant private secretary, was chosen for the role, as the previous incumbent, Lord Wigram, had 'quite early in the new reign [come] to the conclusion that he could not carry on'.[18]

Hardinge was an excellent choice, at least theoretically. As his wife Helen wrote, 'My husband felt, above everything else, an obligation to the nation and Empire that then existed . . . The crown was for him the symbol of national and imperial unity.'[19] He was an unbending man of principle, priggishly so,* and believed the crown to be the metaphorical pin in the grenade when it came to society. Should it be removed, the entire thing would explode. This set him up in opposition to Edward's more radical and self-absorbed impulses from the outset, and could only spell disaster as his reign wore on.

Hardinge despised his master, and had done since before his accession. As he later wrote, 'He appeared to be entirely ignorant of the powers of a constitutional sovereign, and of the lines on which the King's business should be carried on.' Angrily he condemned Edward's 'unpunctuality, inconsequence, lack of consideration and self-conceit', complaining that they 'created every possible difficulty for those who served him'. Nor was he impressed by the new

---

* Lascelles praised his administrative talents, but also noted his 'complete inability to establish friendly, or even civil, relations with his fellow men'.

king's wish to modernise, dismissing it as both 'a desire to change merely for the sake of changing' and 'a dislike, amounting almost to hatred, of the regular methods of his Father', and criticising him on the grounds that 'He [could not] see that this regularity was less a choice than a necessity for the proper discharge of his duties.'[20]

Hardinge also sniffed that 'His main preoccupation . . . was finance, and his primary concern how money could be saved.'[21] After the king found out about the financial snub he had received in his father's will, he became despondent. Wigram noted that 'The King was much perturbed that his Father had left him no money and kept on saying "Where do I come in?" We tried to explain that the late King felt that his eldest son, as Prince of Wales for 25 years, ought to have built up a nice surplus out of the Duchy of Cornwall . . . we failed to comfort the new King. He kept on saying that my brothers and sister have got large sums but I have been left out . . . it was later discovered that he had tucked away over a million sterling . . . His Majesty continued to be obsessed about money.'[22]

Although he was far from poor, with the Duchy of Cornwall making him wealthy beyond his subjects' most grandiose expectations, he did not have the financial security that he had promised Wallis, and this rankled. From the outset of his reign, he was both an unsuited and a reluctant monarch, unwilling to compromise his own happiness for the sake of a symbolic role that he barely believed in.

While he later acknowledged that 'I might not have conspicuously chosen the throne as the most desirable goal of all my aspirations', something echoed by John Simon, who wrote that 'he did not really want to be King',[23] Edward denied Lascelles' assertion that, financially thwarted, his thoughts turned to abdication immediately. Instead, he maintained that 'I wanted to be a successful King, though a King in a modern way.'[24] It did not help his case that this 'modern way' was summarised by Monckton as his being 'a man . . . determined to be himself. He would be available for public business and public occasions when he was wanted, but his private life was to be his own, and was to be . . .

lived in the same way as when he was Prince of Wales.'[25]

However, Edward was able to offer an initial appearance of statesmanship, although not to everyone. The former prime minister, Ramsay MacDonald, who saw him at the Accession Privy Council, believed that 'His first appearance as King was decidedly promising – a little nervous & slight in his ways, but already with an increased steadiness & self-possession.'[26] The Archbishop of Canterbury, Cosmo Lang, was less impressed. Lang had been close to George V, and the two had discussed the prince's wayward behaviour in their interviews together. When he met the new king, Lang may have remembered the scene at the end of *Henry IV, Part II*, when the Lord Chief Justice, fearful that the former wastrel Hal, now Henry V, will exact revenge upon him, states, 'Your Majesty hath no just cause to hate me.' The archbishop sought to reassure Edward that, while he had made frank comments in the past, it was with an aim to the new king's spiritual welfare. This was ecclesiastical humbug at its most disingenuous, and Edward was not taken in by it, believing that Lang was opposed to his 'friendship' with Wallis. 'Hiding my resentment [at this] . . . I could not seem to impress him . . . No doubt he was as relieved as I was when the audience came to an end',[27] he later wrote. It soon became clear that the conservative, affectedly moral Lang and the modernising monarch were not to find common ground.

It was no wonder that, during another encounter, Edward 'shooed the Archbishop of Canterbury out of the house'.[28] As Ziegler says, 'Edward had no Christian faith, and, even when he was at his most popular while Prince of Wales, he viewed the idea of a religious ceremony for assuming the throne with horror, especially the paraphernalia of it – the dressing-up and being respectable.'[29] Hardinge noted that 'on approximately two occasions only did the King attend Divine Service'.[30] Edward was unafraid to make enemies, or, as he put it, to approach 'an irreconcilable conflict';[31] he was king, after all. What were these pygmies to the might of the monarchy? Yet a more humble or reserved man might have considered his actions more carefully. There is a famous line in

Henry IV when the old king laments, 'Uneasy lies the head that wears a crown.' The weight of responsibility that came with kingship was one that Edward was always uneasy with, despite his occasional flurries of energy and action. It was not simply the irritation at his life no longer being his own that stymied his ability to be a ruler worthy of the title, however; it was the vacancy that lay at the centre of his being. He was neither a good sovereign nor a good man, and it would be this ultimate failing that led him to become such easy prey for his enemies and comforters alike.

After a short and reluctant break ('I am sad because I miss you and being near and yet so far seems so unfair'),[32] Edward resumed his association with Wallis in the first weeks of his reign. He spent weekends with her at Fort Belvedere for his zealously guarded 'private life', as well as heading to the Simpsons' flat at Bryanston Court when the opportunity allowed. An irksome responsibility he now faced was carrying official paperwork with him, or, as he described it to Wallis, 'those damned red boxes full of mostly bunk'.[33] Baldwin, who was fully aware of the king's affair, spoke for many at the highest levels of society when he sighed to Duff Cooper, the Secretary of State for War, that 'if she were what I call a respectable whore, I wouldn't mind', and asked Cooper if he might persuade her to absent herself from England for the foreseeable future. An unimpressed Cooper, himself no unskilled Lothario, wrote in his diary that 'I shall certainly do nothing of the kind.'[34]

From the outset, Baldwin could see the possibility of trouble, but, mere weeks into the new reign, he did not wish to take overt action himself. Lang wrote to Wigram, 'I agree with you that SB is the man to deal with the special difficulty which may but I earnestly hope not occur. The mere thought of it is like a nightmare to me.' Nonetheless, his feelings about his ally were mixed. In the same letter, he complained that 'Unfortunately his temperament disposes him to postponements and to action only when a crisis has arrived.'[35] Given what happened later in 1936, this proved an accurate judgement of Baldwin's character.

The royal relationship continued to be an unequal one, conducted with the unlikely involvement of Wallis's husband, the most obliging of cuckolds. Ernest knew Sir Maurice Jenks, Lord Mayor of London, and in 1935 had been admitted by him to his Masonic lodge, although not before the Prince of Wales, also a member, had sworn that he was not having an affair with Wallis. It was widely believed that this was a lie.

On 4 February 1936, Jenks visited Wigram to tell him that Ernest had informed him that the king wished to marry Wallis, and that he would like to see the prime minister to discuss it with him. Wigram called the situation 'so comic that I collapsed in my chair. I had had to tackle some grim situations in my time, but this was the limit.' Jenks and Wigram decided that Ernest's intention was blackmail, but bemoaned that 'Unfortunately Mr S was a British subject, and it would be difficult to deport him.'[36] Simpson also informed Jenks that 'When Prince of Wales, HRH had talked about renouncing his claim to the Throne in order to marry his wife, and for this purpose had remitted a large sum abroad', although Wigram commented that 'This did not tally with my information that HRH had put in trust over a quarter of a million for Mrs S out of the Duchy of Cornwall revenues.' The 'very worried' Ernest believed that if Edward could not marry Wallis, 'when free, he would abdicate'.[37] In this, at least, he was prescient.

Ernest's Masonic initiation had gone ahead in 1935, but it would have been better if it had not. Edward's assistant private secretary, Godfrey Thomas, described the sparsely attended ceremony as a 'humiliating fiasco' and wrote that 'Many abstained from voting and hardly any of the Masonic big wigs from outside, who were invited, came to it. HRH "has violated his Masonic oath" . . . ES merely wished to become a Mason for business reasons and . . . HRH, to keep him quiet about WS, was more or less blackmailed into sponsoring him. This incident, I am told, has done an immense amount of harm; it is known now throughout the body of Freemasonry and has alienated the loyalty of them all as far as HRH is concerned.'[38]

In a remarkably candid letter, possibly unsent, that Thomas wrote to Edward, he concluded that 'You have succeeded with the cooperation in some way of Sir M Jenks in "forcing" on a Lodge a candidate whom the majority of the members didn't want, so in doing so have pretty well disrupted the Lodge, judging by what is said to have happened at the initiation meeting and the number of indignant resignations that are expected. Worse than that, people are saying YRH cannot be ignorant of the strain that this "put up job" has caused, not only in the Lodge concerned but in Masonry generally, so you couldn't possibly, as a free agent, have wished to force on a Lodge . . . anyone who you knew would be unwelcome to the majority of the members and who, without YRH's intervention, would undoubtedly be rejected. So, let me say that clearly, in this case you are in the humiliating position of doing it because you've got to; because Mr S, for obvious reasons, has you under his thumb – and that what he says, goes.'[39]

The journalist Bernard Rickatson-Hatt, a friend of Ernest's, lunched with him and Edward at York House in February 1936, and was privy to an unusually intimate conversation between subject and monarch. As Rickatson-Hatt prepared to leave, Ernest pressed him to remain, before candidly saying to Edward, 'Wallis will have to choose between us. What do you mean to do about this? Do you mean to marry her?' The irritated king stood up and replied, 'Do you really think that I would be crowned without Wallis by my side?'[40] Rickatson-Hatt was no admirer of Wallis, observing that 'she was incapable of being in love with any man . . . She likes the good things of the earth and is fundamentally selfish . . . She was flattered by the advances of the Prince of Wales and the King and enjoyed his generous gifts to her.'[41]

It seemed, for a short time, as if Edward might be able to reconcile duty and pleasure. Even as Hardinge complained that 'the King always speaks first without thinking',[42] he busied himself with his ceremonial responsibilities, taking particular pride in his role as head of the armed forces. He also continued to impress the Privy Council. Ramsay MacDonald praised him for being 'young, lively, talkative ... more informal & conversational [than George V], promising & nothing really essential lost'.[43] If he had needed to have politics, they would have been Conservative; as he wrote in his memoirs, 'I believed ... in private enterprise, a strong Navy ... a balanced budget, the gold standard and close relations with the United States.'[44]

Still, if he cut a forthright and modern figure in his official engagements, he also ran the risk of private ridiculousness, due to a regal lack of self-awareness. Diana Cooper, visiting the Fort again in February 1936 with her husband, wrote to her friend Conrad Russell, with knowing irony, that 'his Majesty's evening kilt was better than ever ... I think it was a mourning one, tho' he denied it ... On Sunday, by request, he donned his "wee bonnet" and marched around his table, his stalwart piper behind him playing "Over the Sea to Skye" and also a composition of his own.' She waspishly added that 'It's clever to have chosen the pipes as one's "shew off" for which one of us can detect mistakes, or know good from bad artistry?'[45] It is possible that her scorn was partially dictated by an incident when, late for dinner and profusely apologetic, she was interrupted by Wallis peremptorily saying, 'Oh cut it out, David and I don't mind.'[46]

On the same visit, Diana saw the heavy, and indeed politically embarrassing, hand of Wallis. 'I had rather she had not said to him at dinner that she wanted to encourage his reading his papers and documents, that he was inclined to have them read to him ... but that it was essential he should learn to master the points in them quickly.' The musical monarch was quick to demonstrate his subservience - 'Wallis is quite right, she always is' - but not before Diana noted that while his 'pupil ways are so winning', there was also something 'very pathetic about his childish ... belief in his capacity for learning'.[47]

Edward had always enjoyed cultivating popularity with his public - anyone who opened a gate to him on his estate while he was out hunting when he was Prince of Wales, for instance, could have expected a handsome tip - and so his first broadcast to the British Empire, delivered on 1 March 1936, St David's Day, was more significant for him than for his predecessors. Hardinge dismissed this as '[his belief] that what counted was the popularity that springs from democratic actions, commonly called "stunts". Respect meant nothing to him - and in this, as in most other estimates of the working of the British mind, he was profoundly wrong.'[48]

The king was expected to read out a long, dry statement of intent - 'a noble example of Whitehall rhetoric' - but he rewrote it in 'my own simple style'. He attempted to add a paragraph of man-to-man, all-in-it-together fellowship - 'I [have] had the opportunity of getting to know the people of nearly every country of the world, under all circumstances and conditions . . . Though now I speak to you as the King, I am still that same man who has had that experience and whose constant effort it will be to promote the well-being of his fellow men'[49] - but this did not make the broadcast, nor did his well-intentioned but politically embarrassing statement of solidarity with Indian nationalism. Lord Crawford, the former Conservative chief whip, noted, not without sympathy, 'We have to deal with a very opinionated man who probably feels much more resentment than anybody knows at the restraints and restrictions which have surrounded him hitherto.'[50]

The new king knew what the family business entailed, and resented it. He described the day-to-day routine of monarchy as 'an occupation of considerable drudgery', and commented how, 'from long observation of my father's activities, I knew only too well what I was in for. The picture of him "doing the boxes", to use his own phrase, had long represented for me the relentless grind of the King's daily routine.' When one official attempted to sympa-thise with his task, commenting, 'I'm afraid, sir, signing all these papers isn't very interesting', he brusquely declared, 'Oh well, it's work.'[51] Some of this ill-feeling may have poisoned his relationship with Wallis, who fled to France for refuge. A letter of 8 March 1936 to Aunt Bessie from Paris referred enigmatically to feelings of 'exhaustion, rage and despair', and added, with understandable weariness, 'that little King insists I return and I might as well [be there] with the telephone about 4 times daily – not much rest'.[52]

Edward tried to be an innovator in a modest way, and, in an even more modest fashion, occasionally succeeded. He later stated that 'all I ever had in mind was to throw open the windows a little' and 'to broaden the base of the Monarchy a little more',[53] which in practice meant that he successfully dispensed with the requirement for the Yeomen of the Guard to grow beards in full Tudor splendour, and was able to create a division of the air force in his name, the so-called 'King's Flight'. Sometimes his innovations were coupled with personal vanity. He asked that the coins that would be minted with his face bear his left profile, rather than his right, because he believed it was more flattering. When this was questioned, he grew angry, saying, 'It is *my* face that is to be used . . . isn't it only reasonable that I should have the privilege of deciding which side is to be put on public display?'[54] The coins were never produced, save as specimens, making this point of precedent moot.

He did at least try to be King of England, rather than merely a London lounge lizard. He visited Clydebank in early March to inspect the largest ocean liner ever constructed, the *Queen Mary*, and was cheered by the shipyard workers. He also won some popularity by going round the filthy and cramped housing and offering his sincere sympathy to those unfortunate enough to live there. Moment to moment, he was certainly interested in the lives of his subjects. It was unfortunate that, bound for London and Wallis again, he quickly forgot his earlier concerns. He had the Fort to live in, rather than a slum.

Yet he also chafed against the dual restrictions of protocol and a hungry public desperate for news of their new king. He was photographed with a member of his staff, Admiral Sir Lionel Halsey, walking from Buckingham Palace in the rain, holding an umbrella and clad in a bowler hat. This would be unexceptional for anyone else in the country, but it was considered infra dig for the ruler to behave in such a way (as it no doubt would to this day), and Edward later wrote that Wallis was asked by a 'prominent Member of Parliament and confidant of the Prime Minister' to ensure that it did not happen again. As the unnamed politician complained, 'The monarchy must remain aloof and above the commonplace . . . We can't have the King doing this kind of thing',[55] Wallis shrugged and calmly suggested to her interlocutor that, as an American, it would be presumptuous of her to attempt to lecture an Englishman – let alone the king – as to how to behave in his own country.

Her regal paramour, meanwhile, was capable of acting pettily as well as magnanimously. He was not deaf to the whisperings at Buckingham Palace and Sandringham that he was unsuited to his role. Helen Hardinge reported, 'nothing but a ghastly conversation with [two old members of the household] about how awful the new King is',[56] and there was a general perception that he did not care for the concerns of his staff. He chose not to eat lunch as a rule, given his lifelong obsession with keeping his weight down – one shared by Wallis – and so was irritated that other people might want to interrupt their day to do so. He kept, as Hardinge put it, 'strange hours', and would often start on his routine of 'going through the boxes' well into the night, telephoning his private secretary four or five times to clarify some point or other. As Helen Hardinge lamented, 'His whole world had come to exist only in and for Mrs Simpson.'[57] Everything else was but a passing distraction.

If his courtiers dared to suggest that he was behaving in an in-appropriate or unbecoming way, they were summarily dismissed, regardless of their seniority or length of service. Godfrey Thomas chose to retain a dignified silence, just as Hardinge did for the moment, but it was not forgotten that Halsey, Edward's equerry and companion in the 'umbrella incident', had often been critical of Wallis when he was Prince of Wales, telling him to his face that she was damaging his reputation and the country. Then, he would have been unable to act without incurring his father's displeasure, but now he was king, and he could behave as he wanted. Thus, Halsey was fired, abruptly and meanly. Edward even attempted to deny him a pension, despite his decades of distinguished service to him and his family, to say nothing of his country.

Hardinge wrote angrily that Halsey's 'only crime was that he would not condone an intrigue which 98 per cent of the country were shortly to condemn ... What can really be said for a man who threw out, without even a handshake, a close friend of twenty years or more, whose only crime was a loyalty to old friends sadly and plainly lacking in his employer?'[58] John Aird mused, 'This trait in HM's character of no sign of gratitude for past work is a very nasty one.'[59] Surprisingly, one courtier who remained in favour, for the time being, was Lascelles, who was intelligent enough to remain on side. Aird believed that 'Tommy ... has fallen under W[allis]'s control almost completely', but, given what he knew of Edward's previous behaviour, his true agenda only became apparent much later.

Wallis was expensive. Trips to Paris and the finest haute couture were substantial costs to be borne, and Edward, who now considered himself a relative pauper, cast about for ways of finding the money to pay for his paramour. He reserved an especial horror for the costs of running Sandringham, which he had no affection for* – he visited it only once, briefly, during his reign, preferring the Fort as a refuge – and dismissed it as a 'white elephant'. He commissioned a report that suggested that a quarter of the staff, a hundred servants, should be dismissed in order to keep the £50,000 annual costs down, and began proceedings to sell off the neighbouring farms, which were only stopped due to his abdication. He would have dispensed with Sandringham itself if he had had the chance. It was, along with Balmoral, his own private property, in the terms of his father's will, and in his hands to do as he pleased with.

All the same, Edward begrudged his inamorata nothing. On one trip to Windsor, he was shown a much-prized crop of peach blossom, which he insisted, to the head gardener's dismay, be

---

* In a letter that he wrote on 23 December 1919 to Freda Dudley Ward, he gave his address as York Cottage, Sandringham, writing viciously underneath, 'Fuck it!!!!'

cut and sent to Wallis as a gift. ('Caligula himself can never have done anything more wanton',[60] a courtier remarked.) As suspicions percolated through Downing Street that his involvement with her might become a source of political and national embarrassment, he relished his opportunities to show her off.

One spectacularly awkward occasion occurred on 28 March, when Hardinge, Wigram and their wives were invited to Windsor Castle to meet some of Edward and Wallis's friends, including a woman called Mary Raffray (neé Kirk), whose nickname was 'Buttercup' Kennedy. Wallis was said to be in a 'teasing' mood, and suggested that Buttercup might one day make a fine match for Ernest, much to the consternation of those present. After watching a couple of films, the 'very agreeable' Mrs Simpson and Edward walked in the Grand Corridor with their guests, drawing particular attention to the portraits of George IV along with his mistress Maria Fitzherbert. Theirs had been a similarly scandalous relationship a century and a half before, involving a secret and legally invalid marriage (and a simultaneous disastrous union with Caroline of Brunswick). Edward and Wallis took care to drop 'hints and talk about them', and it became clear to the company that they 'bristled with unspoken confidences about the present, as we discussed the personal affairs of George IV'. The weight of the past bore down on Helen Hardinge, who wrote in her diary that there were 'too many ghosts at this party'; Alec, meanwhile, pronounced himself 'very much depressed at HM's irresponsibility'.[61]

This irresponsibility took many forms. It was commonly known that Edward left confidential state papers scattered about Fort Belvedere as if they were of no more import than the previous day's newspaper; Hardinge complained that 'There was no responsible person in charge of them, and it was usually days, and sometimes weeks, before they were returned. Who among the "exotic circle" has had access to them can only be a matter of conjecture.'[62] Robert Vansittart fearfully told Baldwin that 'Mrs Simpson is one of the key points in this country as the King discusses everything with her ... The Foreign Secretary is anxious lest the [Foreign Office] cypher be compromised, as Mrs S is said to be in the pocket of the German ambassador.'[63] Wigram went so far as to suggest that 'I did not think the King was normal, and this view was shared by my colleagues at Buckingham Palace. He might any moment develop into a George III, and it was imperative to pass the Regency Bill as soon as possible, so that if necessary he could be certified.'[64]

Although these fears were probably groundless, there was increasing irritation that the king was not behaving in a fashion either regal or becoming of a gentleman. Lord Crawford moaned, 'One hears these stories of engagements being chucked or of outrageous examples of tardiness. He doesn't yet realise how much trouble is taken on his behalf nor what inconvenience is caused by his thoughtlessness and vacillation.'[65] He was especially embarrassed by a fellow peer's comment that any decent London club would have blackballed Edward for his actions.

Most, if not all, of these thoughtless and inconsiderate instances were caused by the king blithely disregarding his responsibilities and duties in order to be with Wallis as much as he could. He did not attempt to hide his grand passion from those around him. Baldwin reported to John Reith, the director general of the BBC, how he entered the room while Edward was talking to Mrs Simpson on the telephone to find him in an 'ecstasy', with his face 'as if he had seen a vision'. All he could say from his trance-like state was 'She is the most wonderful woman in the world.'[66] Hardinge wrote, with scorn, that 'It was scarcely realised at this early stage how overwhelming and inexorable was the influence exerted on the new King by the lady of the moment . . . Every decision, big or small, was subordinated to her will – from her sprang the meanness which characterised his every action and alienated all around him – from her the repellent hardness, the disloyalty to old friends of both sexes; and so too the converse, which brought him among people for whom a few short months before his contempt had been outspoken. But it was she who filled his thoughts at all times – she alone who mattered – before her the affairs of state sank into insignificance. Such was the unhappy atmosphere in which the new reign began.'[67]

Still, he could, on 28 March, dismiss the idea of the king marrying Wallis as 'too wild to even be considered',[68] although it was reported that a piece of paper had been found at the Fort bearing the words 'to our marriage' in Wallis's handwriting. Others at court, such as Wigram, believed that it was all but an inevitability that Edward would somehow find a way to go against centuries of protocol, not to mention Wallis's marriage vows. Edward might have found his consort to be all-consuming, in all senses – Osborne, the butler at the Fort, wrote that 'after a night . . . with Mrs S, the King was absolutely limp and a rag'[69] – but he remained besotted with her, and damned the consequences of his impropriety. He might have done well to heed the words of Ramsay MacDonald to the politician and diarist Harold Nicolson, after Wallis had been sent to Ascot in a royal car: 'The people of this country do not mind fornication, but they loathe adultery . . . Nobody would mind about Mrs Simpson were she a widow and the King not so obstinate and tactless.'[70]

On 2 April, Nicolson himself dined with Edward, Wallis, Ernest and others at Bryanston Court, which was festooned with 'many orchids and white arums'.* He wrote in his diary that the King was 'very alert and delightful', that Wallis was 'a perfectly harmless type of American' and that 'her husband is an obvious bounder', but had the candour to note that 'something snobbish in me is rather saddened by all this . . . the whole setting is slightly second-rate . . . She makes him happy, and that should be enough, but I do not myself want to be drawn into that set if I can help it.'[71] This was echoed by Geoffrey Dawson, who wrote in his diary on 24 April that he had lunched with the 'celebrated Mrs Simpson', but professed himself neither impressed by 'Mrs S's strong American accent, or . . . her charms', even as he described her as 'pleasant, quiet and sensible'.[72] His opinions, like those of many others, would evolve throughout the year.

On 27 May, Edward hosted his first official dinner at York House

---

* A kind of lily noted for its scarcity and expense.

in St James's Palace. The guests included leading figures in politics and society, such as the Baldwins, the Mountbattens and the Wigrams, along with more unexpected attendees, such as Mr and Mrs Simpson and Wallis's friend Emerald Cunard.* It was a typically rash and ostentatious thing to have done, and although Wallis had expressed her hesitation at its propriety, Edward blithely said, 'It's got to be done. Sooner or later my Prime Minister must meet my future wife.'[73]

The evening was a disaster, not least because Wallis was given precedence in the seating arrangements, when protocol demanded that that honour should be accorded to the prime minister's wife. Helen Hardinge wrote that Mrs Simpson 'was not nonplussed by [the guests'] barely-concealed and not entirely friendly curiosity',[74] and as one contemporary gossip magazine, *The King and the Lady*, put it, 'proper and homely Stanley and Lucy [Baldwin] sat awkwardly through the dinner, but their embarrassment was nothing to the apoplectic rage of duchesses and a few dukes when they saw in the sacred Court Circular the list of guests – including Mrs Ernest Simpson'.[75] Edward had taken personal responsibility for the Court Circular, much to the dismay of those around him; Reith believed that the inclusion of the news of the dinner in *The Times* was 'too horrible and it is serious and sad beyond calculation',[76] while Hardinge shrieked that 'the folly of flaunting [his] liaison [and] blazoning it in the Court Circular was almost incredible'.[77]

Now that the king's 'friendship' with Wallis was, officially, a matter of public record, it had to be dealt with, even as he shrugged that 'secrecy and concealment were not of my nature'.[78] As Baldwin and Lang attempted to tell him that he was acting in a way that could not be countenanced by protocol, he angrily repeated that his private life was his own affair, that nobody had any right to interfere in his business, and that he would continue to associate

---

* A disapproving contemporary police note stated solemnly that Emerald 'is reputed to be a drug addict', and that her 'notorious' daughter Nancy 'is very partial to coloured men [and] caused a sensation some few years ago by taking up residence in the negro quarter of New York'.

with Wallis as he pleased. His attitude towards being scolded, as he saw it, was one of such disdain that, seeing a stern-faced courtier approaching, he once climbed out of a ground-floor window and fled to avoid what he believed would be another interminable wigging. Yet as Helen Hardinge wrote, 'Once the King had started the process of turning Mrs Simpson into a public issue . . . he could not stop it just because it suited his whim . . . If he refused to discuss it with those responsible to and for him, it did not mean they could ignore the situation.'[79]

A few months into Edward's reign, the battle lines, such as they were, had been drawn. Many of those who met Wallis either disliked or feared her, believing that she was a toxic influence upon the king. Their condemnation usually took the form of pointedly faint praise, such as Samuel Hoare remarking on her 'sparkling talk, and sparkling jewels with up-to-date Cartier settings . . . [Wallis was] very attractive and intelligent, with little or no knowledge of English life.'[80]

One notable exception was Winston Churchill, who met her at a dinner at York House on 9 July. He believed that too much fuss was being made about her presence in Edward's life, and that, leaving aside questions of morality, it did not matter whether she was present at dinners and events. This did not mean that he could not make a point, however heavy-handedly. That same evening, he gave a semi-formal speech about the relationship between George IV and Mrs Fitzherbert, after which the Duchess of York* remarked, perhaps in an attempt to defray any awkwardness, 'Well, that was a *long* time ago.'[81] Nobody made the point that history had a habit of repeating itself.

The question of what to do with the vexatious king was dominating Whitehall and St James's Palace alike throughout the first half of 1936, even as he ingratiated himself with some of his subjects. Nicolson, for instance, reported after a dinner on 10 June that, despite being half an hour late, 'he has infinitely improved

---

* Better known today as the Queen Mother.

since the old Prince of Wales days . . . He seems almost completely to have lost his nervousness and shyness, and his charm and good manners are more apparent than ever.'*[82] A few days later, at a lunch party at Bryanston Court, Emerald Cunard attempted to flatter Edward by calling him 'the most modernistic man in England'. He blinked, and replied 'with the utmost simplicity' that 'I am not a modernist, since I am not a highbrow. All I try to do is to move with the times.'[83]

It was the speed of this movement that concerned his courtiers. Hardinge met discreetly with his old school friend Walter Monckton in June to discuss legal and political matters in the abstract. The ever-loyal Monckton, however, was mostly in India, advising the Nizam of Hyderabad, and was unable to do more than offer general counsel at this point. Edward, meanwhile, seemed surprised that after the first appearance of Wallis in the Court Circular, the press showed greater interest in him than before. On one appearance in Portsmouth, to view the yacht *Nahlin*, he told a waiting gaggle of photographers that they had no right to take pictures of him in his private sphere, and that they must leave immediately. On this occasion, his wish was granted. Yet he seemed genuinely irritated that he, as monarch, did not automatically have the power of veto over the press.

As far back as 1927, Lascelles had expressed the treacherous hope that Edward might break his neck riding in a point-to-point race, and thereby save the country from his reign, something that Baldwin agreed with. The reality was almost worse than they could have imagined. The king was not merely a besotted boy, but someone capable of active harm to the institution of the monarchy and the country. As courtier and politician alike breathed the nightly prayer, 'Will nobody rid us of this troublesome ruler?', an unlikely source of deliverance appeared on hand. His mission was a simple one: to kill the King of England.

---

* He did also remark on Edward's 'appalling obstinacy' in his diary of 13 July.

Chapter Three

God Save the King

At about quarter past eight on the morning of Thursday 16 July, a short and unprepossessing-looking man left the basement flat of 215 Gloucester Terrace in Bayswater. He claimed to be thirty-five, looked a decade older, and wore the kind of nondescript brown suit that any undistinguished lower-middle-class man might have dressed in for his Sunday best. The house he lodged in, a shabby white stucco-fronted Victorian terrace, was typical of the area. Near to Paddington station, it had been divided up into inexpensive rented housing for the down-at-heel and previously better-off. He had said goodbye to his wife Rose earlier that day. Her husband's nervous and agitated behaviour would have given another woman cause for concern, but she knew his eccentricities all too well, and made no comment.

She did not know that he was carrying a loaded revolver, with five rounds in its chambers, and another cartridge in his pocket, nor that he was bound for Constitution Hill on a dangerous and treacherous mission. He had little expectation of coming home alive from it.

If they had walked by, an onlooker might have seen George McMahon, as he called himself, standing on the steps of the house and looking back at it with an anguished expression. He had lived there for more than three years, and it had offered him some stability amidst the turbulent chaos of his life. Now, that chaos was about to reach its apotheosis. He glanced quickly up and down the street, half expecting to see the Special Branch officers he had run into the previous night. They had assured him, as they had done before, that everything would be absolutely fine as long as he did precisely what he was told. Yet nobody was on Gloucester Terrace. He was alone.

He hurried over to the agreed meeting place, the Express Dairy café by Marble Arch, where he was met by the two men he had come to know. Eventually, as the morning wore on, McMahon saw seven other members of his party assemble; each of whom stuck to their respective small groups to avert suspicion. He kept glancing around anxiously to see if MI5 or Special Branch were on hand, as they had promised to be. Nobody came.

By now, his companions were beginning to suspect that the twitchy McMahon was up to something, so when he asked to be allowed to telephone Rose from a public box, they accompanied him. He dialled two numbers: the 'secret' number for MI5 that he had been given, and the private home number of the Home Secretary, Sir John Simon. The first call was unanswered, and the second was received by Simon's wife's private secretary, who blandly took his name. No *deus ex machina* was at hand to save him. Then it was time to walk over to Hyde Park and confront the inevitable.

As McMahon and his associates reached the spot where the act was to take place, near the luxury hotels of Park Lane, they found that a large number of the seats had been reserved, removing their target from the effective range of gunfire. It was decided to head nearer to Buckingham Palace, so that access was easier, but as the morning drew on, McMahon panicked. Terrified of what he was about to do, he went into a nearby toilet and removed the first cartridge from the chamber of his revolver, meaning that his attempt would be foiled for a valuable second or two. Yet he knew that two armed men accompanied him, neither of whom would hesitate to act if he did not. Emerging, they walked to Constitution Hill, where, incongruously, they ate an early lunch in the nearby Alexandra Hotel, before McMahon and his fellow conspirators took their stand beneath Wellington Arch. They did not anticipate a long wait. The gun in McMahon's pocket still held four bullets; more than enough, if he did not lose his nerve, to commit the act of regal assassination on which he was bound. Every bullet counts, he told himself.

The sixteenth of July was a glorious summer's day, putting the king in a fine humour. After his usual morning appointments and business, he settled into the main activity of the day, an inspection of the ranks of the Guardsmen in Hyde Park. Edward had once served in the Guards, and retained a great affection for them, writing, 'Although I had been through the ceremony many times and this one deviated in no detail from the drill as laid down in standing orders of the Brigade of Guards, I was nevertheless deeply stirred.'[1] The ceremony went according to plan, with spirits lifted by the weather. The battalions formed three sides of a square, and Edward dismounted from his horse before the chaplains consecrated the army colours. The king gave a short speech, made appropriately stirring by a late polish by Churchill, and then remounted, with Major General 'Boy' Sergison-Brooke riding to his right, and the Duke of York, in his role as Colonel of the Scots Guards, on his left.

As McMahon saw the trio drawing nearer, amidst the cheering and pageantry of the day, there seemed to be a great flashing of colour as the bayonets caught the sun and the scarlet tunics of the Guardsmen set off the green foliage of the trees. In the few moments he had before Edward was in sight, he scribbled a brief note on a piece of newspaper, which said, simply, 'May, I love you.' The first sound of exultation led him to think that his moment had arrived, but it was instead Queen Mary with Princesses Elizabeth and Margaret, bound for Buckingham Palace. Then another, louder cheer let him know that the time had come.

As the trio of riders approached his position, he asked a nearby mounted policeman to move so that he could have a better view of the procession. The policeman obliged, but McMahon's anxious, excitable demeanour was not that of a proud patriot, and it drew the attention of a nearby woman, Alice Lawrence, who had been waiting to catch a glimpse of the king. She watched McMahon's actions with increasing interest. She had seen him in conversation earlier with a man she described as 'tall and well-dressed, with a moustache and hat'. There was, she thought, something odd about this agitated character.

At half past twelve, Edward's horse drew near, and McMahon prepared himself. He held the gun in his right hand, covered in a newspaper, and his left hand twitched nervously against his leg. Amidst the noise of the massed bands of the Guards regiments, and the cheering and clamouring, there was a moment of still concentration. Then he walked quickly into the line of sight of the king, lowered his newspaper, produced his revolver and made ready as if to fire.

Alice instinctively grabbed his arm in panic, and a nearby special constable named Anthony Dick swiftly moved forward and punched McMahon in his lower arm, knocking the gun out of his hand. It fell into the road, first under Edward's mount, which it briefly struck, and then under Sergison-Brooke's. Alice cried, 'He has thrown a bomb.' The king himself felt a brief moment of terror as he braced himself for an explosion, before realising that he was safe. As McMahon shouted, 'Here you are, I am the person', he was bundled away by three policemen, while a shaken Edward continued on his procession. The usually fearless Sergison-Brooke looked over at the king to see how he was faring, and remarkably, given the circumstances, he managed a nonchalant response: 'Boy, I don't know what that thing was, but if it had gone off, it would have made a nasty mess of us.'[2] The whole incident was over in a few seconds.

The royal party carried on as if nothing had occurred, eventually arriving back at the Palace, where Edward was informed that it was not a bomb that had been thrown at him, but a revolver. Bemused, the king asked, 'A revolver? But if that man wanted to kill me, why didn't he shoot? Why did he only throw the revolver?' His equerry responded, 'He apparently meant your Majesty no harm. He only wished to cause a scene.'[3] Edward later wrote to Sergison-Brooke to say, 'We have to thank the Almighty for two things: firstly, that it did not rain, and secondly that the man in the brown suit's gun did not go off!'[4]

Once it became clear that there had been a near-miss of some kind, a grateful nation gave thanks for Edward's deliverance. Geoffrey Dawson's description of it as 'an alarming incident of a man [with] a revolver . . . the whole country was agog all afternoon'[5] summed up public feeling. It was not remarked upon at the time, but nearly a century before, on 10 July 1840, there had been a similar attempt on the lives of Queen Victoria and Prince Albert by a madman named Edward Oxford: he was sentenced to be confined indefinitely. Although Harold Nicolson's comment that 'on arrival at the House [of Commons], I hear that it is nothing serious, but merely the act of some lunatic'[6] was typical of the political reaction to the moment, it was still considered important enough for the Labour leader Clement Attlee, in the Commons, to ask the Home Secretary to make a formal comment about the incident. Simon, still apparently in ignorance of who the would-be assassin was, replied that 'The whole House will be profoundly thankful that the risk to which His Majesty was exposed was so promptly averted.'[7] Halifax made a similar statement in the House of Lords.

That evening, a burst of relief and patriotic fervour saw several theatres launch into spontaneous renditions of the National Anthem, while it was also sung in cinemas at newsreel footage of the king taking the salute in Hyde Park that morning. Even foreign leaders offered their good wishes. A telegram from Hitler stated, 'I have just received news of the abominable attempt on the life of your Majesty, and send my heartiest congratulations on your escape.'[8]

As the agent of the 'abominable attempt' was taken away, with a certain degree of force, Chief Inspector Sands read him his rights, and asked what his intentions had been. McMahon replied, 'I did not try to shoot the King . . . I only did it as a protest. I could easily have shot him, but I only threw it', and asked, with what he claimed was concern, whether Edward had been harmed in any way. It was later argued at his trial that this remark was in fact a statement of disappointment that someone had not finished the job that he had been frustrated in doing. He then reportedly said, 'It would have been better if I had shot myself.'[9]

The truth behind what happened on that mid-July day has long been unclear. The accepted version of the events, as depicted by historians and by Edward himself in his memoirs, is that McMahon was a confused attention-seeker who never had any serious intention of doing any harm to the king. He instead had a grievance against the Home Secretary because he had been frustrated in his attempts to publish a magazine called the *Human Gazette*. Thus, he staged a demonstration in the most public of fashions, which inevitably resulted in his subsequent arrest and imprisonment, albeit with a considerably lighter sentence than a suspected royal assassin would usually merit. Edward himself did not take the attempted outrage especially seriously, lightly referring to it as 'the dastardly attempt' – a phrase used by an outraged courtier – and later commented, when it was suggested that he had been assisting his would-be assailant in some way, 'He is about the last man I would help . . . McMahon got all the front pages and the headlines and nobody read my speech.'[10]

This is a neat enough summary of what occurred. Yet it is not wholly accurate. Officials wished to suppress the details of what really happened, only a few months into the new reign, and their attempts led to this bland disinformation becoming the accepted story. However, recently declassified MI5 files, to say nothing of an extraordinary autobiographical document, *He Was My King*, written by McMahon himself, offer a stranger and more complex narrative, in which a succession of half-truths and acts of subterfuge give a glance into a febrile, paranoid time, just a few years before the outbreak of World War II, in which anything – even a royal assassination – seemed possible.

George Andrew McMahon was born Jerome Brannigan around 1901. There was some confusion as to where he came from, which was variously suggested to be either Govan, a poor district of Glasgow, or Cookstown in Northern Ireland. He later claimed that, as a schoolboy, he had a mysterious accident 'which disabled me for life, and prevented my obtaining a school education . . . I am entirely self-educated.'[11] He drifted around between odd jobs for a while, indulging a heavy drinking problem, and was eventually imprisoned for embezzling money while a travelling salesman for a printing firm. After his release, he adopted the pseudonym of McMahon and spent some time in Dublin and Liverpool, working in a succession of dead-end sales roles, before he moved to London in 1933. Here, by his own account, he became secretary to a sports club and made some success out of it, until police intervention saw him fired once again.

In his story, the 'disgraceful conduct of two CID officers, of which definite proof had been supplied to me,'[12] led him to make a formal complaint, which he was advised not to take any further. Upon his refusing to comply, he was arrested, charged with libelling the police, and imprisoned again for twelve months. It was then that he first came to the attention of MI5, as he wrote to the chair of the Communist Party, care of its newspaper, the *Daily Worker*, in August 1933, vehemently proclaiming his innocence and announcing a claim for £4,000 in compensation that he was launching against the Home Secretary.

After being released on appeal after a couple of months, he attempted to claim his compensation, but without success. He then struggled to find work, but eventually founded a small advertising agency, which he stated employed 'some hundreds of men in many parts of the country'.[13] How accurate this statement is remains uncertain, but somehow McMahon found the funds to launch his own newspaper, the *Human Gazette*, which then folded because 'additional capital which I had been promised did not materialise'. This became a major grievance of his, and also 'resulted . . . in my forming a number of associations which subsequently had very serious consequences for me'.[14]

After declining an opportunity to relaunch the *Human Gazette* as an explicitly anti-British periodical, McMahon acted as a gun-runner to Abyssinia, during which he became known to the Italian embassy. Their policy of offering him large sums in cash for information pertaining to the destination and quantity of these armaments baffled him, but he was happy to take their money. Before long, he practically had the run of the Italian military attaché's office, or so he suggested. Yet by September 1935, it had dawned on McMahon, by no means the most perceptive or self-aware of men, that he had become party to something else that he barely understood. As he described it, 'I now realised that I was unwittingly being used to obtain and pass to a foreign power information that would be prejudicial to my own Country's well-being.' The particular incident that triggered his conscience was his being asked for details relating to an RAF plane 'of particular value to the British Air Force and regarded as one of a highly secret type'.[15]

It is impossible to separate fact from fantasy in McMahon's autobiographical accounts. He was clearly something of a Walter Mitty character, prone to exaggerating his achievements and accomplishments to a degree whereby it became difficult to distinguish simple falsehood from enthusiastic embellishment. Considerable alcohol intake did not aid his recall. Yet the recently declassified MI5 files reveal a surprising degree of correlation between his stories and their own activities.

While his first approach to them in September 1935 was inconclusive, a letter of 18 October 1935 from Special Branch to the Home Secretary, referring to a meeting held the previous day between McMahon and John Ottaway, a Detective Superintendent and MI5 agent, details a string of names of contacts at the Italian embassy with suspected fascist sympathies. Although a note on McMahon's file suggests that some of this 'flow of information' had been 'absolutely useless', it also records that 'He did however . . . give us the name of Mrs Ponte at the Italian Embassy, telling us she was responsible for receiving intelligence reports intended for the military attaché . . . we were definitely able to ascertain that [she]..was being used for certain intelligence work.'[16] Another confidential document affirmed that some of what he was feeding them was 'undoubtedly accurate'.

After decades of not being of any obvious use to anyone, McMahon had now established himself as, of all things, an informant for MI5. Yet even then, the account of his operations was tinged with scepticism. It was noted, for instance, that the cash payments of five-pound notes were exchanged at his habitual haunt of public houses, such as the Hog in the Pound on Oxford Street. The drinking that had ruined his earlier attempts at employment had not ceased. However, he could now write with pride that 'I was to act thenceforth under the direction and supervision of the Military Intelligence Department.'[17]

McMahon boasted that 'I had gained a reputation amongst [the Italians] as a useful dupe and one whose services could be easily purchased.'[18] He was assisted in this subterfuge by his Irish background, and the near-continual failure of his business activities meant that he was both in constant need of cash and poorly disposed towards 'them', the amorphous mass of policemen, bureaucrats and politicians he held responsible for frustrating his plans and ambitions.

He was indulged by his Italian contacts and taken out to private clubs for expensive dinners and wine. He gleefully noted that 'It often gave me food for thought that, within the very place which even Royalty sometimes visited, and rubbing shoulders with distinguished Englishmen, were these people whose only object in life was to cause destruction and disaffection.'[19] When, 'after a substantial repast', his handler asked him what his attitude towards the British government was, 'My reply came readily . . . I detested the whole regime.'[20] Despite his later protestations that he was always acting as an undercover agent for MI5, McMahon had impressed the Italians sufficiently for them to make him a lucrative offer: to act in the assassination of the king.

Accounts as to what subsequently happened differ dramatically. McMahon's lengthy story detailed a series of meetings that he had with the Italian military attaché and his staff, information from which he regularly fed back to MI5. Official records show that he met with intelligence services frequently throughout late 1935 and early 1936, although no record exists of what, if any, payment he demanded for his services. In December 1935, he showed Ottaway a pistol and informed him that he had been given it by the foreign power's representatives for his protection. Ottaway merely told his informant to obtain a licence from the police if he planned on carrying it around London.

McMahon enjoyed his double life. He asserted that 'As I was acting under their instruction . . . I was able to enter into the full spirit of the conspiracy, knowing in my heart that I was only performing a duty and the more enthusiastic I appeared, the more likely I was to obtain full information which would enable the dastardly deed to be frustrated.'[21] A contemporary MI5 account is less effusive. It states that 'On the 17 April McMahon approached Mr Ottaway, and informed him that he was in possession of information regarding a Communist plot to assassinate the monarch.'[22] Ottaway's own account stated that McMahon assured him that nothing was due to happen until the summer.

Given the accuracy of some of McMahon's previous intelligence, his statement was taken seriously, and was passed to Norman Kendal, head of the Criminal Investigation Department. However, his demand for £1,000 for his information was ignored. He was instead informed that 'he would no doubt be compensated for its value, and . . . every protection by the authorities would be afforded him'.[23]

A meeting was then arranged with McMahon on 20 April, which he described as having 'put my mind at complete rest', with the policeman being in full knowledge and approval of him retaining a revolver and ammunition that he had been passed by his confederates. This meant that 'I [had] to carry this weapon at every moment of my waking day that I might have to defend myself with it.'[24] MI5 viewed the interview differently. Ottaway was given instructions 'gradually to break off his association with McMahon

. . . While we have had some use out of him, he was too unreliable to be of real assistance.'[25] As McMahon reported increasingly incredible theories regarding the conspiracy that he had been drawn into – 'the full resources of the Vatican were eventually to be at the disposal of the country' – he was warming to his role of royal assassin. At one meeting, when asked whether he was willing to execute the *coup de grâce* himself, he replied with bravado, 'What did you give me a gun for?',[26] to be greeted by a chorus of cheering and approval.

McMahon's lengthy and detailed account of the preparations for the assassination attempt may well be entirely fantastical. Yet if it is fictitious, it has an uncanny consistency with many of the official records, even if his self-regarding belief that the police and MI5 were following his every movement with interest was erroneous. He claimed that an initial attempt at assassination by Horse Guards Parade during the Trooping of the Colour ended in farce when a nearby sightseer, attempting to take a photograph of the king, overbalanced and fell flat on his face, attracting a large amount of unwelcome attention. He was alarmed that there was no overt police presence – 'unless perhaps they were instrumental in staging the apparently accidental postponement'[27] – and so, when it was decided that the next attempt would take place when the king was receiving the Regiments of Guards, he panicked.

On 13 July, McMahon telephoned Ottaway 'in an excited condition'[28] and informed him that he had 'full particulars of the discussions and arrangements made'.[29] The two met that evening at Victory House in Victoria Street, and Ottaway stated that McMahon showed 'signs of nervousness' and believed 'that he would not be alive after Thursday 16 July . . . Arrangements had been made that he and a companion should assassinate the King on Thursday.' Ottaway, mindful of McMahon's reputation for unreliability, 'endeavoured to dissuade him from any such action, and failed to obtain from him anything to assist investigation'.

The reluctant assassin stated that 'nothing could prevent him carrying out his part of the plan, and that he had made the necessary arrangements . . . in the event of his death'.[30] One of these 'arrangements' was to write to the Home Secretary. McMahon insisted that this was a scheme dreamt up by the conspirators, 'referring to my persecution by the police . . . and demanding cessation of this – failing which I would take some desperate action'. He seemed to believe that 'the production of this letter, in the event of the worst happening, might mitigate my offence, by drawing attention to the fact of my great grievance which had not been redressed in spite of my constant endeavours to this end'.[31] He was incorrect.

McMahon asked Ottaway to meet him at 8 a.m. on the morning of 16 July, suggesting that, should he help frustrate the planned assassination, he would make a name for himself. He also asked him to ensure that Special Branch followed him. Ottaway demurred, telling him that it was a police matter rather than a security services one, and so McMahon asked that an Inspector Clarke come and meet him on the 14th, in exchange for which he would give him full details of the planned attempt. He also suggested that the previous attempt at assassination, during the Trooping of the Colour, had been prevented by some intervention. Ottaway enquired what had happened to the pistol that he had waved around on an earlier occasion, and McMahon told him that it had been disposed of.

This, along with much else that he said, was untrue. Ottaway noted that 'McMahon's story was altogether different to that told me in April, but no promise or occasion was given him on the last occasion',[32] and his unreliability was commonly accepted. And so the events of 16 July, with their own bizarre inevitability, took place. Yet as soon as McMahon appeared in court, charged with 'unlawfully possessing a firearm and ammunition to endanger life', 'presenting near the person of the King a pistol with intent to break the peace' and 'producing a revolver near the person of the King with intent to alarm his Majesty', the whole saga moved into stranger and murkier territory altogether.

In his memoir, McMahon detailed a series of Kafkaesque betrayals and reversals in the run-up to his trial, in which he was repeatedly beaten and threatened by the police, and his previous involvement with MI5 denied by everyone he encountered. He remarked that when he, with a 'dishevelled appearance', stood up in court in September 1936, 'to my surprise, a Jewish solicitor, whom I knew and had some dealings with previously . . . arose and said that he had been instructed to represent me'.[33] This solicitor, Alfred Kerstein, was more astute than his client, and as McMahon expressed his surprise that he was not released from prison immediately ('I was given to understand . . . that His Majesty the King, ever mindful of those in trouble, had sent a message to the prison authorities that I was to be made as comfortable as possible'), Kerstein began doing his best to prepare a defence. He was considerably more committed to his client than McMahon's barrister St John 'Jack' Hutchinson was. Hutchinson blithely commented to Harold Nicolson after the trial that McMahon 'was not a lunatic, but he was a man of such inordinate conceit that he will undoubtedly go mad'.[34]

Hutchinson's view of his client's espionage activities was breezy. 'He has certainly been in touch with the German Embassy but of course they have not urged him to stage an assassination of the King.'[35] This was true. Yet the McMahon case was considered sufficiently serious to be prosecuted by none other than Sir Donald Somervell, the attorney general. There was also a division of the charges that McMahon faced. The possession of the firearm with intent to endanger life charge was relatively minor, coming under the scope of the Firearms Act of 1920. The other two charges were more serious, and came under the Treason Act of 1842. What then ensued was a masterclass in obfuscation and backstairs dealing, the vast majority of which remained hidden to its principal actors, including McMahon himself.

As reported in the press, Somervell's case for the prosecution was straightforward: namely that McMahon did not intend to kill the king, but that 'it is, perhaps, difficult to imagine any act more calculated to create a disturbance than an act of this kind'. If it seems strange that he was not charged with attempted murder

- a crime that would have been punished with hanging, had he been convicted - then it was at least consistent that the witnesses called, including Lily Yeoman of Leytonstone and Samuel Green of Sidcup, testified to McMahon throwing the pistol on the ground, rather than levelling it at Edward himself. McMahon, in the dock, twitched with irritation at what he saw as both contradictory and false information. One word from MI5, he thought, and he would be discharged without further ado. Perhaps his much-desired compensation would be received as well.

As the case ground forward, it became increasingly clear to McMahon that the evidence seemed damning. Special Constable Dick, described in court as 'the hero of the occasion',[36] testified to knocking the pistol out of his hand, and there was much interest as to why, exactly, McMahon had been holding a picture postcard of the king when arrested. (He claimed that he had tried to 'protect an unusual photograph of His Majesty'.)[37] Hutchinson briefly raised the question with Chief Inspector Sands as to why the accused was in possession of a gun - 'Did . . . McMahon say . . . that, at the end of 1935, he was doing certain work imparting information to the authorities which necessitated him carrying a revolver for his own safety?' - but Sands offered bland denials of any knowledge, which Hutchinson barely pressed him on.

Yet as it became clear that McMahon had been in contact with the police before 16 July, the judge, Justice Greaves-Lord, was driven to intervene to stop Hutchinson's line of questioning, suggesting that 'This is quite contrary to all the rules of evidence. You cannot ask a witness to say something that he does not know.'[38] Nonetheless, a question was percolating in court. The man who had behaved so strangely in front of the king was clearly a fantasist, and the question at hand was how much of a danger he was. Why, then, was this senior policeman unable simply to deny these outlandish claims?

McMahon later wrote that 'When, no doubt, the true facts were brought to the notice of [the] high authorities, who had taken the decision to make the first charge, they were in a quandary.'[39] It was not without satisfaction that he reported that 'They were faced with the fact that, unless some very special steps were taken, all the facts which I have related previously would come out in evidence.' This related, in his mind, 'the association of a foreign power with a conspiracy to assassinate the King', which, as he said, 'might cause international complication at a most inconvenient time'. As great a threat to national stability was his observation that 'Although the authorities had full information regarding this, they had not taken the essential steps to prevent the occurrence.'[40]

He was correct. Regardless of whether he was simply a madman acting alone, or a hapless pawn in some wider conspiracy, he had gone out of his way to warn Special Branch of the likelihood of an attempt on the king's life on 16 July, and the letter he had written to Simon, warning of how 'within 24 hours . . . I will exercise my own prerogative, and obtain the necessary satisfaction which I, in my tortured mind, consider adequate', was produced in court. It was no coincidence that Mr Justice Greaves-Lord, on a flimsy pretext, asked that the jury find McMahon not guilty of the more serious charges of 'presenting near the person of the King a pistol with intent to break the peace' and 'producing a revolver near the person of the King with intent to alarm his Majesty', thus removing the possibility of his being found guilty of a treasonous offence. McMahon claimed that he was asked by his counsel to plead guilty in the expectation of a light sentence, refused, and insisted on taking his turn in the witness box. It would be disastrous for him.

His own account of his testimony was that 'I was placed in the witness box to make a statement. Had I been allowed to make this statement my own way, all would have been well. But immediately I started to speak, my counsel began to interject questions to me which . . . confused the issue and destroyed the cogency of my story.'[41] A contemporary press account of what occurred seems more impartial and accurate. It described how McMahon spoke 'hurriedly and excitedly', and uttered long sentences that were inaudible or incomprehensible to the court, as he outlined the same story he had given to Special Branch, namely his recruitment by agents of a foreign power, for cash, from October 1935. He claimed that he was offered £150 to assassinate the king – a sum that Hutchinson, in cross-examination, belittled as 'a small amount to risk your life for'. Ottaway was present, described as 'Major KC' and 'a gentleman from the War Office', but did not give any evidence. McMahon was clear that he did not wish to kill Edward, but instead to save him.

Although Hutchinson, knowingly or otherwise, touched upon the essentially true facts of McMahon's story, such as alluding to the treacherous Mrs Ponte in the Italian embassy, he did not manage to suggest that the saga was anything other than a series of exaggerations and fabrications dreamed up by a mentally ill malcontent – much as he suggested, privately, to Nicolson. The attorney general was therefore able to suggest 'that the story of the plot is the product of your imagination'. McMahon responded, 'You did not want me to come in and give evidence . . . The offer was made to me, if I pleaded guilty, I would get off with a light sentence. Why was that offer made to me but to hide the bungling of other people?'[42]

After McMahon left the witness box, sweating heavily, Somervell described him as a 'wholly unreliable person', and mocked his 'Edgar Wallace story'. Even as he grudgingly accepted that 'McMahon had been employed by a foreign power', he set great store by his Irish background, which 'to foreigners [meant] Irishmen were supposed to have been nurtured in hatred against Great Britain'.[43] Castigating him as 'an absolute down and out', he left the jury in little doubt that they were dealing with a fantasist, compounded by the judge's highly partial summing-up – 'Does a man who wants merely to make a protest go into a public place with a revolver loaded in four chambers out of five?'[44]

McMahon was convicted and sentenced to twelve months hard labour, as the judge described him as 'one of those misguided persons who think that by notoriety they can call attention to [their] grievances'. Greaves-Lord loftily informed him that the comparative lightness of his punishment was because 'I am not going to make you into a sort of fancied hero . . . I am not going to pass a sentence that would have any tendency to do that.'[45] Would-be royal assassins, after all, did not get a year's imprisonment; that was the punishment for fantasists and troublemakers. As the prison doctor at Brixton reportedly said to McMahon, 'in an unpleasant way', 'You're lucky to have got off so lightly after pleading not guilty.'[46]

Those who had had any dealings with McMahon over the previous year might have been relieved that he had disappeared into the prison system once again, with his story rubbished and his credibility destroyed. They had reckoned without his solicitor. Kerstein, unlike Hutchinson, continued to believe that there was some substance to McMahon's statements, confused and contradictory though they were, and he wrote to the Home Secretary on 15 October to explore the veracity of what Ottaway had, or hadn't, said. McMahon declared that he had been told, 'It's alright Mac. No matter what happens you will be looked after and protected, only my superiors cannot suggest the advisability of putting anything in writing.'[47] Kerstein suggested, 'We appreciate that even if such promise of immunity from legal proceedings was given, that promise has no effect in any criminal court . . . however, if you satisfy yourself . . . that our client is telling the truth, this will further help prove to you that our client was not actuated by any criminal or unpatriotic motive.'[48] He made it clear that he was not operating under instructions from McMahon, but out of a desire to see justice done.

As McMahon descended into a paranoid belief that Kerstein had stolen hundreds of pounds from him ('from parties who published libellous statements regarding me and the revolver incident'),[49] various memoranda from Carew Robinson of the Home Office strike an indignant note. Describing Kerstein as 'very confused', he recounted the solicitor's central argument: that McMahon's story was substantially true, that its appearance at the Old Bailey would have imperilled international relations, that McMahon would be similarly unable to tell his story at the court of appeal, and that he deserved a free pardon as a result. As Robinson allowed that 'McMahon has been in communication with the Communist Party about his personal grievances', he did not mention his earlier dealings with MI5, nor his supplying of information relating to the Italian embassy. Mysteriously, the 'foreign power' that he claimed was employing him had switched from Italy to Germany in the recounting. Robinson wrote that 'It seems perfectly clear that there is nothing in his stories about a plot to assassinate King Edward', but instead suggested that 'There was reason to believe that McMahon's story was financed by newspapers, and that Mr Kerstein was expected to conduct it on lines that would provide good "copy".'[50]

Robinson was especially keen that nothing sensational or shocking be allowed to enter the public domain, and as a result, no appeal was allowed for McMahon, who suffered through his prison sentence until he was released on 13 August 1937, to be met by his wife and Kerstein. The presence of the latter was surprising, given the paranoid ranting that his client had engaged in. Due to the unusual amount of attention around his case, he was released at night, with the utmost secrecy, rather than the traditional early morning.

He was ruined. The notoriety surrounding him meant that any chance of returning to a lawful occupation was impossible, even if he had wished for it, and he returned to drinking. His only public statements were hugely contradictory. His long attempt at self-justification, *He Was My King*, praises Edward throughout, just as an 'appeal' that he produced in September 1938, in which he compared himself to Captain Dreyfus and Oscar Slater,* calls him 'England's greatest Monarch', and eulogises him as 'GREAT KING, GREAT GENTLEMEN [*sic*] and GREAT HUMANITARIAN', while continuing to insist upon his own intelligence work.

---

* A victim of a notorious miscarriage in Scotland in 1908, whose innocence became a *cause célèbre* supported by the likes of Sir Arthur Conan Doyle and Ramsay MacDonald.

It was unfortunate, then, that the subsequent times that he came to the attention of MI5 were during World War II, firstly for writing a letter on forged War Office paper that called for the expulsion of the 'rascally Jew Horeb-Elisha' (Leslie Hore-Belisha, then Secretary of State for War) and described Edward, whom Hore-Belisha had supported, as 'the exiled traitor Windsor'. McMahon was then closely associated with the Anglo-Saxon League, or the so-called 'People's Alliance', an organisation of British fascists, and continued to write to Oswald Mosley long after the end of the war. As one despairing Special Branch staff member wrote, 'I should think that he is the sort of man who is perpetually thinking out magnificent schemes, but who has very little ability to execute them.'[51] He was sent to prison again in 1951 for three years, this time for falsely obtaining £1,600 for a non-existent company called Modern Society Publications, and eventually died in 1970, forgotten and penniless.

It is impossible to be sure as to what really happened on 16 July 1936, and why. Yet one detail remains intriguing and under-explored. The note that McMahon wrote shortly before he stepped out into infamy, 'May, I love you', was widely believed to be to his wife. Yet his wife's name was Rose, and nowhere in any of their correspondence (including a letter that she wrote to Wallis Simpson in 1938, begging for help finding a job) is she referred to as May. It is therefore no coincidence that one of McMahon's neighbours in his Bayswater flat was May Galley, herself an associate of Edith Suschitzky, the Russian émigré and recruiter for the Cambridge spy network. It is quite likely that they were lovers.

Although the usually loquacious McMahon was silent on the topic of the 'other' May, it does not take Special Branch's finest minds to piece together an intrigue involving a coalition of disaffected Communists, Italian spies and fellow sympathisers, whose ultimate aim was to cause a high-profile outrage involving the new King of England. It was their good fortune to find as their patsy a fantasist who could be fed a mixture of accurate and false information, and who could then involve the security services; it was their bad luck that he was so unstable and unreliable a character. Yet it is tempting to believe that when McMahon stood in front of Edward for a second that July day, he genuinely had no idea what he was about to do. Had he fired, and killed his monarch, then his name would be notorious, rather than a footnote in a wider saga.

Given what occurred during the rest of 1936, it might have been better for all concerned if he had acted so decisively.

Chapter Four

'Flatterers, Sycophants and Malice'

Around the time of World War I, it was suggested that Diana Cooper - then known as Lady Diana Manners - would make a suitable wife for the Prince of Wales. She was widely believed to be the most desirable woman in England, possessed of both enviable beauty and wit. In many respects, she was a more glamorous figure than Edward was. When, safely married to Duff Cooper, she re-encountered the prince at a luncheon party, Duff was able to patronise him as 'wonderfully charming', explaining that 'There is a leaven of snobbery, or I should prefer to call it loyalty, which magnifies the emotion one feels about him', and damned him with the accolade of being 'shy but [having] beautiful manners'. He said of his wife, in the full uxorious glow of a new union, 'Diana was singularly self-possessed, because she did not find the Prince in the least intimidating.'[1] He did not need to mention that the former Lady Manners seldom found anyone intimidating, regardless of their status.

A friendship of sorts continued between the Coopers and the Prince of Wales. On one occasion while they were in Wales in the twenties, Edward, possibly in his cups, became maudlin. He described Buckingham Palace as mired in gloom, 'how he himself and all of [his family] "froze up" whenever they got inside it; how bad-tempered his father was [and] how the Duchess of York was the one bright spot there'.[2] As in most areas of his life before Wallis, he seemed desperately unhappy about his situation. He complained about how miserable his life was, with a particular nadir coming when, finally allowed a day's hunting, he was deprived of the chance to murder beasts of the hedgerow and field because Andrew Bonar Law, the former prime minister, had been selfish enough to die and thus spoil his sport.

When Diana was summoned to join a royal cruise in the late summer of 1936, she was therefore surprised to find that the prince, who had formerly given a passable imitation of Young Werther, was a rejuvenated figure. He sported the unusual attire of straw sandals, grey flannel 'spick-and-span-little'[3] shorts and two crosses on a gold chain around his neck; Wallis wore the same crosses around her wrist. Edward was stripped to the waist, leaving royal dignity behind along with his shirt and jacket. It was an open invitation for any passing photographer or journalist to get the scoop of the year, but even if they had, it would not be printed. The reason for Edward's modesty being thus spared lay largely with one man: Max Aitken, the first Lord Beaverbrook.

In later life, Beaverbrook was asked whether he had any regrets about the abdication crisis, and his role within it. The newspaper magnate responded that 'I wouldn't have missed it on any account, because of the fun I got out of it.'[4] Yet for a man who would become one of Edward's most committed supporters – albeit out of pragmatism as much as sympathy – their relationship began inauspiciously. Beaverbrook attended Edward's swearing-in ceremony at St James's Palace in early 1936. 'I struggled into the uniform of a Privy Councillor [for] the second time I had worn the uniform in twenty years, and it was a tight fit.'[5] He paid the necessary homage, writing that 'A new reign, with a young and independent-minded sovereign, excited my imagination . . . I believed that Edward VIII would set a fresh tone and give a colourful leadership in the country',[6] and then went home.

He had dined with Edward while he was still Prince of Wales, and noted approvingly that he had managed to antagonise two of his own foes: the prime minister and the Archbishop of Canterbury. The prince, he observed happily, 'made enemies among politicians by his habit of discussing them in free and unflattering terms with no regard as to who might be listening'.[7] Baldwin 'appeared to be strong and confident of himself', but he had irritated Edward before ('the King found Baldwin something of a bore, and he suffered from his flow of unwanted information during a Canadian tour which they undertook together')[8] and so, in the spirit of befriending his enemy's enemy, Beaverbrook took Edward's side. This magnanimous impulse was strengthened by the knowledge that one of Baldwin's closest friends was Geoffrey Dawson, editor of Beaverbrook's rival paper *The Times*.

Even as it was reported by Harold Nicolson that 'Beaverbrook is becoming very mellow in his later age, but that his personal vendettas seem never to diminish', the newspaper magnate continually repeated, 'Remember that every friend is a potential enemy and every enemy a potential friend.'[9] It was not immediately clear in which category he placed the new king, who was given to speaking his mind from the outset of his reign, regardless of how undiplomatic or unhelpful his interjections might be. Beaverbrook wrote cheerily that 'The inner circles [of power] were distressed and even dismayed by the freedom of Edward VIII's opinions openly spoken on many political issues, and usually hostile to the Administration.'[10] It is little wonder, given his Machiavellian scheming and delight in stratagems, that Ziegler describes Beaverbrook as 'bad, in fact I'd say evil – one of the few people I would use that word about'.[11]

Nonetheless, he and his fellow newspaper proprietors stuck to their unwritten rule: no public criticism of the king and his attitudes, however bizarre or unhelpful his actions. A different man could have achieved a huge amount without unwanted scrutiny. Yet as Beaverbrook observed, 'the threat to the throne was to come from quite another source. While the popularity of the King was unchallenged and appeared to be unchallengeable, there were rumours in Fleet Street.' Even as the grateful nation, led by its press, rejoiced at Edward's deliverance from whatever McMahon had planned, it was becoming increasingly clear that, as Beaverbrook put it, 'the people were soon to hear much more of Mrs Simpson'.[12]

It did not help that a photograph had appeared in the papers, apparently innocently, 'of a small group at a window of St James's Palace watching a ceremonial parade'.* This group consisted of 'an intimate gathering of the King's close friends, but there was a woman among them whose face was unfamiliar . . . Inquiries were at once set on foot and her identity was promptly discovered.'[13] Wallis's inevitable presence, as Edward's closest friend, was one that could be suppressed for a short period, but not indefinitely.

Neither did it help that Ernest Simpson was becoming a lecherous liability. Diana Cooper, along with her husband Duff, then Minister of War, was a guest at Blenheim Palace in June 1936 ('I'm not actually unhappy [to be there] . . . the house [is] of a breathtaking magnificence . . . [although] it is rather disfigured by huge infernal machines')[14] and found herself in an unfortunately intimate situation with Ernest, who had 'asked me to promise to come out and look at the light in the garden'.

After Diana's excuses failed to deter him, his 'dogged determination got me out . . . We walked along the terrace in the dark, me talking hectically, knowing that if I stopped there would be some advance . . . which indeed there was . . . not a pounce . . . at least not for the face but arms, hands and palms . . . very embarrassing; there was a great deal about my being his goddess. The worst was when we came in 20 minutes later . . . all the men were gossiping together . . . Duff, through embarrassment at my being there at all, and of my doing anything out of the usual, behaved like only very jealous husbands do.' Diana ended her account of her time at Ernest's hands by writing that 'I slunk up to bed as tho' I had been caught stealing',[15] but the blame lay with the most famous cuckold in England rather than her.

Evenings like this offered a pretext for Wallis to instruct the solicitor Theodore Goddard to represent her in divorce proceedings, but she acted with some reluctance. Edward had written to inform

---

* See p 32

her that 'My talk with Ernest was difficult this evening but I must get after him now or he won't move', and referred to their predicament as 'all so unsatisfactory until it's all settled and WE are really one'. Allowing that 'I can't bear your having to hear unpleasant things said, as I'm just as sensitive as you are'[16], Edward nevertheless insisted on a course of action that would inevitably lead to his beloved divorcing for the second time. There was giddiness to his actions; Wallis was invited to another dinner and named in the Court Circular once again, this time without her husband. Chips Channon wrote sympathetically that 'The Simpson scandal is growing, and she, poor Wallis, looks unhappy. The world is closing in around her, the flatterers, the sycophants, and the malice.'[17]

As custom demanded, it was necessary for Ernest to be discovered in an adulterous scene by detectives hired by Wallis's solicitors, and then for her to send him a formal letter announcing her intention of filing for divorce. He accordingly registered at the Hotel de Paris, an expensive and exclusive establishment in the Thames-side village of Bray on 21 July, under the pseudonym 'Ernest A. Simmons', joined by Buttercup Kennedy. Her presence was an inevitability given her previous meeting with Ernest in Wallis's company. The pair were photographed in bed together, although the carefully stage-managed production of the evidence came close to not taking place. When the divorce petition was filed and served, the hotel management, realising who Ernest was and his reasons for being there with La Buttercup, were aghast at the thought of unsavoury publicity. They attempted to remove the staff who had witnessed the scandalous scene by dismissing them. Thankfully for the divorce, Goddard was experienced in these matters, and ensured that the servants were handsomely reimbursed for their testimonies in due course, as well as being put up at a nearby inn, away from the press.

It was a given that when the divorce case was heard in court, Wallis's letter to Ernest of 23 July would attract some attention. Therefore it was intentionally blandly worded, almost certainly on the advice of Goddard: 'Instead of being away on business as you led me to believe you have been staying in Bray with a lady. I am sure you realise this is conduct which I cannot possibly overlook and must insist you do not continue to live here with me . . . I am therefore instructing my solicitors to take proceedings for divorce.'[18] Yet the traditional *omertà* of British press silence when it came to the private life of royalty was an invaluable asset for WE. As Beaverbrook wrote, 'As the publicity was due to her association with him, he, for his part, felt that he should protect her. These reasons appeared satisfactory to me. And so I took part in the general suppression of the news.'[19]

This generous attitude was not, unfortunately for the king and Wallis, shared by the American newspapers, which were happy to speculate as to the motivations, propriety and actions of the couple. It was an infamous cruise aboard the yacht the *Nahlin* in August that would lead to growing public disdain for 'the unrespectable whore' and 'the playboy king' and set in motion a series of events that would lead to a breakdown in constitutional and political norms, and spark the greatest royal crisis of the century.

Edward felt that he deserved a holiday, as he was exhausted by the responsibilities and duties that he had undertaken over the previous six months. The McMahon business had not helped his equanimity, nor had an embarrassing incident at Buckingham Palace on 21 July when a summer garden party designed to act as a 'coming out' parade for various debutantes was ruined by a sudden downpour of rain. Edward's unilateral decision to cancel the event therefore looked like a snub for those unfortunate girls who had not yet been presented to him. His initial intention for a holiday was to head to a villa near Cannes, but its proximity to the Spanish Civil War made it a poor idea, so a cruise was decided upon as compensation.

Preparations for the trip began. The *Nahlin*, hired at short notice from Lady Yule, was described by John Aird as 'furnished rather like a Calais whore-shop'.[20] Its library was thrown out and replaced with a Bacchanalian quantity of drink, and a portable pool was installed on the boat deck. As for the company that assembled, it included, at various points, the Coopers, the Earl of Sefton and his paramour, the married socialite Josephine Armstrong, and Wallis's acquaintance Herman Rogers, along with his wife Katherine: she had encountered the pair during her Chinese sojourn. Lascelles, who accompanied the trip, described it acidly as 'outwardly as respectable as a boatload of archdeacons, but the fact remains that the two chief passengers were cohabiting with other men's wives'.[21] The king and Wallis occupied the best suite at one end of the boat, in separate rooms, while the other guests were expected to make themselves as comfortable as they could in this quasi-Gallic brothel at the other end.

There was soon a tension between the stated purpose of the voyage – a holiday for the king and his friends – and the expectation that a monarch travelling round Europe would perform some diplomatic functions. Thus, even as Edward attempted to preserve his anonymity by calling himself the Duke of Lancaster – a façade that did not last long – his itinerary became encumbered by the obligations of a head of state. Hardinge bemoaned that 'The King, in complying with [the Foreign Office's] views, found himself engaged in a series of semi-official visits to the countries of Eastern Europe ... It should never have been undertaken on such lines, without the Foreign Secretary being in attendance.'[22]

When he visited Turkey, Edward met its absolute ruler Kemal Atatürk, who drove him to the British embassy in a top-down car and received Wallis with all due attention. Their encounter was, as Atatürk's biographer Lord Kinross described it, 'an exercise in cordial diplomacy to rank with the foreign excursions of his grandfather, King Edward VII',[23] even if the Foreign Office were surprised by Edward blithely inviting the Turkish ruler to London as if asking him to pop in at his club. The king received a similarly warm reception in Athens and Belgrade, where the American minister spoke highly of the visit's effect on national feeling, even as he acknowledged that the king's primary interest was his own enjoyment and that 'the political consideration was an afterthought, albeit an important one'.[24]

Atatürk, who himself led an eventful and exciting romantic life, was struck by how completely in thrall to his American companion the king was. He admired his visitor's 'uncommon charm', as well as his 'simplicity and directness',[25] but feared that the role of ruler was incompatible with that of adoring supplicant. He let it be known to Percy Loraine, the British ambassador, that he was pleased that he had seen Edward in the more informal context of a meeting than the rigmarole of a state visit, but did not expect to encounter him again, as it seemed an almost foregone conclusion that he would have to give up his throne if he persisted in his romance.

The tour continued, and so did the sense of unreality, as the entire holiday took on a strangely theatrical feel. An intimate romantic escape for the king and his mistress was diversified by the presence of a bevy of friends, staff and hangers-on, two destroyers, and tens of thousands of inhabitants of the nations they visited. The royal glamour and charm led to the diplomatic aspect of the trip being a success, and even Hardinge acknowledged that 'The effect of these visits to the Balkan States was undoubtedly - even if only temporarily - good.'[26] The British minister in Vienna, Sir Walford Selby, summarised the mood when he wrote that 'The impression made by His Majesty was reflected in the send-off he had last night. The Ringstrasse was a seething crowd and he was cheered again and again . . . His Majesty met all official needs to a degree which would satisfy his greediest servant.'[27]

Certainly, the novelty of seeing the new king excited the sensibilities of those he encountered on the trip. After being denied the opportunity to dock at Venice by the Foreign Secretary, Anthony Eden - perhaps with memories of McMahon's claims of Italian hostility in mind - the yacht had departed from Šibenik in Croatia on 10 August, accompanied by the vessels the *Grafton* and the *Glowworm*. It was estimated that as many as twenty thousand Croatians greeted them when they arrived at Dubrovnik, with a mighty cry of '*Zivela ljubav!*' which can be loosely translated as 'Hurrah for the lovers!' Wallis, for her part, was pleased that they were being received with such fervour at the first public recognition of them as a couple, saying, with a touch of condescension, 'It delighted both of us that strangers of uncomplicated hearts should wish us well.'[28]

When Diana and Duff Cooper joined the *Nahlin* at Split, she – no possessor of an uncomplicated heart – was able to witness the whole caboodle with a cynical, though not unkind, eye. She wrote to her friend Conrad Russell that the young king was 'radiant in health . . . he [wore] no hat . . . *espadrilles*, the same little shorts and a tiny blue-and-white singlet bought in one of [the Croatian] villages'.*[29] Diana almost immediately became ill with tonsillitis, but recovered in time to see Edward make his regal progress through the streets of Ragusa in Sicily, where the populace 'were cheering their lungs out with looks of ecstasy on their faces'.[30]

He enjoyed the attention – 'the King walks a little ahead, talking deafeningly to the Consul or Mayor, if possible in German, and we follow adoring it'[31] – and Diana observed that he was 'utterly unselfconscious . . . That I think is the reason of why he does some things, that he likes doing, superlatively well, but it means that he can't act, and therefore makes no attempt to do anything he dislikes well.'[32] Edward believed that the world, wherever he was, revolved around him. Diana reported how, in Ragusa, 'In the middle of the procession, he stopped for quite 2 minutes, doing up his shoe. There was a knot, and it took time – we were all left staring at his bottom. You and I would have risen above the lace until the procession was over, wouldn't we, but it did not occur to him, so the people say "Isn't he human? Isn't he natural? He stopped to do up his shoe like any of us!"'[33]

There were soon differences of personality. Diana reported, perhaps with some exaggeration, that 'The King loathes me – but Helen [Fitzgerald],† who I know he likes, feels the same about herself', and calmly shrugged that 'It doesn't grieve me.'[34] As she noted

---

* An expurgated and sanitised account of the voyage – wrongly dated June, rather than August – was published in Diana's autobiography, but the contemporary letters offer a more engaging and vivid tale.
† A friend of Wallis's.

his pettiness, even when it came to ordering drinks – 'Unlike us . . .
he asked, in German and English, for whisky, water, cordial – but
not sparkling – lemon rind, gin, vermouth, ice, and a shaker, &
must make the cocktails himself' – she also observed his complete
lack of self-consciousness: 'How he spoils everyone's fun.' At one
point, he remarked, in a blasé way, 'I think we'll stay here a day or
two, and relax', which led Diana to muse sardonically, 'I longed to
know what we'd been doing the last few days!'[35]

Edward's major activity was pleasing Wallis, who knew her
power over him. They made a strange pair: Edward permanently
eager to accommodate her whims, and she offering her patron-
age with a mixture of *noblesse oblige* and a similar absence of self-
awareness. Diana told Russell of how 'We went [ashore] to discover
a sandy beach for Wallis; [Edward] asked her to go with him, she
said it was too hot. She looked all day a figure of fun, in a child's
piqué dress, [and] a ridiculous baby's bonnet . . . As her face is an
adult's face "par excellence", the silly bonnet looked grotesque.'[36]
Helpfully, she drew an illustration of the bonnet for Russell, which
bore a distinct resemblance to something that the god Hermes
might have donned while off duty. Edward, meanwhile, was ridiculed as 'this hot tow-headed little nude in their midst'. So much
for his regal dignity.

They encountered other royalty on their odyssey, not least the
King of Greece, who Wallis entertained at a formal dinner along
with 'six common English intimates, including a very good-looking
mistress called Mrs Jones'.[37] Mrs Simpson showed her inimitable
skills as a hostess. 'The voice rasping out, the wisecracks following
in quick succession, the King clearly very admiring and amused
– perhaps a little politically so.'[38] The presence of Mrs Jones led
Wallis to ask, with some incredulity, why the Greek king didn't
simply marry her, and it had to be explained to her, as if to a child,
that it was against all conceivable protocol that a ruler could wed a
commoner, and one already married to boot.

Afterwards, Mrs Simpson was 'embarrassing . . . Wallis was very
lit up, successful in all things . . . she'd done well with the foreign

King. She talked everyone's head off . . . [and] the King was fussing over her proudly, going down on hands & knees to pull her dress from under the chair feet.' Things swiftly went awry, as Diana and the others were treated to a first-hand display of the power dynamic within their relationship. 'She stared at him as one would a freak, [saying] "well that's the *maust* extraordinary performance I've ever seen", and then she started picking on him for having been silent & rude to Mrs Jones.' It was quite a performance – 'On and on she went, till I began to think he had perhaps talked too long & too animatedly to Mrs Jones.' Edward 'got a little irritated and sad', and Diana left, 'almost in protest, knowing it was not going to be dropped all night'.[39]

The following day, still feeling unwell, Diana encountered Wallis 'in a sulky humour', and she soon shared her feelings that the voyage had not been a happy one. 'I felt the sooner the trip ended for us, the better . . . It's impossible to enjoy antiquities with people who won't land for them and who call Delphi Delhi. Wallis is wearing very very badly. Her commonness and her Becky Sharpishness irritate.'[40] After one of the ship's captains was injured in an accident off Delphi, Diana saw how pathetic Edward could be in adversity. Even as she allowed that he was 'greatly upset', she reported how he said, 'I've told them not to worry about us if we're delayed, it doesn't matter a bit. I thought that's what you'd like me to say, Wallis. Of course Wallis has always been perfectly right about motor boats – you've always said they were dangerous, haven't you?' With understandable weariness, Wallis replied, 'Yes sir, I have.'[41]

Diana's comments about the cruise have to be taken with some caution as a wholly accurate record of the event. She was writing to entertain as much as to inform, and some of her complaints, not least the £15 she was expected to fork out in tips ('That could not happen in a hotel, far less in a country house, least of all staying with a King – I hope it staggers you'),[42] seem dictated by weariness and torpor brought on by a mixture of the heat and illness. Yet her first-hand account of the relationship between Edward and Wallis has a valuable immediacy lacking from more prolix descriptions of their love affair. As Ziegler puts it, 'Diana Cooper was a highly sensible and intelligent woman, and her attitude towards the Windsors was an accurate one. Her husband took a very informed interest in the whole thing, and between them, they got it more or less right.'[43]

Her instinct was that, rather than witnessing two people very much in the throes of passion, Edward had made himself look ridiculous and small – very much 'the little man' – by his infatuation, and Wallis was growing weary of the entanglement, not least because she had now realised that she was at risk of becoming a subject of international fascination herself. As Diana wrote, after a further outbreak of temper caused by Wallis refusing to go bathing, 'The truth is she's bored stiff by him, and her picking on him and her coldness towards him, far from policy, are irritation and boredom.'[44] Duff had already decided of Wallis as far back as January that 'She is a nice woman and a sensible woman – but she is hard as nails and doesn't love him.'[45] Chips Channon was surprised to find Cooper, after he returned to England, 'revolted by the King's selfish stupidity',[46] and, along with his wife, thoroughly sceptical about the likelihood – even the possibility – of a marriage between two such obviously mismatched people.

Others were equally unimpressed. Sir Sydney Waterlow, the British ambassador in Greece, wrote to Hardinge on 1 September; Lascelles later appended a note to the letter that 'This seems, in retrospect, to me a very shrewd diagnosis.' Waterlow, while acknowledging that 'You will see from my official dispatches that the visit has been a great success', nonetheless sighed, 'I am left with a certain feeling of depression ... made up partly of uneasiness as to the ultimate results of our prestige abroad if the King should persist in being surrounded on his travels by ... people of little or no standing (I was very sorry that the Duff Coopers had to leave halfway through the stay at Athens) and partly of the effect produced on me by the atmosphere of the jaunt; which was of an almost unbelievable vapidity, quite without any taint of raffishness indeed, but equally with no dignity and no spark of intelligent interest in anything seen or heard.'

Waterlow had the opportunity to take a long mountain walk with the king, and noted that 'It seemed to me that his character is in an unformed and fluid state - almost a case of arrested development* - with great possibilities for good, which may be lost without some strong, sympathetic & womanly understanding. Influence can be brought to bear which, without imposing itself, would canalise the energy now going to waste in a restless treasure-hunt that brings no satisfaction (he is so obviously, and pathetically, worried, anxious, pre-occupied all the time) & help him to build up some sort of central control. Otherwise I should say that, lacking the usual background of educated people (I hadn't before realised how completely this is absent), he will find less and less satisfaction in himself as time goes on, and that this, combined with his great native obstinacy, will open up the possibility of serious trouble.'

The ambassador was fair-minded about Edward - 'There is something appealing about him - something really charming & good, with much good intention' - but he despaired of his companion. 'The moment one sees them together it *sauté aux yeux*† that Mrs S is essentially the response to his craving [for domesticity], and, I think, a serious response. For that reason, and also because it was borne in on me that they are temperamentally well-matched, I was left with a quite definite impression that she has come to stay.' He was unimpressed by Wallis: 'The problem must be hopeless; for the characteristic marks of this type of American female are precisely those which ... must aggravate the situation - perpetual restlessness and a vacuum as complete as that of the prairie or small town from which it originally descends. What can be hoped from mating restlessness with restlessness, vacuum with vacuum?'

Waterlow concluded his 'indiscreet remarks' by writing, in a

---

* This was vigorously underlined by Lascelles.
† Meaning 'it will be obvious'.

determined spirit of optimism, 'I shouldn't like to say, from my brief glimpses of her, whether anything of this tough, bleak, unsophisticated moral American stain, so alien to our own standards, so unintelligible, persists in this particular little person; but I did distinctly "take" to her, I fully understand HM falling for her, and I ended by wondering whether this union, however queer & generally unsuitable & embarrassing for the State, may not in the long run turn out to be more in harmony with the spirit of the new age than anything that Britain could have contrived.'[47] Months before the abdication crisis tore the monarchy apart, this diagnosis was shrewd, accurate and prescient. Had the sentiments in it been acted upon in time, the results could have been very different.

During the cruise, Edward and Wallis paid little heed to conventional strictures about not being photographed together. Even before they boarded the boat, they wandered around Strasbourg like tourists: prey for anyone who possessed a camera and fancied making a few pounds from the papers. Wallis found it irksome, complaining to her Aunt Bessie that 'It ruins exploring and closely resembles the Pied Piper.'[48] Yet the English press still retained its discretion. The first picture of Edward was printed by the *Daily Sketch*, owned by Lord Camrose, before its proprietor forbade any more to be published. Beaverbrook, aware of the intense public interest in the king's journey, compromised. His papers, the *Evening Standard* and the *Daily Express*, continued to print pictures of the king, but Mrs Simpson was deliberately omitted from them. As for Lord Rothermere's *Sunday Dispatch*, an edict was given out that no pictures or stories of the *Nahlin*'s voyage were to be published, 'unless these contain matter of proper national interest'.

A rather different attitude was taken by the American press of the day, who took delight in publishing such stories as 'King's Playmate Big Problem to British' and 'All Europe Buzzing Over Mrs Simpson'. Without meaning to, Wallis became a celebrity in America, albeit in the most scandalous of registers. Her expensive clothing and jewellery, her 'friendship' with Edward, and, of course, her two living husbands were spread across supplements and magazines for the public to gawp over, helped by a constant supply of new pictures from the cruise. Whether it was an image of Wallis and Edward in a boat together, with her holding his arm and he gazing adoringly at her, or a photograph of the two of them travelling through Athens together in an open-topped car, any attempt at concealment was set aside, as an excited America bought the latest developments in their romance by, quite literally, the boatload. The *Sunday News* even commented on the absence of information given in British newspapers by tartly observing in its standfirst that 'Only the press fails to see Mrs Simpson, ever at ruler's side.'[49]

It is hard to say whether the lovers were blithely unaware of the attention that their actions had excited, or, in Edward's case at least, whether months of concealment and being expected to play an unaccustomed part had given way to boredom and a desire for transparency. Yet he remained king, whereas Wallis, for all the favour that she had been granted, was still a commoner, and one subject to the vagaries of public opinion. Thus, when the cruise came to an end on 14 September, and Edward returned to England from Zurich, Wallis arrived at Le Meurice hotel in Paris to be made uncomfortably aware of the press coverage about her. She later claimed to be 'distressed and shocked' at how her actions were 'a topic of dinner-table conversation for every newspaper reader in the United States, Europe and the Dominions'.[50]

It is impossible not to feel some sympathy for her. She did not reciprocate Edward's grand passion for her, and began to believe that she was trapped within the most gilded of cages. Accordingly, she wrote a 'difficult letter' to the king on the night of 16 September from Paris. Even as she allowed that 'we are so awfully congenial and understand getting on together very well', she stated that 'The possession of beautiful things is thrilling to me and much appreciated but weighed against a calm congenial life I choose the latter.' She made it explicit that she wished to return to Ernest, saying, 'I have the deepest affection and respect for him. I feel I am better with him than with you – and so you must understand.' There is a tacit acceptance of her culpability – 'In a few months your life will run again as it did before and without my nagging' – but also the considered realisation that they could never be truly happy with one another: 'I am sure you and I would only create disaster together.' She ended by saying, 'I am sure that after this letter you will realise that no human being could assume this responsibility and it would be most unfair to make things harder for me by seeing me. Good-bye WE.'[51]

A man more committed to his crown might have accepted the inevitable parting of the ways, and also been grateful for the opportunity to avoid any further scandal. Yet Edward, who had had a similar conversation over the telephone with her, simply refused to acknowledge Wallis's concerns. He wrote to her as if he were a petulant small child – 'Why do you say such hard things to David on the telephone sometimes?' – and seemed to blame her clear-sighted wish to end their relationship on an illness that she was suffering from. As he gushed, 'I do love you so entirely and in every way, Wallis. Madly tenderly adoringly and with admiration and such confidence',[52] as well as coining the nauseating nickname 'pooky demus' for her, there was also a darker and more histrionic side displayed. Lascelles believed that the immediate effect of receiving her letter was for him to threaten suicide unless she joined him at Balmoral.

She accepted the inevitable. She had tried to escape from an intense and claustrophobic entanglement, but without success. If she had read Evelyn Waugh's A Handful of Dust, published two years previously, she might have felt some sympathy with the ultimate predicament of its protagonist Tony Last, who ends up marooned in a remote part of South America, fated to read Dickens every day to a madman, without hope of rescue. Wallis had a rather more pleasant existence, but she had no more chance of flight than Tony Last did. It was with resignation, then, that she read the Court Circular on 24 September, which announced her arrival at Balmoral the previous day. She was given the best spare bedroom, with

Edward occupying an adjoining room, doubtless for the late-night cups of cocoa that both enjoyed.

The king, then, had triumphed. He had once again reassured himself of the commitment of his beloved mistress, who he hoped could still become his wife; had enjoyed a lavish holiday during which he had been able to behave as if he were still Prince of Wales while simultaneously being hailed as a consummate ambassador for Britain; and could now set about his reforming plans for his country with renewed energy and commitment. Even Queen Mary did not create any awkwardness when they met upon his return, with the most pertinent question she asked being 'Didn't you find it terribly warm in the Adriatic?'[53] A less impulsive man could have enjoyed the status quo for the moment, and behaved with greater discretion. Yet this was not in Edward's character. As he wrote in his memoirs, 'I flew home . . . to deal with a personal problem which it had become increasingly clear could not be held much longer in abeyance.'[54]

This problem, and its resolution, would occupy the remainder of his brief reign.

Chapter Five

'Power Without Responsibility'

Throughout the thirties, any society host or hostess who knew their claret from their Beaujolais would invite the author Osbert Sitwell to their table, and during 1936 he was one of London's most popular guests. Although his most recent book, 1935's *Penny Foolish*, was subtitled 'a book of tirades and panegyrics', the witty and charming Sitwell was an invaluable addition to any gathering. His quips, carefully honed throughout many of these evenings, were barbed enough to nick the skin, but never any more. As a consequence, he was considered the most desirable of house visitors, even if he felt himself, in T. S. Eliot's words, to be 'Full of high sentence, but a bit obtuse.'[1]

Sitwell chafed against his 'safe' reputation, although usually behind closed doors. He had begun his writing career with experimental poetry and satirical novels such as 1925's *Before the Bombardment*, but he had been subsumed into a middlebrow world of popular biographies and respectable journalism. Even as he willingly sang for his lavish suppers, wearing his 'blank, bland mask',[2] at the salons of the likes of Margaret 'Aunt Maggie' Greville, one of the best-connected women in London, he stored up resentments against those he considered patronising towards him. The man who topped his list of grievances was the king.

The two had served together in the Brigade of Guards at the close of World War I, where Sitwell wrote pacifist-leaning poetry for the likes of the *Spectator* and the *Nation*, much to the then prince's contempt; Sitwell wrote of his 'cold blue eye reflecting disapproval'.[3] It was equally the case that as his career continued, Edward remained a disappointment to his fellow officer. Sitwell lamented that the prince had not 'desired to break away from the traditional court circle of those who bore the historic names of England', and never 'surrounded himself with poets, painters and musicians', but instead took his company from those the author sardonically ridiculed as 'the Golden Horde' and 'the Fun Brigade'.[4]

Edward was not an intellectual. Sitwell mocked him for how he would produce 'the same opening sentences, obviously prepared beforehand and carefully calculated to interest . . . [Lady Desborough] his hostess, whom he knew to be a discriminating amateur of literature'. Unfortunately, this took the form of the prince enthusiastically saying, 'I'm reading *such* an interesting novel. I think it would appeal to you: it's called *Dracula*!'[5] This echoed John Simon's judgement that '[Edward] read nothing of weight or value.'[6] Sitwell was similarly dismissive of Ernest Simpson – 'an outrageous bounder . . . unconsciously dressed for the part for which nature had so plainly cast him' – and Wallis, who he sneered at for having been 'the mistress of a Chinese [man] . . . in search of local colour' during her time in Beijing, and for having 'induced King Edward to take up an attitude of coldness, and sometimes of rudeness, to [Queen Mary]'.[7]

Sitwell disliked the 'dull and unpleasant' couple, but he reserved equal contempt for the 'riff-raff of two continents' with whom Edward had sailed on the *Nahlin* and who now holidayed at Balmoral with him. He vigorously ridiculed them as 'a wisecracking team of smartish, middle-aged, semi-millionaire Americans, with the usual interchangeable names, and over-life-size faces, customarily to be seen in bars and in hotels in Paris and the South of France – the rootless spawn of New York, Cracow, Antwerp and the Mile End Road . . . never a doubt except of their own position, and continual loud laughs bottled in alcohol and always on tap'.[8] He went so far as to ask his friend, the novelist Michael Arlen, 'whether the British Empire is to be governed from Buckingham Palace, Westminster and Whitehall, or from the Ritz Bar in Paris'.

Later in 1936, Sitwell summoned up some of his youthful vigour to write a scathing satire on Edward, Wallis and their circle, *Rat Week*. It was never published in his lifetime, for fear both of libel and of destroying the reputation that he had acquired as 'a good guest'. Yet it has an anger and charge to its specific accusations that make it a fascinating contemporary account of those whom Edward and Wallis chose to spend their days with.

The fascist sympathiser Emerald Cunard habitually referred to the king as 'Majesty Divine' – noted with contempt by Sitwell – and Lady Colefax, 'a beige-looking product, with an indeterminate skin [and] beige eyes that looked like knapped flints', was jeered at for her 'iron cage of curls'.[9] The king's friend Johnny McMullen, former editor of *Vogue* magazine, was said to have been 'engaged for the past few decades in a hopeless struggle to look young [and] be amusing' and so had kitted himself out with 'a great many false teeth, glass eyes, and even, it was said, artificial limbs [in] his careful presentation of himself'.[10]

It was Sitwell's contention that this 'nameless, faceless, raucous gang' were a series of Falstaffian figures, guzzling and quaffing for all they were worth, and ridiculing the king and Wallis when they were not paying enthusiastic lip service to their efforts to be sophisticated. Edward's attempts to play the pipes were mocked by Sitwell, as they had been by Diana Cooper, as he asserted that 'Even the most musical/Admired the bagpipes' horrid skirl/When played with royal cheeks outblown/And royal feet tramping up and down.'[11] He wrote of how the 'gay, courageous, pirate crew' believed the king to be nothing more than 'weak, and obstinate and vain', and devoid of either taste or breeding; a charge, naturally, that could be levelled, with interest, at all of these habitués of the Ritz Bar.

Sitwell sneered at the 'jolly crew' gracing 'Balmoral's Coburg towers', in which they 'danced to the gramophone'.[12] This proved to be a mild description of what occurred at Edward's Scottish seat when he, Wallis and their friends arrived there in September 1936. Some aspects of Sitwell's description were tainted by anti-Americanism, but nonetheless the Balmoral visit was a largely disastrous one, as Aird had anticipated when he wrote, 'Heard today that W is to be at Balmoral. Thank God I shall not be there.'[13] Rather than the usual dignitaries who would have been expected to be present, such as the Archbishop of Canterbury and the prime minister, the king instead decided to invite his friends for what he described as 'my first house-party'.

As with so much in his reign, his arrogant carelessness saw the holiday begin terribly. Edward decided to eschew his royal responsibility to open the new Aberdeen Infirmary on 23 September in favour of driving to the station to collect Wallis, on the spurious grounds that he was still in official mourning for his father. The Aberdeen *Evening Express* pointedly juxtaposed the headline 'HIS MAJESTY IN ABERDEEN SURPRISE VISIT IN CAR TO MEET GUESTS' with the picture of the royals who had been dragooned into undertaking the responsibility instead, despite the theoretical period of mourning: the Duke and Duchess of York, Bertie and Elizabeth. Helen Hardinge moaned that 'if this was to be the pattern of his future conduct, then the outlook was infinitely depressing',[14] and her husband called it 'folly ... an act which antagonized at a blow the whole of Scotland'.[15] The Scots dealt with the snub in robust fashion. The citizens of Aberdeen chalked their walls with the slogan 'Down with the American harlot!'

Edward at least had one constant counsellor in Bertie, his younger brother and heir presumptive. Even as he chafed against the influence of his father, George V, the king acknowledged that Bertie was 'in outlook and temperament very much like my father ... with the steady swing of habit taking them both year after year to the same places at the same time and with the same associates'.[16] While Edward's younger brothers, Prince George, Duke of Kent, and Prince Henry, Duke of Gloucester, were, respectively, a hedonistic libertine whose licentious existence was only checked by his death in wartime and an amiable but drunken nonentity best known for his affair with the aviator Beryl Markham,* Bertie was a decent and principled man whom Edward envied, despite his debilitating stammer and the pronounced sense of shyness that resulted from it. His father wrote to him that 'You have always been so sensible & easy to work with & you have always been ready to listen to any advice . . . I feel that we have always got on very well together (very different to dear David).'[17]

Edward initially placed inordinate faith in Bertie's judgement. He insisted, perhaps in an attempt to share the burden, that his brother was kept abreast of all relevant court papers and matters of state. Yet this trust did not extend to his dealings with Wallis. The two brothers, who had hitherto been close, began to drift apart. The Duke of York had a happy domestic life with his beloved wife and daughters, Elizabeth and Margaret; the king did not. Sometimes their different approaches caused tension. After their visit to Aberdeen, the duke and duchess stayed at nearby Birkhall. Aware that the Archbishop of Canterbury should have been invited to Balmoral, they took it upon themselves to invite him to their home instead, in what was either a generous gesture of friendship or a calculated rebuke to the king, depending on one's interpretation.

As a result, the relationship between the two brothers grew distant. Helen Hardinge wrote, 'The situation at Balmoral had been like a nightmare . . . [Bertie] felt that he had lost a friend and was rapidly losing a brother.'[18] His useful grasp of protocol was especially missed. Hardinge had attempted to explain to Wallis, early on in the holiday, that regardless of whether she eventually married Edward, 'certain things would not be acceptable', such as

---

* His youngest brother, Prince John, who suffered from epilepsy, died in 1919, aged 13. He has been described as the 'Lost Prince'. His sister Mary remained close to him after the abdication, often to the chagrin of the rest of the family, but her limited role within these pages reflects the lack of agency that a female royal faced in this era.

her becoming queen. As Helen wrote sadly, 'Such things did not seem to penetrate her mind.'[19] A mistake that Wallis had made* was to assume that the king somehow occupied a similar position as the President of the United States, without being subject to the necessity of democratic elections. A by-product of her error was to believe that she herself was second only to Edward in terms of standing in the country, and possibly not even that.

This misapprehension was exposed in the most awkward of fashions on 26 September, when the Yorks visited Balmoral for dinner. There was some residual ill-will already, both because of the Aberdeen incident a few days before, and because Edward had shown no previous interest in visiting or maintaining Balmoral. This led Bertie to write, 'I do hope he will realise that he must go slow, as he does not know anything or anybody . . . I do think it such a pity that David will never listen to anybody.'[20] Yet Wallis made the situation markedly worse through a mixture of her own carelessness and arrogance. Precedent and etiquette dictated that visiting royalty should and could only be welcomed by the official host, namely Edward, but Wallis took it upon herself to greet the Duchess of York when she entered the Balmoral drawing room, in what one onlooker called 'a deliberate and calculated display of power'.[21]

Wallis had already made her influence known in Scotland, albeit in relatively minor ways, such as sending Edward off like a servant to fetch champagne while she played bridge, and by demanding that the kitchens serve a new American invention of chicken and bacon in toasted bread: a club sandwich. He continued to hand her confidential papers to read in full view of the other guests, and, as the Earl and Countess of Rosebery remarked, 'All her judgements were acclaimed by him with ecstatic admiration.'[22] However, as the Duchess of York stood in front of her that evening, it was soon made clear to Wallis that not everyone was as subservient as the King of England. Elizabeth pointedly ignored the interloper, saying

---

* As had Ribbentrop and Hitler.

'as if to no one in particular', 'I came to dine with the King', and her intervention had the desired effect. Edward, looking 'rather startled', extricated himself from his nearby conversation and the evening proceeded in a smoother fashion, even if Bertie was 'embarrassed and very nervous' at the clash.[23]

Even as Edward later wrote of this eleven-day sojourn at Balmoral as a glorious time ('Despite the rumblings abroad, life within the castle was extremely pleasant . . . My guests enjoyed themselves as much as I did')[24] and took pride in being the first member of the royal family to play the bagpipes there, others had had a more uncomfortable experience. The Duchess of York wrote to Queen Mary to say that despite the clement weather, 'there has been a great sadness and sense of loss for us and all the people. It will never quite be the same for us . . . David does not seem to possess the faculty of making others feel *wanted* . . . I feel that the whole difficulty is a certain person. I do not feel that I *can* make advances to her and ask her to our house, as I imagine would be liked . . . The whole situation is complicated and *horrible*.'[25] Almost without knowing or caring, Edward had managed to estrange himself from his entire family. This carelessness would eventually prove catastrophic.

On 1 October, the king and Mrs Simpson parted ways, albeit temporarily. After both of them arrived in London – on board the royal train, naturally – she moved into a suite at Claridge's while waiting for a house in Regent's Park to be finished to her specifications. He, more reluctantly, took up residence in Buckingham Palace for the first time in his reign. Queen Mary had spent the previous months moving her household from there to Marlborough House, and once they had gone through the formalities of lunch, Edward was left alone, in a place that he loathed.

It is hard not to feel sympathy for the king as he spent the following days trudging miserably around a palace that he associated with his unhappy youth, and of which he was now the custodian. As he later wrote, 'I took up residence in that vast building without pleasure; the dank, musty smell I had always associated with the building assailed me afresh the instant I set foot inside the King's Door.'[26] He set up camp in the Belgian Suite on the ground floor, named in honour of Queen Victoria's uncle, Leopold I, King of Belgium. It had traditionally been used by visiting kings and queens, and now, as he realised the enormity of the monolithic institution of which he was now part, Edward mused, 'I had a feeling that I might not be there very long.' Defeated by the idea of making any significant additions or flourishes of his own – 'One never tinkers much with palaces; like museums, they seem to resist change' – he later wrote, 'I never got over the feeling of not quite belonging there. I felt lost in its regal immensity.'[27]

In America, meanwhile, the interest engendered by pictures of Wallis on board the *Nahlin* continued. The *New York Times*, regarded as the country's authoritative bastion of contemporary reporting, lived up to its reputation of publishing 'all the news that's fit to print' by running a carefully worded column in its 4 October issue. It described Edward's 'very friendly terms with Mr and Mrs Simpson', and skilfully deployed a series of archly worded euphemisms in its note that Wallis, 'a witty and sparkling conversationalist', shared many interests with the king, not least being 'expert dancers of the tango' and aficionados of 'hot jazz'. It slyly revealed her presence at Fort Belvedere most weekends by describing their keen mutual passion for gardening, and declared that 'The world which knew him so well as the Prince of Wales should not have been taken by surprise at his desire, as King, to have around him people of the same democratic type.'[28]

This stately respect was not shared by titles such as the *New York Woman* and the *World-Telegram*, which delighted in publishing stories with headlines like 'The Yankee at King Edward's Court' and tantalised its readers with gossip about Queen Mary disapproving of Wallis and how Edward had bestowed £200,000 worth of jewellery upon her. Simpson's first wife was tracked down, and obligingly gave hungry journalists the damning quote that 'The present Mrs Simpson has enough of "what it takes" to steal a man.'[29]

The stories made excellent financial sense; the 8 October issue of the *New York Woman* alone sold 100,000 copies to Wallis's insatiably curious countrymen.

As a result of this publicity, disgruntled expatriates began writing letters to the *New York Times*. One lengthy epistle, from G. W. Johnson of New Jersey, complained that 'The doings of the King, as reported in the American press, have in the course of a few months transformed Great Britain, as envisaged by the average American, from a sober and dignified realm into a dizzy Balkan musical comedy attuned to the rhythm of Jazz.' After noting that the King, 'a hopeless case [and] an irresponsible jazz-mad cocktail shaker', was regarded as 'a pitiful and bemused lover who is completely enslaved by Mrs Simpson's charms', Johnson concluded that 'The really serious, even tragic aspect of the affair is not so much what is said of the King as an individual but what repercussions these stories have upon the international scene.'

He pithily summarised the situation by writing, 'George V was an invaluable asset to British prestige abroad; Edward VIII has proved himself an incalculable liability', and concluded: 'Nothing would please me more [than] to hear that Edward VIII had abdicated his rights in favour of the Heir Presumptive, who I am confident would be prepared to carry on in the sterling tradition established by his father . . . [This should happen] before the disquiet has progressed to the point of calling in question the institution of monarchy itself.'[30]

Nor was this interest confined to America. Nicolson wrote in his diary on 6 October of an evening with Sibyl Colefax, amongst others, where the Balmoral trip was discussed. It was widely felt to have been an error of judgement ('there is a fine old row on') and Sibyl remarked that 'Up until last July, there was no indiscretion at all . . . Wallis seemed really to understand the responsibility of her position. But since the *Nahlin*, things have gone more recklessly.' Wallis's many ostentations ('the new house in Regent's Park') were bemoaned, and Robin Maugham even presciently stated, 'The whole thing is really serious and will shake the foundations

of monarchy.' For his own part, Nicolson professed himself saddened, 'since I like Wallis Simpson and why should she not have a
love affair with her white-eyed coon if she wants?'* Nonetheless,
recognising that the king's intimates were unwilling to intercede
with him, Nicolson acknowledged 'there is seething criticism
which may develop into actual discontent'.[31]

Wallis and Edward were briefly reunited for the weekend of
9 October, when they visited the Fort together, and then she was
bound for an altogether less salubrious destination, namely the
small coastal town of Felixstowe in Suffolk, where lodgings had
been temporarily arranged for her. It was an unpleasant change
from the finest hotels in Europe and Balmoral. As she wrote,
'There is nothing drearier than a seaside town after the season.'[32]
Her divorce hearing from Ernest had been set for 27 October
at the Ipswich Assizes, both for reasons of convenience – the
London courts were full until well into 1937 – and to avoid the
attention that would have accompanied a hearing in the capital.
A hundred years before, Edward might have got his wish, but the
advent of motor cars and trains meant that Ipswich was nearly as
easily accessible from Fleet Street as the Chancery courts would
have been. Wallis would be represented by Theodore Goddard
and one of England's most celebrated and flamboyant barristers,
Norman Birkett. As Goddard's clerk Robert Egerton wrote, 'if you
wanted to rake up all the dirt, you briefed Sir Patrick [Hastings]
and if you wanted the case conducting in a dignified manner, you
briefed Birkett.'[33]

The king and Wallis regarded the divorce differently. For him,
it was no more than another chore to be dealt with. He wished
to marry her before his planned coronation date of 12 May 1937,
and, after a statutory period of six months had elapsed, he would
be able to achieve his aim by the end of April the following year.

---

* The use of what is traditionally a racial slur to describe Edward is surprising.
Either Nicolson is making some sly point regarding his interest in jazz, or there
is an altogether different allusion being made. In any case, the line was omitted
from Nicolson's published diaries.

She, however, felt an encroaching sense of doom and misery, knowing that what little privacy she still maintained would be inexorably stripped from her. On 14 October, she wrote to Edward from Felixstowe – still using Claridge's writing paper – to plead for clemency. Saying, 'This is really more than you or I bargained for', she suggested that '[the divorce] will hurt your popularity in the country.' She informed him that at one cinema, the traditional performance of 'God Save the King' had been enlivened by a wag shouting, 'And Mrs Simpson!' Once again, she asked him, 'Isn't it best for me to steal quietly away?' and added poignantly, 'I feel like an animal in a trap . . . Together I suppose we are strong enough to face this mean world – but separated I feel eanum* and scared for you.'[34] She also knew that without bodyguards and an ever-vigilant police force watching her every move, she was more vulnerable than Edward, and ended the letter by observing, 'I might easily have a brick thrown at my car.'[35]

Both Wallis and Edward understood the fickleness of public opinion. The crowds who had assembled a couple of months before in Europe, cheering their every appearance and shouting, '*Vive l'amour!*', were not very different to the king's own subjects. The mob was tolerable, even likeable, when in good-hearted spirits, but if they were to turn on the monarch and his concubine, then all the bodyguards in the world could not save them. It was the media of the day that was responsible for fermenting approval or disapproval, and the all-powerful barons who owned the papers could direct the populace, far more than any politician or churchman, into either hearty bellows of approval or equally lusty shouts of anger, merely with a few well-chosen words blaring out of their front covers.

The king's reaction, therefore, was not to consider abandoning or even delaying the divorce, but instead to ensure that it received as little publicity as it could. On 16 October, the day after he received Wallis's letter, he met Beaverbrook at Buckingham Palace.

---

* Her term for 'uncertain and frightened'.

There had been none of the usual circumlocution that court etiquette demanded. He had called the newspaper magnate directly on 13 October and asked for his counsel, effectively saying 'name your own time' when Beaverbrook enquired when might be convenient, which led the latter 'to believe that he was exceedingly anxious for the interview'.[36] Ziegler argues that 'The only person who Edward listened to was Beaverbrook - if he had said to the King, "you are making a ghastly mistake, you must stop and think about this", then it might have sunk in. He may not have accepted his advice, but he would have listened to it.'[37]

After delaying his visit for a couple of days - he pleaded toothache, but a meeting with Ernest Simpson on 15 October suggests otherwise - Beaverbrook found Edward calmly insistent that he wished to suppress all news coverage relating to Wallis's divorce, both before and after the event. As the king later wrote, 'My one desire was to protect Wallis from sensational publicity',[38] and Beaverbrook concurred, ensuring, in association with Edward's friend Esmond Harmsworth, the chairman of the Newspaper Proprietors Association, that the British press would operate under an unusual and significant amount of discretion when it came to the impending divorce.* Yet Edward offered no hint to Beaverbrook, or anyone else, that he wished to marry Wallis, and thereby spark a constitutional crisis.

The man who should have known about such a plan was Stanley Baldwin, who had resumed parliamentary duties in mid-October after taking two months' rest following the end of the summer session. His aide (or *éminence grise*, if his enemies were to be

---

* This was despite a document sent to Special Branch on 23 October 1936 by the chief constable of the Metropolitan Police, which suggested that 'It is being said in Fleet Street that Mrs Simpson encourages photographers to take pictures when she is with the King, because it satisfies her vanity and provides a means of developing certain commercial undertakings in which she and her friends are interested directly or indirectly.' If accurate, Wallis anticipated the complicity of minor celebrities with the popular press by several decades.

believed) Sir Horace Wilson - a man who was said to hold power 'unequalled by any member of the Cabinet' - wrote that 'During the summer of 1936, the Prime Minister became increasingly anxious about the King's association with Mrs Simpson', although without firm proof of such an association, Baldwin was left to hope that 'the traditional instincts of the Royal Family would come to the King's aid . . . [and] that the only course open to him was to do his utmost to be that King which the people of this country had come to expect'.[39]

While it had become clear that Edward's obsession with Wallis made this unlikely, Baldwin was occupied with other matters, such as the outbreak of the Spanish Civil War and continued tensions with Germany. These, coupled with his delicate health and a natural reluctance to pry too deeply into his sovereign's private life, meant that the king's affair seemed only a modest cause for concern. Hardinge went so far as to write that 'It was seemingly impossible to persuade him to address his mind at all to the serious situation which we, who were in the King's personal service, knew to be developing.' Still, as Hardinge admitted, 'No constitutional issue could arise as long as Mrs Simpson remained married to Mr Simpson.'[40]

Nonetheless, on 12 October, Wilson and Baldwin discovered that both written and oral accounts of Edward's activities - including 'the most unfavourable comment throughout Scotland'[41] as a result of his snubbing his royal duties to collect Wallis from Aberdeen station - were highly critical of the king. While Baldwin understood that 'before very long, public opinion would be provoked to an outburst', his intentions of investigating the matter further were superseded by a summons to an audience with His Majesty. On this occasion, the matter was routine, with Edward inquiring solicitously about his prime minister's health, but when Hardinge was informed by the Press Association on 15 October about Wallis's impending divorce case, he begged Baldwin to intercede with Edward and see if there was any possibility of halting proceedings, as well as ensuring that their entanglement should not be so public in the future: no more Court Circular appearances.

It was Hardinge, rather than Baldwin, who made the running in arranging the next interview between the two, telling Edward that the prime minister needed an audience 'on an important and urgent matter'. He had already informed Baldwin on 14 October that 'in my opinion the day would come when [the PM] would have to intervene and he agreed, though he said that he hoped to stave it off until after the Coronation', something that he returned to a few days later, saying that '[you are] the only person who could intervene with effect – that intervention would have to come sooner or later, and that the longer it was left the more serious it would be . . . I suggest that [you] ask . . . that divorce proceedings should be stopped [and] that in future the association should not be flaunted in public.'[42]

The king, who was shooting at Sandringham, was irritated by the interruption, and initially demanded Baldwin's presence in Norfolk, before being advised by Hardinge that this might cause 'undesirable gossip'. Thus, with ill grace, he returned to Fort Belvedere, where he and Baldwin met at 10 a.m. on 20 October. It was the first of eight occasions on which the two would meet in the last few months of 1936, and established the pattern on which the subsequent, increasingly charged, encounters would take place.

The two men were so distinct from one another as to represent different eras. Baldwin was a wealthy industrialist who had been involved in politics for decades. He first became an MP in 1908 and had already served as prime minister twice before under George V. He was a mild-mannered, avuncular figure, known as 'Honest Stan' and in the One Nation tradition of the Conservative Party. Ziegler describes him as 'a thoroughly honourable, decent, limited, unimaginative man – on the whole he was a good thing'.[43] Conscientious and fair-minded, he had nevertheless made implacable enemies of Beaverbrook and Lord Rothermere, the *Daily Mail*'s proprietor (and Esmond Harmsworth's father), whose publications he had criticised in 1930 as 'not newspapers in the ordinary acceptance of the term . . . [but] engines of propaganda for the constantly changing policies, desires, personal wishes, personal likes and personal dislikes of two men'. In a devastating line written by his cousin Rudyard Kipling, he railed against their proprietors by claiming their desire was 'power without responsibility, the prerogative of the harlot throughout the ages'. The slight would not be forgotten.

At this stage, the sovereign and his prime minister conversed in an affable enough fashion. Edward recalled that his visitor was 'friendly, casual and discursive' and that 'he might have been a neighbour who had called to discuss a dispute over a boundary fence'.[44] This was intentional. As Wilson wrote, Baldwin felt that more would be achieved if he talked 'as [Edward's] friend and as one who knew that the King had confidence in him, in his friendship and his judgement'.[45] A nervous Baldwin asked for a whisky, to Edward's undisguised surprise - 'I never take a drink before seven o'clock in the evening'[46] - and then the two reluctantly discussed the urgent matter that had brought them together.

Their recollections of the conversation differed. Edward recalled contemptuously that Baldwin seemed 'not so much a generous Prime Minister trying to help his sovereign through a personal situation of almost indescribable complexity as . . . a political Procrustes determined to fit his regal victim into the iron bed of convention'.*[47] Baldwin, who subsequently gave the House of Commons his own account of their encounter, stressed how much he liked Edward as both his ruler and a man, and, while acknowledging that 'you might think me Victorian' with his outdated views, told him, 'I believe I know how to interpret the minds of our own people . . . [they expect] a higher standard from their King. People are talking about you and this American woman, Mrs Simpson. I

---

* Procrustes was a bandit and blacksmith who, in Greek mythology, was notorious for lengthening or shortening his victims' legs so as to fit them to the length of an iron bed. He was eventually killed in the same fashion by Theseus. The erudition of the allusion reminds one that the Duke of Windsor - and his ghostwriter Charles J. V. Murphy - produced a royal memoir (to date, the only one written by a king) of considerable literary sophistication and interest.

have had many nasty letters written by people who respected your father but who don't like the way you are going on.'[48]

Edward and Baldwin spoke for an hour, with the prime minister doing most of the talking. He stressed that 'there would be a risk of factions growing up in a matter where no factions ought ever to exist', and that 'the risk would be intensely increased by the institution of Mrs Simpson's divorce proceedings'.[49] The king dealt with the interview with a mixture of charm, condescension and boredom, until it dawned on him that Baldwin's real object was to persuade him to prevail upon Wallis to withdraw her divorce petition.

For Baldwin was no naïve blunderer. Noting his sovereign's lack of engagement, he deliberately used one of Edward's own much-loved phrases, 'I don't believe you can go on like this and get away with it', which shocked his interlocutor. When the king asked, indignantly, 'What do you mean, not get away with it?', Baldwin replied, 'I think I know our people. They'll tolerate a lot in public life, but they will not stand for this sort of thing in the life of a public personage, and when they read in the Court Circular of Mrs Simpson's visit to Balmoral they resented it.'[50]

Edward's response was that Wallis was his friend, and that he did not wish to sneak her in by the back door, but saw nothing to be ashamed of. This was at odds with his saying of his belle that 'She wore such a look of beauty as . . . might have lighted the face of a young knight who had caught a glimpse of the holy grail',[51] and that 'She is the only woman in this world; I cannot live without her.'[52] Nonetheless, he asked the prime minister whether he had not carried out his duties – his onerous, personally tiring duties – with suitably regal dignity.

Baldwin acknowledged that he had, but that matters were heading for a point of no return, where the press's silence could not hold and where gossip and tittle-tattle would become accepted fact. At last, breaking with politeness, he asked 'almost bluntly', 'Cannot you have this coming divorce put off?'[53] Edward was angered by this impertinence, but attempted to hide his irritation beneath his usual suavity, saying, 'I have no right to interfere with the affairs of an individual. It would be wrong were I to attempt to influence Mrs Simpson just because she happens to be a friend of the King's.'[54] This was a lie. Baldwin, realising that a breakthrough was not imminent, prepared to end the interview and urged Edward to persuade Wallis to go into temporary exile for six months or so, to which the king did not respond. He later recalled that he was surprised Baldwin did not ask him as to his intention to marry Wallis once she was divorced.

The two men parted with some innocuous conversation about the best way to replant a herbaceous border, but no seeds of mutual comprehension had been effectively sown. Baldwin initially believed that his veiled warnings had made some impact, but Wilson learned afterwards that Edward let it be known to his intimates that they had had a friendly chat, 'and that so far from endeavouring to oppose the King's wishes, the Prime Minister had shown every sympathy with the King's personal difficulties'.[55] Little wonder that Wilson was 'much perturbed' at what he heard Edward saying after the interview, as 'it did not seem to square at all with what the Prime Minister had told me he had said to the King'.[56] Edward had won this particular round. As he later wrote, 'Rising to leave, [Baldwin] mentioned something about being glad the ice had been broken . . . It was on the tip of my tongue to say that so far as I could see, the only ice that had been broken had long since melted in his drink . . . but Mr Baldwin's sense of humour being intermittent and unpredictable, I thought better of it.'[57]

The prime minister now realised, with Wallis's divorce hearing imminent, that tact and diplomacy alone – to say nothing of simple truth – would not sway his monarch. Hardinge wrote that 'the Prime Minister spoke with frankness, though it would not appear as if the danger to be apprehended from any suggestion of marriage was sufficiently emphasized. In any case the warning was completely disregarded, and the divorce allowed to proceed.'[58] Yet there was a tough determination underneath the romance. As sovereign and premier parted, with only a week to go before 'the royal whore' obtained her divorce, Edward made his position clear in a manner that was as much threat as command. 'You and I must settle this matter together. I will not have anyone interfering.'[59]

Chapter Six

'The Most Serious Crisis of My Life'

Sir Anthony Hawke was in a bad temper. The sixty-seven-year old former politician and High Court judge was suffering from a cold on the morning of 27 October 1936, which placed him in an unsettled state, but his ill health was as nothing compared to the bafflement with which he greeted the hoopla that had begun to take place outside his courtroom at Ipswich County Hall. Despite the elaborate planning that had gone into the arrangements for the day, nobody had bothered to inform him of the upheaval his court would face, and so practically the first words he spoke, testily, were 'Why has the case been brought here?'[1]

Mr Justice Hawke may, or may not, have known something of the background to the exceptional divorce case that he was about to undertake, which would set in motion the extraordinary events that dominated the news for the remainder of the year. Yet he had not been a member of the High Court of Justice for the past eight years without acquiring a keen knowledge of both the law and the way in which those who came before him - on both sides of the dock - attempted to manipulate it. Thus there was something amiss, in his eyes, about the smartly presented middle-aged American woman who stood before him, resplendent in an expensive dark navy woollen suit. Her nervousness and unsettled demeanour seemed to suggest that something was very much amiss. She had written to Edward on 14 October to suggest abandoning these divorce proceedings because of the reputational damage that they might cause, and had fretted 'Also I'm terrified that this judge will lose his nerve'. The meaning of this ambiguous sentence may have been that Hawke was approached beforehand to ascertain whether he would grant the decree without undue influence from gossip or rumour, although this would have been done discreetly, if at all.[2]

One reason for Wallis Simpson's trepidation was the baying presence of rabid packs of the international press, who had taken up residence nearby from early morning. The journalists jostled for space outside the courtroom, or as close to it as they could get. The police, knowing the extraordinary situation they had on their hands, had closed St Helen's Street in the town, which immediately adjoined the building where the assizes were to take place, in an attempt to minimise press access to the court. The dozens, or more,* of writers and photographers who had flown, driven or sailed to Ipswich were not to be denied their scoops, however, and managed to get themselves into buildings on St Helen's and nearby Bond Street from early in the morning. Yet despite their best efforts, there was a prevalent sense that day that justice was neither being done nor being seen to be done, but that instead a grubby charade was being enacted with the complicity of the highest in the land, for their own convenience.

Wallis had, unsurprisingly, spent a sleepless night in Felixstowe, from where she was to be conveyed to her place of reckoning. As she wrote in her memoirs, 'I paced the small floor for hours, wondering whether I was doing the right thing, whether my recklessness of consequences had betrayed me, whether I was right in my confidence that what I was about to do would bring no harm to the King.'[3] Early that morning, with appropriate trepidation, she dressed in dark, fashionable clothing, knowing that she would be photographed despite her protector's best efforts, breakfasted lightly and then left Beach House, her home for the previous six weeks. She was met by Edward's chauffeur, George Ladbroke, in

---

* Wallis speculated 'perhaps twenty or so' in her memoirs; this seems an understatement.

a black Buick sedan car, which then whisked her to Ipswich at an impressive speed, outstripping opportunistic photographers who were hoping for a glimpse of the soon-to-be divorcee.

She did not know, in all likelihood, that her imminent court case had been dominating the international press for days, with speculation reaching a climax the day before. According to the news magazine *Cavalcade*, 'Four thousand words . . . were put across the cable to the United States by the Associated Press in the last few days . . . of a story of which not one word was printed in British newspapers.' Wallis was a hot property; a police report stated that 'any information respecting Mrs Simpson finds a ready market in newspaper circles abroad, especially in America'.[4] The *New York American* newspaper announced that it was inevitable that Edward would marry Wallis in eight months' time, and the New York *Daily Mirror* even boasted that she would be married in the Palace, in a photo entitled 'Royal Fiancée'. There was, surely, no correlation intended between that story and another story's adjacent headline, 'RAID RICH VICE NEST'.

John Simon described the American papers' motives concisely. 'A Royal romance interests everybody, but a romance between the King of England and the daughter of the proprietor of a Baltimore boarding-house roused to a frenzy the inhabitants of a Republic dedicated to the proposition that all men are created equal. American editors found that the opportunity for pandering to vulgarity and tuft-hunting snobbery was too good to be lost.'[5] Reporters from the snobbish papers, and dozens of others, were all waiting in Ipswich for Wallis's arrival, and desperately hoping for some piece of scurrilous or revelatory news. They were soon disappointed, despite the efforts of one intrepid cameraman who attempted to leap onto the Buick in order to take a photograph; for his pains, the waiting police smashed his camera. Wallis, accompanied by a detective, her solicitor Theodore Goddard and her counsel Norman Birkett, was hustled swiftly through a side door, and then the police locked and bolted the front of the building. The latest act of this peculiar drama would be played out in private.

The extraordinary secrecy within which the divorce itself was conducted was the result of a direct royal entreaty from the king to the chief constable of Suffolk, an unparalleled usage – some might even say abuse – of royal powers. His intention was to avoid any unnecessary embarrassment, but also to ensure Wallis's safety. One anonymous letter received at New Scotland Yard around this time called Edward 'a rotten swine asking us to pay for emerelds [sic] and fine things for his ugly whore', and, while allowing him 'to go to the parliament for his ma's sake', threatened that 'if that Yankee harlot does not get out, we will smash her windows and give her a hiding'. The letter ended, ominously, with the words 'We have warned you.'[6] A similar epistle, from an American named Joe Longton, was rich in homophobic and racial slurs, but spoke for a growing section of US opinion when it described Wallis – who was denigrated as a 'mofradite [hermaphrodite] of the introvert type' – as 'the Queen of the Golden Grummet',* and her relationship to Edward as 'a blind or a stall to cover his own sexual malformation'.[7]

The subject of this innuendo, meanwhile, entered a virtually empty courtroom, from which the majority of spectators had been banished. The few who were allowed in were witnesses who were integral to the case, along with around twenty journalists sitting in the two front rows of the court's public seats. It was said of Wallis by one reporter, perhaps with a touch of poetic licence as she took her seat, that she was 'like [a] living portrait Whistler might have painted . . . [she was] a chick [sic] woman with chiselled delicate features'. She was said to outshine all others 'like [a] flower against [the] flame'.[8] The judge had not yet arrived, leading to wild speculation outside the courtroom that the case was to be held wholly in camera, or that there was some legal deficiency that meant the divorce could not be obtained, but his lordship soon made an appearance, and the case began.

---

* A 'knight of the golden grummet' was contemporary slang for a homosexual, especially one who took the passive role. Edward himself was thus doubly denigrated in the same letter.

Hawke's irritable enquiry as to why his court was virtually empty, and why Wallis's case was taking place in Ipswich rather than London, was answered in a whispered aside by the clerk of assize. Whatever explanation he offered partially placated the judge, who said, 'Yes, yes, I see', but his suspicion remained obvious as an uneasy Wallis took the witness box. Birkett, the man who was once hailed as 'the greatest legal discovery of the year', kept an unaccustomed state of silence until Hawke indicated that he could begin cross-examination, which he duly did.

The first answers, delivered in 'unruffled' fashion, were straightforward enough. Wallis confirmed that she lived at Beach House in Felixstowe, with a town address at 16 Cumberland Terrace in London. Birkett then asked, 'On Christmas Day, 1934, did you find a note lying on the dressing table?' Wallis confirmed that she had, and Birkett, with a more restrained flourish than usual, produced the note, which Wallis identified as having the look of being in a woman's handwriting, and agreed that it had caused her considerable distress. That her evidence was so far almost entirely false was not challenged by anyone in court.

Birkett allowed her to trot out a boilerplate account of how her marriage to Ernest had been happy until the autumn of 1934, at which point she complained that he became 'indifferent', went away for weekends on his own, and did not respond to her complaints about his behaviour. Yet this continued, in her version of events, until Easter 1936, when she received a letter informing her that her husband was conducting an extramarital affair. She then wrote to him to confirm her intention of divorcing him on the grounds of adultery - 'conduct I cannot possibly overlook' - and her plans to instruct her solicitors immediately. She identified her husband from a photograph, and his handwriting in the register of the Hotel de Paris in Bray, using the pseudonym 'Arthur Simmons'. She was then allowed to step down from the witness box, where she had been for around fourteen minutes.

Her words, as coaxed from her by Birkett, were essentially untrue, and it is not going too far to say that she committed perjury in her testimony, to say nothing of the fabricated letters. This, how-ever, was hardly unusual in divorce cases. It was also obligatory for the petitioner to be asked if she herself had committed adultery; as Egerton wrote in his memoir of the case 'it was expected that the judge would overlook one or two lapses for which the petitioner was suitably contrite, but it took a brave man, and an even braver woman, to list a large number of 'acts of adultery'.[9]

Many chose to bypass this requirement, claiming ignorance if it became an issue, but the solicitor was legally obliged to ask his client if adultery had taken place, which Wallis denied. Egerton observed 'it will surprise many people that Mrs Simpson should have, in effect, denied that she had committed adultery with the King',[10] and noted that 'there had been numerous occasions when they had been alone together in circumstances that constituted *prima facie* evidence of adultery'.*[11] He was not alone in speculating: 'Could any love idyll have been so perfect for two people without sex coming into it?'[12]

There followed the corroborating evidence of two waiters and a hall porter, who testified to seeing Simpson in bed with a woman not his wife – 'both of them occupied . . . it was a little bed' – and then the case was placed before Mr Justice Hawke, with Birkett saying: 'On that evidence, my Lord, I ask for a decree nisi with costs'. The judge hesitated a moment, and then said, 'I don't know.' Egerton described this as 'one of those moments which solicitors dread, when what appeared to be a cut-and-dried case suddenly strikes an awkward snag.'[13] On the surface, this was an adultery case like a thousand others, and yet none of those had necessitated the extraordinary arrangements that had prevailed in court that day, nor warranted the clamour that had temporarily turned Ipswich into a simulacrum of a Barnum & Bailey circus for the morning. Wallis,

---

* He also noted: 'it would be extraordinary if there were not dozens of people able to testify that the King's infatuation had led to the pair being alone in circumstances which provided an opportunity for adultery and that would have been enough to satisfy the court in an ordinary case in the absence of a satisfactory denial and explanation by the parties'.

guessing what was on his mind, wrote, 'For a terrible moment, I felt sure that he was determined to deny me my divorce.'[14]

Birkett broke the silence with 'I think I know what's on your lordship's mind', to which Hawke testily replied, 'How do you know what's on my mind?' Birkett answered apologetically, 'I was wondering if your lordship wanted to know why the other lady's name has not been mentioned in the case.' Hawke agreed – 'That is so' – at which Birkett, with the faintest glimmer of the flourish that he was so renowned for, suavely asserted, 'My lord, the name of the lady is plainly disclosed in the petition, and the lady has been served with a copy of the petition. I now ask for a decree nisi.' Hawke responded, 'very casually', 'Well, I suppose I must grant it in these unusual circumstances.'[15]

Birkett then asked for, and was awarded, Wallis's costs against her now former husband,* and the case was at an end. Hawke felt obvious discomfort at his part in the affair ('he had not liked what he saw of Mrs Simpson in the box'), and Egerton observed that 'he was showing his feeling that in this particular case he would have liked to find a way out of presiding over what was palpably a judicial farce.'[16] His own impression of the royal couple was that 'Mrs Simpson was an experienced woman and a social climber with no pretence to superior moral standards' and that 'the King was obsessed with her to the exclusion of everything else.'[17] After the statutory six-month interim period, her divorce would be made absolute on 27 April 1937. She left court quickly, got into the Buick once again, and headed off to London with Goddard, who 'exuded an air of quiet triumph'. A police car obligingly blocked the road for a further ten minutes so that she would have a clear run before the inevitable pursuit began. Wallis felt 'no triumph – only

---

* These would have been astronomical; Egerton lists some of them as being 'a leading KC, a conference at Fort Belvedere, keeping witnesses for several weeks at an inn, lavish hotel bills for solicitors' staff, dealings with the police and press and many other exceptional activities by the two partners'. Ernest's contributions, if he made any, would have been 'negligible', and almost certainly reimbursed later – which itself amounted to collusion if so.

a sense of relief'. And she knew that that was to be short-lived.[18]

Edward had had an eventful morning. First he held a Privy Council at Buckingham Palace, during which some of his courtiers, including Hardinge, were sworn in as privy councillors, and then he met the prime minister of Canada, W. L. Mackenzie King. The Canadian politician knew what was occurring between the monarch and Wallis, and Hardinge had asked him to discuss the matter during his reception, stressing that Edward's behaviour was causing ructions in his dominions. He later described this request as arising from 'becoming increasingly alarmed at the effect on the Empire at large of the humiliating comments appearing in the foreign, and particularly the American, press, and at the harm that was being done to a monarchy which for so long had been without reproach. This period of drift was, in my opinion, one of growing and incalculable danger.'[19]

Ever the statesman, the Canadian answered, 'If the King raises the matter, I will speak with perfect candour. But only then; I will not take the initiative myself.'[20] In the event, there was no such opportunity, but it is doubtful that anything he said would have made any impact. By his own admission, Edward 'was preoccupied with what was taking place at Ipswich',[21] and his anxiety did not abate until he received a message from Goddard after lunch, informing him that the decree nisi had been successfully granted.

That evening, the king and Wallis were reunited at her new home in Regent's Park. It was, initially, a joyful occasion, with Edward giving his lover the opulent gift of a hugely expensive emerald ring, inscribed 'WE are ours now, 27.X.36'. Yet it soon became clear to Wallis that Edward saw the events of the day entirely differently to her. He had spent days, if not weeks, obsessing over the possibility of the divorce not being granted and his name somehow being dragged into the saga – or, worse, Wallis deciding that she no longer wanted to be part of the whole affair, as she had frequently suggested to him since the *Nahlin* cruise. Now, once the decree was granted, he saw, in the words of Dickens, 'no shadow of another parting from her'.

Yet Wallis was able to play the worldly Estella to Edward's besotted Pip. While the king revelled in his triumph, Wallis, already in a heightened state of nerves because of the morning's events, saw a plethora of problems bounding in their direction, not least the six-month wait before the divorce could be finalised. As Edward confided in her about his audience with Baldwin a week before, Wallis was initially bewildered, then appalled, as she realised that the prime minister had taken active steps to frustrate a marriage between the two of them. She was also, with good cause, more frightened than Edward at the possibility that the *omertà* that currently existed in the British press would come to an abrupt end if the reporting of the existence of her divorce petition were felt to be in the public interest. Even as Edward reassured her of the 'gentleman's agreement' that he had come to with Beaverbrook and Harmsworth, and that Baldwin could be managed, she felt an uneasy scepticism that even his promise 'Don't be alarmed; I'm sure I can fix things'[22] did not succeed in quashing.

Although Beaverbrook and Harmsworth ensured that their papers did not print anything noteworthy about the events at Ipswich, there was no chance of the news not percolating into the consciousness of the country at large. Official government documents noted that, on 28 October, 'The pictures of the King on his holiday in the Near East [were] received unfavourably; shouts coming from some of the audience "Why does he not abdicate" . . . Some pressure had to be brought to bear to secure the singing of "God save the King"; working women in their Lancashire dialect muttering and saying "the new King is not like the good old King".'[23]

Harold Nicolson wrote in his diary the same day that, at a dinner given by Sibyl Colefax, 'I discuss with [the Duchess of Rutland] the great Simpson question . . . There are very serious rumours that the King will make her Duchess of Edinburgh and marry.' The gossip soon intensified to the posing of a single question; as Nicolson noted, with some alarm, 'The point is whether he is so infatuated as to insist upon her becoming Queen.' Although the Duchess of

Rutland reassured him that 'he would [not] really do anything so foolish', the matter was sufficiently serious for Nicolson to write, 'I gather from other people that there is considerable danger.'[24]

Queen Wallis. The words seemed unbelievable, even risible, when placed together. However, it was clear to the politicians and courtiers who observed the king at close quarters during this time that he was by now so in thrall to his sweetheart as to ignore affairs of state entirely. Helen Hardinge saw her husband's work become essentially impossible as Edward took little interest in his official business, cancelling arrangements on a whim.

Nonetheless, he could still dazzle, when he chose to. On the few occasions that he could be bothered to undertake a commitment, such as a reception he gave at Buckingham Palace on 30 October for the Argentine foreign minister, he was charming, suave and even slightly irreverent, turning 'a rather nervous ceremonial' into 'an enjoyable men's party',[25] in the words of the historian Philip Guedalla. And even Nicolson admitted that when he opened Parliament on 3 November, 'he did it well . . . he looked like a boy of eighteen'[26], even if he also felt that Wallis's influence could be found in an unusual area. 'The King's accent is really terrible. He speaks of Ammurica.'[27] If this was for his consort's benefit, it was wasted. The former Mrs Simpson chose instead to spend the day shopping at Harrods.

Yet there were greater problems than Edward's newly transatlantic diction. The American press spared no time constructing ever more lurid and inventive headlines – an especially vivid one was 'KING'S MOLL RENOED IN WOLSEY'S HOME TOWN',* somehow combining a strange mixture of erudition and slang[28] – and there was widespread speculation that, as a divorced woman, Wallis would now be free to marry Edward once the six-month period that the decree nisi required was up. However, a mistake

---

* To be 'renoed' was, unsurprisingly enough, to be divorced; the name came from Reno, in Nevada, then America's divorce capital. A few decades later, it was also, of course, the place where Johnny Cash 'shot a man, just to watch him die'.

that both of them made was to assume that it was an inevitability that the divorce would be granted after the court case. In fact, matters remained more fluid than either would have liked.

Horace Wilson wrote that 'representations had been made to the King ... as to the probable state of opinion in this country and in the Empire', and stated hopefully that 'these would not be without effect; for example, Mrs Simpson might go away out of the country'. Inevitably, 'such was not to be the case', with the result that 'Every day public opinion, though not vocal, became more and more disturbed and there was ever-increasing evidence that before very long the storm would break.'[29] One fashion in which this could take place was in a suspicion, one undoubtedly shared by Mr Justice Hawke, that the divorce had been obtained altogether too easily, in circumstances that reeked of all manner of backstairs dealing.

It therefore fell upon the King's Proctor, as the Crown's legal representative, to be prepared to investigate any complaints made by members of the public, any of whom were at liberty to write a letter pointing out the various oddities in the case, such as Wallis's short-lived residence in Felixstowe, her frequent presence at Fort Belvedere and elsewhere with the king, and, most perplexingly, the complete failure of Ernest Simpson to offer any defence regarding the allegations against him. While none of these on their own indicated illegality, the sense in the country that a crisis was coming – 'One cannot prevent people discussing and gossiping and speculating on this one subject the whole time', as Helen Hardinge observed – meant that the chances of a 'concerned citizen' causing a great deal of trouble for his or her monarch were growing by the day.

Whether Edward knew the extent of public dissatisfaction with his behaviour, or remained blithely ignorant, was unclear. He would later affirm that 'The role of a successful constitutional monarch consists in no small measure of appearing to be not only above politics but also above life.'[30] Nonetheless, he was not so rarefied as to avoid a meeting with Beaverbrook, who was summoned to Buckingham Palace once again on 5 November. The newspaper magnate was beginning to feel compromised. He no longer believed Edward's assurances that he had no intention of marrying Wallis, and 'as a newspaper proprietor, I wanted to stand down from intimate consultations with the King and to regain my liberty of expression in my own newspapers'.[31] He had had enough of being dictated to as to what he could and could not include in his publications, and so he attended the appointment with the scepticism of a true newspaperman.

In the event, he could report that 'the dinner was most interesting', thanks to the presence of Mrs Simpson. Beaverbrook's cameo of her is compelling, all the more so for its relative impartiality. Saying that 'she appeared to me to be a simple woman', and one 'plainly dressed', he added that he 'was not attracted to her style of hairdressing', even if her smile was 'kindly and pleasing'. (In deleted passages from his memoir, he also wrote that 'She had a mole on her face, which I believed to be unattractive . . . [and] she shaved the back of her neck, which did not appeal to me at all.' He also toned down a description of her 'too affable' smile, eventually describing it as 'agreeable'.)[32]

She made a great show of her ignorance of politics and inexperience of world affairs, coupled with 'declarations of simplicity of character and outlook', but this did not last throughout dinner. When she did engage in political conversation, 'she showed a liberal outlook, well maintained in discussion and based on a conception which was sound'. He was also 'greatly interested' in an example of her increasingly regal behaviour. Wallis received six women 'with appropriate dignity', and five of them greeted her with a kiss. 'In no case did she return it.'[33]

Edward spoke freely in front of Beaverbrook, regarding him as an ally, and made overt criticisms of several of his ministers. Given the two men's mutual animosity towards Baldwin, it was inevitable that the prime minister was one of those discussed, although Beaverbrook does not offer details. The king dropped hints that there was some assistance that the magnate could offer him, but Beaverbrook, believing that Edward wanted him to modify the coverage of him and Wallis in the American newspapers, suggested that this now lay in the hands of Walter Monckton. As he wrote, 'I was glad to be out of the affair, for negotiations with the Americans promised to be both difficult and tedious, and quite likely to end in failure.'[34] Although the king would have wished for Beaverbrook's input into this, it was not a subject of pressing concern. That matter would have to wait until their next encounter, when it would be a far more dominant problem.

'I have grown to hate that woman', Stanley Baldwin lamented to the civil servant Thomas Jones in early November. Inevitably, he was speaking of Wallis, who dominated public discussion in a way few others had ever managed to. If Jones's account is accurate, the prime minister lambasted her, saying, 'She has done more in nine months to damage the monarchy than Victoria and George the Fifth did to repair it in half a century.' Gloomily - and accurately - speculating that Edward had been profligate with the royal purse, Baldwin offered a terse summation of matters as they stood constitutionally. 'If he marries her she is automatically Queen of England. I would then hand in my resignation and I think my colleagues would agree to do so. Of course he may offer to abdicate.' He concluded that 'The best thing that could happen just now would be that he should be received in silence in the streets.'[35]

At the same time as Baldwin's despair was mounting, Hardinge was being invited to turn traitor to his monarch, or, as he put it, 'to see a draft of an official submission to the PM to make to the King on the subject of his association with Mrs Simpson'.[36] The concern that existed was that a formal request for Edward to end his relationship with Wallis would lead either to his abdication, or to the collapse of the government. The nature of constitutional monarchy was that the king was obliged to act on the advice given by his prime minister and Cabinet. Should he refuse to do so - and it seemed inevitable that he would - then the consequences would be unparalleled.

Neither Baldwin nor Hardinge wanted to bring about the

Ragnarök that loomed before them, and so the draft of the letter was toned down, on Hardinge's advice; he stated that 'A submission . . . contained formal advice from the Government that the association must be terminated forthwith. This seemed to me very drastic, and I made some suggestions for keeping the matter on a more informal footing.'[37] Rather than stating, 'Unless steps are taken promptly to allay the widespread and growing misgivings among the people, the feelings of respect, esteem and affection which Your Majesty has evoked among them will disappear in a revulsion of so grave and perilous a character as possibly to threaten the stability of the nation and the Empire', the revised version now asked that 'In view of the grave dangers to which . . . this country is being exposed, your association with Mrs Simpson should be terminated forthwith.' Yet even here, animosity towards the situation still lingered. The final suggestion, 'If Mrs Simpson left the country forthwith, this distasteful matter could be settled in a less formal manner',[38] dripped with official disdain.

Baldwin did not see these drafts until 13 November, but he was anything but deaf to the widely held view that 'the scandal was doing no end of harm to this country's prestige'.[39] He believed that his conversation with Edward the previous month had been useful, and made arrangements to see him again for another avuncular session of pipe smoking and advice. Hardinge, who was more attuned to the manner in which Fleet Street, frustrated by not being able to sell papers with details of the most significant news story in the country, was preparing to end its unofficial policy of silence, had been liaising with Geoffrey Dawson. The editor had brandished an incendiary leader article he had written and informed him, during the course of what he termed 'a long and rather depressing talk',[40] that 'the Press could not be held for more than a few days longer, and . . . *The Times* should be in the forefront'.[41] Hardinge, atypically, 'expressed no views'.[42] Dawson wrote that Hardinge 'is . . . attempting the argument himself, but is bringing in big guns to bear on his master'.[43] It was also known that two affidavits to the King's Proctor, asking for an investigation into possible collusion in the divorce judgement, had been filed. The storm had arrived at last.

Hardinge consulted Baldwin, who asked whether there had been any lessening of ardour from Edward towards Wallis. Hardinge replied that 'Everything was going on just as before, as far as I could see.' As Baldwin, humiliated by the realisation that his cosy chat with the king had been a useless waste of time, made plans to meet his monarch again with some urgency, Hardinge composed a letter to Edward of staggering bluntness and directness.

It could either be interpreted as a desperate act from a patriotic courtier driven to despair by his king's blinkered selfishness, or a cynical and treacherous attempt to bring down the monarch, brokered by a combination of Dawson, who described it as 'most admirable',[44] Baldwin and the general establishment. Monckton later wrote that '[The letter] made it impossible for the King to go on with Hardinge in any such confidential relationship as was proper between King and Private Secretary . . . Hardinge either knew this or ought to have known it.'*[45] Whatever one's interpretation, the message was abundantly clear: Hardinge's loyalty – and, by extension, that of most of Edward's inner circle – was to the office of the Crown, and not to its current holder. His wife may have described it as 'a last bid to enable the King to remain on the Throne',[46] but in hindsight it reads more like a punctilious yet furious outburst, suppressed for months and finally unleashed.

There was little attempt at *noblesse oblige*. Hardinge stated, 'I feel it is my duty to bring to your notice the following facts which have come to my knowledge, and which I *know* to be accurate', and then coldly outlined the situation. 'The silence of the British Press on the subject of Your Majesty's friendship with Mrs Simpson is not going to be maintained. It is probably only a matter of days before the outburst begins. Judging by the letters from British subjects living in foreign countries where the Press has been outspoken,

---

* Years later, he was still advising against its being published in the Duke of Windsor's memoirs, on the grounds that it was 'too well written' and that 'the ordinary reader will be inclined to think that Hardinge was right and courageous'.

the effect will be calamitous.' Whether or not Hardinge knew of Wallis's terror of the country being whipped into a state of excitement by the papers, the statement was bluntly designed to instil fear into his master, and his mistress.

Hardinge proceeded to outline the constitutional situation, suggesting that, should the government fall as a result of Edward's actions, 'Your Majesty [would have] to find someone else capable of forming a government which would receive the support of the present House of Commons . . . This is hardly within the bounds of possibility.' He then suggested that, should a general election thus be called, 'Your Majesty's personal affairs would be the chief issue – and I cannot help feeling that even those who would sympathise with Your Majesty as an individual would deeply resent the damage which would inevitably be done to the Crown, the corner-stone on which the whole Empire rests.' It was unheard-of for the monarch to be threatened, however obliquely, by one of his courtiers, but here Hardinge came close to suggesting that an angry nation would lose no time in turning on the man they believed had despoiled the throne itself.

The solution, such as it was, was presented as an inevitability – 'only one step which holds out any prospect of avoiding this dangerous situation' – and that was for Wallis to flee the country, or, as Hardinge put it, 'to go abroad *without further delay*'. He begged Edward 'to give this proposal your earnest consideration before the position has become irretrievable'. Suggesting that 'the changing attitude of the press' had made the matter one of 'great urgency', he ended the letter by asserting, in a servile manner at odds with the strength of his earlier statements, 'I am of course entirely at Your Majesty's disposal if there is anything at all that you want.'[47]

Hardinge's wife later claimed that 'There was never any question, at any time, of his composing [the letter] in co-operation with, at the instigation of, the Prime Minister, Geoffrey Dawson or anybody else.'[48] This seems unlikely, given that Dawson happened to coincidentally appear at his office 'at this moment of anxiety and distress', and as Hardinge praised the editor as 'a man

[of] discretion, experience and integrity', Dawson spoke similarly highly of the letter as 'respectful, courageous and definite',[49] not least the explicit warning that the gentlemen's agreement relating to the media's silence was about to end. Likewise, Hardinge's presence in 10 Downing Street shortly after the letter was written seems unusually fortuitous. While it may be true that Baldwin and Dawson did not tell him precisely what to write, it is equally undeniable that their aims and agenda were also served by someone as senior as Hardinge composing a letter that could not simply be ignored or shrugged off.

When it was finished, Hardinge sent the letter directly to Fort Belvedere in a red box, marked 'Urgent and Confidential'. The king had spent the previous two days in Portland, inspecting the Home Fleet, and had enjoyed himself, despite the cold, not least because an impromptu speech of his led to 'an unforgettable scene of the wildest and most spontaneous enthusiasm'.[50] He later wrote that 'I was able to put aside for a few hours the burning issue that was pressing for decision.'[51] When he arrived at the Fort, he was in need of a hot bath and a rest, but, curious as to why Hardinge should have felt the urge to write him a letter of this nature, he opened it.

As he later said, clearly with the memory of its receipt still smarting, 'An instant later, I was confronted by the most serious crisis of my life.'[52]

Chapter Seven

'Something Must Be Done'

By 13 November, Wallis felt like a prisoner in the most opulent of jails. If she left Cumberland Terrace or Fort Belvedere, she became an object of fascination, even without any press coverage of her exploits. She had learned from her Aunt Bessie of the hysteria that had enveloped America, and confessed that she found herself 'seriously disturbed' by the reactions she engendered. Edward, however, remained stoic, assuring her that these public humiliations, as she saw them, were relatively fleeting, and worth sticking with until their eventual resolution.

Yet on the day that the king received Hardinge's letter, he was unable to present himself in his usual cheery fashion. After he had read it, Wallis knew that something had gone badly awry, saying of him that 'he was preoccupied and his manner abstracted . . . The dispatch had plainly induced some kind of shock.' Thanks to his 'extraordinary capacity for keeping his inner tensions locked up inside his mind and heart', he recovered some of his bonhomie, and the weekend seemed to pass as normal, seeing friends for lunch and dinner and visiting the Kents for Sunday afternoon tea. Thereafter, Edward mentioned something vague about visiting Windsor Castle to rehang some portraits, and vanished.

When he eventually reappeared, Wallis pressed him on what he had been up to, and he replied that he had lied. In fact he had been at Windsor for a confidential chat with an adviser regarding the letter he had received from Hardinge. He described it as 'very serious', and, handing it to Wallis upon their return to the Fort, said, 'After you've read it, I think you'll agree that there is only one thing for me to do - send for Mr Baldwin.'[1] She offered to leave the country, as demanded, but he batted the idea away, describing the letter as 'an impertinence' and saying, 'On the throne or off, I'm going to marry you.' She begged him to listen to reason - 'for him to go on hoping, to go on fighting the inevitable, could only mean tragedy for him and catastrophe for me' - but once again he ignored her entreaties. She later described how 'Nothing I had seen had made me appreciate how vulnerable the King really was, how little power he could actually command, how little his wishes really counted for against those of his Ministers and Parliament.' She also noted, with no apparent bitterness, that 'David did nothing to disabuse me of these misconceptions.'[2]

Part of the reason for the king's feigned nonchalance was that his considerable pride had been badly hurt. Edward described himself as 'shocked and angry' by Hardinge's statements and suggestions, and only just restrained himself from telephoning him in a state of fury. Allowing that Hardinge had acted within the bounds of propriety - 'As to his right to address such a communication to his sovereign there could, of course, be no question' - and therefore could not be summarily dismissed, he began to wonder why it was written with such 'cold formality', and quickly came to the conclusion that Baldwin was behind the letter and its sentiments.

Wondering what his prime minister wished to achieve, Edward was later able to write, with tough-guy bravado, 'If the real intention was to try to induce me to give Wallis up by pointing at my head this big pistol of the Government's threatened resignation, they had clearly misjudged their man.' Still, even as he gruffly barked, 'They had struck at the very roots of my pride . . . Only the most faint-hearted would not have remained unaroused by such a challenge . . . This was not the crisis of a Prince; this was the crisis of a King',[3] it became obvious that he was not equipped to face the challenge alone. His first instinct was to summon Baldwin for a showdown at the Palace on the evening of 16 November. His second, and wiser, decision was to enlist the help of an old university friend, whose legal expertise would become invaluable to him over the coming weeks: Walter Monckton.

In his unpublished memoir of his involvement with the abdication crisis, Monckton wrote, 'Before October 1936, I had been on terms of close friendship with King Edward, and, though I had seldom met her save with the King, I had known Mrs Simpson for some considerable time and liked her well.'⁴ This may undermine Thomas Jones's assertion that the lawyer sat next to her at dinner 'and came to the conclusion that she was a hard-bitten bitch', or alternatively might reflect Monckton's rare ability to oscillate between opposing viewpoints with ease. Like the lawyer he was, he was able to see both sides of an argument, and place himself upon whichever one was more personally convenient at the time. If it also happened to be the morally, or legally, correct one, that was an added attraction.

Monckton was in a unique position in the events of late 1936 in that he was close to all of the leading players. He had been at Harrow with Hardinge and Sir Godfrey Thomas, Edward's assistant private secretary,* of which he wrote, '[It] made the inherent difficulties of our positions easier where loyalties were hard to reconcile and petty acerbities not always easy to repress.' He then went to Oxford, where he read Classics at Balliol and became president of the Union. It was there that he first met Edward, who, while Prince of Wales, attended a debate at the Union and saw Monckton at his best during an otherwise dull evening. As Lord Birkenhead, Monckton's first biographer, wrote, 'Walter did his best to give the new and royal member a lively impression of the Society by speaking in a poor House with the skill that he usually reserved for great occasions.'⁵ His actions might have arisen from diplomacy, but they were not forgotten.

Thereafter, he had a distinguished career that included serving with great gallantry in World War I despite being virtually blind

---

* As he noted, Baldwin and Churchill were also both Old Harrovians.

in one eye, after which he became a barrister. As with his Union career, his flair for oratory and argument saw him rise to the top of his profession, and in 1932 he encountered Edward once again, when he became attorney general to the Duchy of Cornwall. As Birkenhead wrote, 'What had been a nodding acquaintance with the prince at Oxford ripened into a warm friendship.'[6]

This friendship endured even when Monckton left for India in 1935 to serve as adviser to the Nizam of Hyderabad, where he returned sporadically for the next decade, and their intimacy was sufficiently known for Monckton to be confidentially informed by Lionel Halsey in February 1936 that Edward had told Ernest Simpson that he was in love with his wife and intended to marry her. Monckton dismissed this rumour, not least because 'I was afraid of the possibility of blackmail upon an extravagant basis.'[7] Nonetheless, as the year wore on, he was able to see the continued and strengthening intimacy between Edward and Wallis, but was comforted by Wallis assuring him that 'it was ridiculous to imagine that she had any idea of marrying the King'.[8] She may even have been sincere. Yet by the end of June, Monckton professed himself worried about the continued friendship between the bachelor king and a married woman. He cast about for someone to confide in, and eventually came upon a friend of Edward's, a once-promising politician who was now mired in what he himself called his 'wilderness years'. This confidant was Winston Churchill.

Monckton described Churchill as 'extraordinarily sympathetic and ready to help', when they met at his flat in Morpeth Mansions, Westminster, in early July. Certainly, his account of the then-backbencher suggests a man of great charisma and certainty, given to spouting aphorisms – 'Life is a tease . . . Joy is the shadow of sorrow, sorrow the shadow of joy' – and whose respect for the king meant that he would not dine with those who criticised him. Churchill too was concerned about the state of Edward's friendship with Wallis, and even more worried about the possibility of divorce proceedings, calling her continued marriage to Ernest a 'safeguard'. Although Churchill's own marriage to Clementine was famously resilient and monogamous, he was able to understand the lure of extramarital relations, but counselled caution, suggesting that 'Mrs Simpson ought not to go as a guest to Balmoral, though no doubt if the King wanted to see her whilst he was there she could stay with someone else nearby.'[9] This wise advice was not taken.

When Churchill next saw Edward, on 9 July, he let the king know the substance of his conversation with Monckton, about which Edward was 'surprised but not displeased'. Sending for his adviser, the king once again stated that he 'didn't see why Mrs Simpson should stay tied to an unhappy marriage simply because she was his friend'. In response to Monckton's suggestion that he would do better to keep his friendship with Wallis discreet, Edward replied, 'You should know me better; I am not ashamed of my friendship, and I am not going to hide it or try to deceive people.'[10] It was little wonder, then, that Monckton could write of Edward that 'He knew what he thought right and he had no time for the shufflings and humbug which he saw in the conventional morality.'[11] As a man who himself had had a long extramarital relationship after having become estranged from his wife in 1933, he shared this disdain for 'shufflings and humbug', which made him an ideal ally for the king in the battle that lay ahead.

Monckton flew to India again in early August, intending to return late in the year, but a telegram from Edward in September summoned him back earlier than he had anticipated, and so he arrived in London in early October, ready to be of use to his monarch and friend. It was, inevitably, not long before his expertise was called upon; he was summoned to Windsor Castle after Hardinge's letter had been received, and asked for his advice. Edward let it be known that he bitterly resented his underling's criticisms 'widely and in the strongest terms', and 'regarded the letter as forcing the issue and compelling him either to dismiss Major Hardinge or to take some other action to bring things to a head'.[12]

Monckton's own view of the king's private secretary was a more nuanced one than either Edward or Helen Hardinge displayed. He wrote that Hardinge 'took too pessimistic and critical a view of the

King's conduct' and that 'he expressed his opinion too emphatically and widely to have any hope of retaining the King's confidence when the crisis came'. Nevertheless, he advised Edward against dismissing his secretary, 'as this would at once indicate a breach over Mrs Simpson'.[13] The king accepted his counsel, and instead announced his immediate intention of sending for Baldwin and telling him that he was going to marry Wallis. Hardinge claimed that Monckton advised the king to get the abdication over quickly and leave the country, which seems wishful thinking on the private secretary's part. All the same, the question of who was on whose side was a vexed one, and would remain so until the end of Edward's reign.

As the prime minister headed to Buckingham Palace on 16 November just before 6.30 p.m., he may have recalled a more amicable exchange he had had with Edward four years before. The two of them had travelled from Folkestone to London together after visiting George V, who was gravely ill, and the conversation had been a warm and pleasant one. At its conclusion, Baldwin, mindful of the fact that the prince would soon lose his father, was pleased when Edward, adopting an almost filial tone, said, 'Now you do understand, don't you, that you can always talk to me about everything?'[14]

Such warmth was absent on the chilly evening when Baldwin was ushered into Buckingham Palace to find Edward in a mood that he later told his wife was 'most charming, but [contained] a streak of almost madness'.[15] The prime minister had earlier been with Dawson, to whom he had spoken grimly of 'HM's obsession & determination', and was in the mood, as he told *The Times* editor, 'to [give] him something to think about'.[16] The king had initially asked for Neville Chamberlain and Lord Halifax to attend the meeting, but Baldwin had demurred, believing that the incendiary matters Edward wished to discuss were best kept between themselves, for the moment at least. Both men subsequently provided different accounts of what happened next, although the substance remained the same.

According to Edward's version, he spoke first, saying, 'I understand that you and several members of the Cabinet have some fear of a constitutional crisis developing over my friendship with Mrs Simpson.' Baldwin agreed, and went on to say that he and his colleagues were 'disturbed' by the prospect of the king marrying a divorced woman. He asserted that he knew the will of the British people and what they would and would not tolerate, saying, 'Even my enemies would grant me that.' As Edward sneered, 'He might have been the Gallup* poll incarnate.' Yet behind Baldwin, the king detected the 'shadowy, hovering presence' of Cosmo Lang, Archbishop of Canterbury, who he suspected was acting out of principle: that principle being to ensure that the King of England would never legally be allowed to marry a divorced woman. He was thus faced with a decidedly unholy alliance of Church and State coming together to frustrate his dearly longed-for objective.

Edward, by his own account, spoke 'dispassionately' but clearly to Baldwin at that point, laying down the law and telling him that 'Marriage has become an indispensable condition to my continued existence, whether as King or as man. I intend to marry Mrs Simpson as soon as she is free to marry. If I could marry her as King, well and good; I would be happy and in consequence perhaps a better King. But if, on the other hand, the Government opposed the marriage, as you have given me reason to believe it would, *then I am prepared to go.*'[17]

Baldwin, apparently, was shocked into near-silence, saying only, 'Sir, that is most grievous news ... It is impossible for me to make any comment on it today',[18] and left almost immediately. Edward watched him depart in his ministerial car, which he likened to 'a sinister and purposeful little black beetle', complete with 'portly occupant'. He later wrote, 'When last we separated, the Prime Minister had expressed his satisfaction over the ice being broken ... [Now] the ice had indeed been broken up, and, like

---

* A well-known American polling company, founded in 1935.

Eliza in *Uncle Tom's Cabin*, I found myself facing a perilous dash to shore across the disintegrating floe.'[19] Yet, convoluted literary metaphors aside, the king once again felt a sense of satisfaction at having bested his prime minister. He remained in control. It was with equanimity that he donned white tie and tails and headed to Marlborough House for dinner with his mother, to whom he was preparing, with some trepidation, to divulge recent developments.

Baldwin's account differed substantially in its description of their actions. According to the version he gave his wife that evening, he began by echoing Hardinge's warning that the press would not remain silent for long, and Edward asked, almost eagerly, 'Would my marriage be approved?' When Baldwin told him that, as any marriage that Edward entered into would result in his wife becoming queen, it would not, and that the people would not wear such a course of action, the king became sulky and withdrawn. His torpor increased as the prime minister pointed out that 'The King's wife becomes Queen; the Queen becomes the Queen of the country; and therefore, in the choice of a Queen, the voice of the people must be heard.'[20] This precipitated Edward's response that 'I want you to be the first to know that I have made up my mind and nothing will alter it – I have looked at it from all sides – and I mean to abdicate to marry Mrs Simpson.'[21]

For the first time, a word that had never been used by an English king before hung between the two of them. Baldwin was horrified. A man who described himself as 'a remnant of the old Victorians', he was someone who believed in the idea of duty as sacred, returning to the office of prime minister over and over again despite his increasingly poor health, implacable opposition from the most powerful newspaper publisher of the day and a monarch who clearly found his opinions irritating rather than helpful. Yet here he was, faced with a king who seemed to regard his own responsibilities as considerably less important than the prospect of marrying his mistress – and a twice-divorced one at that. As he later put it to a surprised Dawson, 'HM at the moment wants to quit.'[22]

Baldwin responded, with some understatement, 'Sir, this is a very grave decision, and I am deeply grieved', before pointing out that there was a real risk that the hurried and underhand nature of the divorce meant that it would not eventually be granted. Edward, unsurprisingly, was not pleased by this news. To bring the interview to a close, he said, with studied airiness, 'I have made up my mind and I shall abdicate in favour of my brother, the Duke of York, and I mean to go and acquaint my mother this evening and my family; please don't mention my decision except to two or three trusted Privy Councillors, until I give you permission.' Baldwin knew that Edward could not comprehend the situation he was in, and that there was nobody else who could make him. His account of the conclusion of their meeting has a detail that Edward omits; as they parted, Baldwin extended his hand, which the king held 'for a long time', and as Edward said goodbye, 'there were almost tears in his eyes'.[23]

As the two men went their separate ways, each considered the strength of his respective position. Baldwin, although by no means a universally popular premier, knew that nothing that he had said was inappropriate or untrue. While he was unable to speak as authoritatively about public opinion as he had given Edward the impression he could, he also knew that unsympathetic newspaper headlines, especially where Wallis was concerned, would swiftly transform the largely positive attitude the king's subjects had towards him. He also knew that the likes of Hardinge, Dawson and, especially, Cosmo Lang would be influential supporters of the case that he had outlined. He could only hope that others would follow, and swiftly; the alternative would be the fall of a government that he had been attempting to hold together since June 1935. At a time when an international crisis looked ever more likely, he knew that a constitutional debacle could only play into the hands of England's enemies, whoever they revealed themselves to be.

Whether or not Edward was aware of the depths of the crisis he was about to spark is unclear, although his lack of interest in the finer details of monarchy suggests that he was not. He did not appear to understand that the abdication was not simply his unilateral decision. As John Simon, something of an expert on the constitution in his role as Home Secretary, described it, 'The Crown descends to the heirs of the body of Sophia, Electress of Hanover ... It is impossible that the succession to the Crown should be modified by the mere declaration of its present holder.'

Simon called the constitutional problem 'both novel and exceedingly difficult', with its complication that the Statute of Westminster, passed in 1931, recognised complete equality of status between the United Kingdom and its Dominions, and thus insisted that any law that modified the devolution of the Crown needed the explicit assent and approval of the latter. As the Home Secretary, with understandable weariness, wrote, 'Even though King Edward persisted in his determination and formally declared his abdication, legislation would be needed to give full effect to his desire, and the legislation should be such as to carry with it the consent of the Dominions, expressed either in the preamble to an Imperial Act or by the direct approval of their Parliaments.'[24] In other words, Edward could say what he liked about his intention to abdicate, but there would be an inevitable chasm between his rash statements and any action that occurred.

Baldwin, meanwhile, knew that the silence of the press could only be sustained for a finite period. He had received an elegantly suggestive letter on 12 November from Howell Gwynne, editor of the *Morning Post*, which acknowledged that as 'the senior in my profession' and 'the editor of a newspaper which is the staunchest supporter of monarchical institutions', he was being looked to, in his words, to 'break what they term "the Great Silence"'. While Gwynne acknowledged that 'the press should follow the Government and not dictate to it', he also provocatively proposed that 'it will be impossible to expect this self-imposed silence will last very much longer ... The press in this country is undoubtedly getting very restive ... Each [journalist] has asked me the question "For how long?"'[25]

Edward, meanwhile, lacked widespread and unconditional

support. While he knew that Churchill and Beaverbrook were behind him, as far as anyone could be, other anticipated allies were fading away, although Louis Mountbatten wrote warmly to him after his visit to Portland, saying, 'No visit from any King to his Fleet has ever been more successful. You were "the top" and I was damned proud to be with you and see you do it so well, so very very well', and signing off: 'your dutiful and devoted Dickie'.[26] Samuel Hoare, the First Lord of the Admiralty, offered sympathy but also stressed that Baldwin enjoyed the support of both parties of the House of Commons, and Duff Cooper – who only a few months before had enjoyed Edward's hospitality on board the *Nahlin* – could offer little hope other than a suggestion that the king should attempt to play for time as far as he could. He hinted that, should the Coronation go ahead as planned, Edward would find himself strengthened, but his sovereign refused to 'go ahead with a lie on my lips',[27] and this 'counsel of a sophisticated man of the world',[28] as he called Cooper's advice, was swiftly dropped.

The king had a tense and unproductive interview with his mother on the evening of 16 November, although it could have gone no other way. Queen Mary remembered her late husband's implacable objections to Wallis and his refusal to acknowledge her as his son's consort, and had asked Baldwin at least twice, earlier in 1936, if there was anything that could be done, to which the prime minister had shrugged. To her son, she said nothing, which he may well have interpreted as tacit acceptance of the status quo. In fact, it was the most profound expression of royal authority imaginable. When Edward became king, he was monarch first and son second, and, as he realised, 'to my mother, the monarchy was something sacred'.[29] Consequently, Mary's silence did not indicate a reluctant willingness to accept Wallis as her inevitable daughter-in-law, but instead masked a profound sorrow and disbelief at what she saw as her son's less-than-regal decision to place his own happiness ahead of his duty. As her lady-in-waiting Mabell Ogilvy, Countess of Airlie, later commented, 'She simply refused to accept that, as King, he had any right to a private life of his own choosing.'[30]

When Edward declared that he intended to marry Wallis, she did not fly into a rage or castigate him, but retained her self-control. Her son believed that this indicated some sympathy towards his predicament, despite his realisation that she was 'obviously distressed'. However, he soon understood that she regarded his decision with deep consternation, albeit expressed in the most restrained of ways. He begged to be allowed to present Wallis to her, but what he called 'the iron grip of Royal convention' - to say nothing of her own inclinations - forbade this.

He was probably unaware that she had spent the previous weeks poring with growing horror over the American newspaper accounts of his relationship with Mrs Simpson. As her friend Marie Belloc Lowndes wrote in November, 'Queen Mary is in anguish. She can neither sleep nor eat.'[31] The Duchess of York sympathetically told her that 'I feel quite overcome with horror and emotion . . . One feels so helpless against such obstinacy.'[32] Consequently, Mary's cool parting instruction to her son that she hoped he would make a wise and prudent choice was a piece of theatre that concealed a morass of fear and disquiet.

Her antipathy to the situation could be summarised by her actions of the following day. Before Edward headed off on a tour of the depressed mining villages of South Wales, she sent him a note: 'As your mother I must send you a line of true sympathy in the difficult position in which you are placed. I have been thinking of you all day, hoping you are making a wise decision for your future. I fear your visit to Wales will be trying in more ways than one, with this momentous action hanging over your head.' A less formal approach might be discerned by her exasperated comments to the prime minister, who had visited her at Marlborough House in an attempt to find common ground. She greeted him in a businesslike fashion, saying, 'Well, Mr Baldwin! *This* is a pretty kettle of fish!'[33]

Around the same time, Edward met with his brothers, most notably the Duke of York, who would become king in the event of abdication taking place. (The Duke of Gloucester was 'little moved by what I had to say' and the Duke of Kent 'seemed genuinely upset', in part because he had met and liked Wallis.) Bertie, whose innate reserve and dread of public speaking sat uneasily with his integrity and personal decency, 'was so taken aback by my news that in his shy way he could not bring himself to express his innermost feelings at the time', as Edward later wrote. In fact, it was more likely a combination of horror at the self-centred nature of his brother's actions and dismay at what now, inevitably, lay ahead.

The formal letter that he later wrote, offering his hopes for Edward's happiness, and his belief that 'whatever I decided would be in the best interests of the country and the Empire',[34] was, in its own way, as much of an evasion as his mother's reticence. Faced with the unthinkable, the royal family withdrew into the comforting certainty of protocol, even as it threatened to come crashing down around them. Bertie's wife's feelings were more overt. On 20 November, she wrote to Queen Mary to say, 'It is almost incredible that David contemplates such a step, and every day I pray to God that he will see reason, and not abandon his people . . . It is a great strain having to talk and behave as if nothing was wrong during these difficult days, especially as I do not think that anybody here dreams of what is worrying all of us.'[35]

Despite all the drama of the previous couple of days, Edward, increasingly tenuous though his hold on the crown seemed, remained sovereign, and was expected to carry out his royal duties. Accordingly, he headed to Wales on 17 November, on an excursion that was to become one of the most controversial and wilfully misunderstood events of his reign. He had regularly visited the area while Prince of Wales, and had had his investiture there, at Caernarvon Castle, yet now he was seeing the grimiest and most hopeless parts of it. Pontypool, Merthyr Tydfil, Mountain Ash, Glamorgan; the names, and the utter contrast that their squalid surroundings offered to the glamorous places around which Edward had spent much of his reign, seemed to offer an implicit rebuke to their royal visitor. *This is your kingdom too*, they seemed to say, *and we are your subjects*.

Edward had never lacked the common touch, and one of his

strengths as king was his ability to connect with the ordinary man on an immediate, if necessarily superficial, level. As he travelled around, along with the traitorous Hardinge, he was driven to sympathise that 'Even a king, who would be among the last to feel the pinch of a depression, could see that something was manifestly wrong.' Hardinge described this, ironically, as 'a triumphal progress'· and noted that 'From a personal point of view, it was interesting that the King at that time bore me no malice for my action in writing to him as I did – for I was in attendance on him during the visit to South Wales, and no one could have been more friendly.'*[36]

Accordingly, on 19 November, Edward made the off-the-cuff comment, in the presence of journalists who were hoping for some slip of the tongue about Wallis, that 'these works brought all these people here . . . something must be done to get them at work again'.[37] It was an innocuous, compassionate comment, made without any particular thought or explicit intention. If anything, it showed his relative impotence as king. There was no easy or available fix to deal with the industrial depression that he stood amidst. He later described it as 'the minimum humanitarian response that I could have made to what I had seen',[38] and was correct to do so. Hardinge acknowledged that 'There was no truth whatever in the suggestion of any connection between this trip and the impending crisis . . . Though the personality of the King was to a certain extent that of the stormy petrel, His Majesty's actions throughout were entirely constitutional.'[39]

Yet the press, starved of content about the more compelling events that were currently unfolding, decided to turn his statement into the defining story of his visit. It also offered them a useful means of contrasting royal sympathy with government nonchalance. The *Daily Mail*, under the headline 'The King Edward Touch', talked angrily of Cabinet 'indifference' and of how 'the lot of the

---

* Helen Hardinge noted that Edward showed a 'particular friendliness' towards his private secretary, as if ostentatiously hiding his anger at his betrayal. This was confirmed by Duff Cooper noting that both Hardinge and Edward had spoken bitterly of each other when he had seen them before the Welsh trip.

humblest people has always been [Edward's] nearest anxiety and continual preoccupation',[40] while the *Daily News* blared that 'the man in the street feels that Whitehall stands condemned'.[41]

Even as Hardinge wrote, over-optimistically, to Baldwin to say that the visit had gone off 'extremely well', a debate began as to what, if anything, the king had meant to do. Ramsay MacDonald wrote in his diary that the trip had 'aroused expectations . . . [which] will embarrass the Government. These escapades should be limited. They are an invasion into the field of politics and should be watched constitutionally. Besides he might easily use this method for cloaking the other troubles into which he plunges at present.'[42] Dawson's *Times* used the incident as a means of reminding both politicians and the monarch that the greater story was about to come into focus. Its editorial stated, with commendable restraint, 'The King's ministers are His Majesty's advisers, and to contrast his personal and representative concern for the well-being of a section of the people with the administrative steps of his advisers is a constitutionally dangerous proceeding and would threaten, if continued, to entangle the Throne in politics.'[43]

Edward's statement would mark the beginning of a shadowy, barely recognised entity that was known as the 'King's Party'. Its intentions were unclear, its membership discreet and it never achieved any official status. Yet its *raison d'être* was soon to become clear. When Edward returned from Wales, he was reunited with Wallis at a dinner given by Chips Channon. He was, as Channon noted, 'in a gay mood . . . Nothing could mar his excellent temper.'[44] He cheerily asked Duff Cooper, also present, why the government didn't have greater control over the BBC, and when the nature of its editorial independence was explained to him, he said 'loudly, with a laugh', that 'I'll change that . . . It will be the last thing I do before I go.'[45]

The obvious reason for his (somewhat authoritarian) good humour was that he was once again with Wallis. After a series of awkward and intense interviews with politicians and members of his family revolving around his relationship with her, it reminded him of his rationale for pursuing the path that he had. However, while he had been away, Wallis had been for lunch at Claridge's with Esmond Harmsworth. It had not been a social occasion, but an opportunity for Harmsworth to propose a potential solution to Edward's dilemma that, if successful, would not only enable the two of them to marry, but would also allow him to retain his throne; in simple terms, to have his cake and eat it.

That Harmsworth and Beaverbrook might have their own agenda did not seem to occur to the king.

Chapter Eight

'A Clever Means of Escape'

In 1936, Esmond Harmsworth was a man in the considerable shadow of his father, Lord Rothermere. Although he rejoiced in the grandiose title of chief executive of Associated Newspapers, and had previously been one of the youngest MPs in the House, for the Isle of Thanet, he was aware that he was known as 'Rothermere's boy'. This appellation caused him equal parts pride and embarrassment, not least because his father had been humiliated a few years before for his unseemly haste to support Mosley and the British Union of Fascists. Notoriously, the *Daily Mail* had published an article in 1934 entitled 'Hurrah for the Blackshirts', which was bylined by Lord Rothermere himself and went on to praise Mosley's 'sound, commonsense, Conservative doctrine'.

Harmsworth, who was only thirty-eight years old at the time of the abdication crisis, knew that he had to forge his own, non-Mosleyite, reputation. Like his occasional ally and rival Beaverbrook, he understood that the greatest source of public interest of the day was the king and his relationship with Wallis. In this area, he had a clear advantage over most other journalists and newspaper proprietors: he was friendly with both of them, and had even been a guest at the infamous Balmoral sojourn in September. He was responsible for the *Daily Mail*'s article that had praised Edward's behaviour in South Wales, which was pointedly contrasted with the 'deadweight lethargy' of government. Therefore, when he escorted Wallis to lunch at Claridge's on 19 November, he enjoyed the confidence and candour of an intimate, rather than the stony politeness of an acquaintance. Nonetheless, she was to be surprised when, after some aimless tittle-tattle about how useful Harmsworth had been in suppressing any unflattering stories, he came to the point. 'I know that the King wants to marry you, and of the difficulties involved. Therefore, have you ever considered embarking on a morganatic marriage?'[1]

Wallis later wrote that 'his directness quite took my breath away', and many other men might have felt that they had overstepped any acceptable levels of propriety with such an unusual suggestion. A morganatic marriage, colloquially known as a 'left-handed marriage', is one in which two partners from unequal social ranks are wed, with the explicit proviso that any children from the union will not inherit the title – of king or queen in this case. This therefore would allow Edward and Wallis to marry, but the unacceptable concept of 'Queen Wallis' would be avoided.

It was a masterstroke of a kind, offering a compromise where none had previously existed. It is also unlikely to have originated directly from Harmsworth, who lacked the strategic guile to have come up with the idea. Edward later wrote that Harmsworth told him that it was his father who first suggested it; he in turn had heard it from his adviser, the journalist Collin Brooks, but it was more likely to have originated from Churchill, who had both the inclination and the wide knowledge of royal history to have hit upon it as a potential solution.* It had been discussed informally in high society since Mrs Simpson's divorce, but this was the first time it was proposed in person, so to speak. What Harmsworth did not mention to Wallis at their lunch was that, should it be successful, it would almost certainly result in humiliation for Baldwin, and possibly even a vote of no confidence in his government. This would have been a highly desirable outcome for Harmsworth, Churchill

---

* This was certainly Horace Wilson's impression – he wrote, 'There is some reason to believe that this idea originated with Mr Winston Churchill.'

and Beaverbrook, none of whom would have wept to see 'Honest Stan' removed from Downing Street. In turn, the prime minister was no admirer of Harmsworth; Dawson wrote in his diary on 26 November that '[SB] expressed unmitigated dislike of Esmond H.'² This didn't bother him. A grateful king, happily married and secure on his throne, could be a very useful ally - or puppet - indeed.

Harmsworth, sensing his lunch companion's surprise, acknowledged that this solution 'is not very flattering to you, Wallis, but I am sure that you are one with us in desiring to keep the King on the throne'.³ She found it 'astonishing', and was overwhelmed by its implications, not least Esmond's parting suggestion that she might become Duchess of Lancaster. She wrote, with some justification, 'I knew less than ever of the workings of the British political mind.'⁴ When he asked, 'Would you be willing to marry the King under these conditions', she reserved her answer, saying, 'How the King would marry me, if we are ever to marry, is a question for him to settle with his people.'⁵

When the people's sovereign first heard of the idea - which became known as 'the Harmsworth Plan' - later that day, his immediate reaction was to dismiss it entirely. Wallis herself had called it 'strange and almost inhuman', and Edward, who still held out hope that he might call her his queen, wrote that 'The term itself repelled me as one of the least graceful that might be applied to the relations between men and women.'⁶ He might also have feared that the colloquial phrase, with its faint air of derision, would be used unkindly about a union that was unlikely to result in children. The last time a morganatic marriage had been contracted in the royal family was over ninety years ago, in the case of his great-uncle, the 2nd Duke of Cambridge; it had been, in his words, 'lamentable', as well as probably illegal. Edward therefore told Wallis that 'Whatever the outcome of our situation, I can't see a morganatic marriage as right for you.'⁷

Adversity breeds a willingness to consider previously

unpalatable* ideas, however, and the next day, the king agreed to meet Harmsworth himself in order to discuss the possibility. Wallis reported that he sighed, wearily, 'I'll try anything in the spot I'm in now.'[8] She had also warmed to the Harmsworth plan, and told Edward, 'If there is the slightest possibility that [this] might ease the crisis, and keep you on the throne, then it is our duty to consider it, regardless of our own feelings.'[9] He met Harmsworth, and the magnate was sufficiently persuasive for Edward to agree to take the solution to a next and more critical stage: suggesting it to Baldwin, with the hope that he would then put it to his Cabinet.

One note of caution was struck by Monckton, who had swiftly established himself as the one man who was trusted by all parties in the affair. Relations between Hardinge and Edward had been non-existent since the letter, despite the forced amicability of Wales, and so Monckton became the royal counsellor, a role that he attempted to juggle with pursuing his legal practice. As Horace Wilson wrote, 'He was able to interpret to the Prime Minister what was in the King's mind and went as far as anyone could possibly go to explain to the King the consequences of his proposed actions and at the same time to convey to him the feelings of his many friends as to the unwisdom of his intentions.'[10]

Monckton was able to claim the candour of an old friend and informed Edward that from a legal perspective, the chance of a bill relating to a morganatic marriage passing through Parliament was negligible, in the unlikely event that Cabinet did not veto it in the first instance. The king asked, wildly, whether it was possible to push Wallis's divorce through and make it absolute immediately, and also whether he could bypass government and make her a duchess himself. There was even some absurd suggestion that he should not marry Wallis as king, but in his role as Duke of Cornwall, thus removing the question of whether she would

---

* Although there has been some suggestion that Edward himself had thought of it before. Beaverbrook, albeit an interested party, quoted him as having said, 'I always thought I would get away with a morganatic marriage.'

ever become queen. It was a testament to Monckton's delicacy and tact that, when confronted with these mad ideas, he was able to respond that although of course both instances were technically possible, he was doubtful that success could exist 'in the case we are discussing'.[11]

The prime minister, meanwhile, was bracing himself for a potential abdication, should the Dominions agree to it. Hardinge had earmarked the week beginning 30 November for such a departure, believing that Edward should leave at the same time as announcing his abdication, and that he should not be allowed to make a farewell broadcast 'as there was really nothing that he could profitably say'.[12] Baldwin commented wistfully to Duff Cooper that 'he was not at all sure that the Yorks would not prove the best solution. The King has many good qualities, but not those which best fitted him for the post, whereas the Duke of York would be just like his father.'[13] As Edward knew, and resented, any comparison between him and Bertie was inevitably made to his detriment. Had his younger brother fallen in love with a married woman, the most that would have happened would have been a discreet liaison, which doubtless would have come to a natural conclusion in time.

On 23 November, Baldwin met with Dawson, who wrote in his diary that '[SB's] lips (as usual) were sealed on the subject of HM's intentions, but he was terribly anxious & said he thought of nothing else.'[14] Baldwin had received the first draft of what an abdication bill would involve, but he then discovered via Harmsworth that the king was about to propose a morganatic marriage to him. The meeting was acrimonious, as Harmsworth airily suggested that 'the whole standard of morals is so much more broadminded since the War', and that the British people would look favourably on a morganatic marriage. Baldwin, who again suggested that he, and not the *Daily Mail*, spoke for the British people, responded icily that 'The ideal of morality . . . certainly *has* gone down since the War, but the idea of Kingship has gone *up*.'[15]

Although his reaction to the proposal itself was, as Harmsworth later tactfully reported to Edward, 'surprised, interested and non-committal',[16] Baldwin had already been warned of the impending approach by his adviser and friend J. C. C. Davidson, who then saw him attempt to picture the scene in the House of Commons when he 'had to explain why Mrs Simpson was good enough to be the King's wife but not good enough to be Queen'.[17] Baldwin correctly anticipated that, if the suggestion was to be public knowledge, the nascent so-called King's Party would begin to gather strength and momentum, aided by the Rothermere and Beaverbrook press, and almost certainly led by Churchill, of whom he said, 'You may be sure he is in on this, and does not feel about it as we do.'[18] Although Baldwin was already physically and mentally exhausted – one whip in the Commons described him as being like 'a tired walker on a long road'[19] – he was prepared to retain his principles and resist the suggestion. As he said to Thomas Jones, 'Is this the sort of thing I've stood for in public life? If I have to go out, as go I must, then I'd be quite ready to go out on this.'[20]

Some high-minded support came from the Archbishop of Canterbury, who wrote to Baldwin on 25 November to warn, 'I gather it is becoming more and more difficult to prevent leakage into the press. If so, the leakage will soon become a flood and burst the dam ... If any announcement [of abdication] is to be made ... it should be made as soon as possible. The announcement should appear as a free act.' Lang may have been a man of God, but he was also worldly. His political skill and personal dislike of Edward were clear from his injunction that 'I have reason to think that he does not fully realise that if the course indicated is to be taken, he must leave as soon as possible. It would be out of the question that he should remain until the decree is made absolute ... I understand you are seeing him tonight, and doubtless you could make this plain.'[21]

In fact, Baldwin did not have an opportunity to do so during his interview with the king, which revolved entirely around the discussion of the morganatic marriage proposal. Edward, too, was worn out by the stress he was under; the prime minister informed his Cabinet that 'His Majesty had a bad cold and was not looking as fit as usual.'[22] When asked whether Parliament would pass the necessary legislation for the marriage to be approved, Baldwin offered his informal advice that it was unlikely, or, as he put it to Cabinet, 'If he thought he was going to get away with it in that way he was making a huge mistake.'[23]

As with their previous, and subsequent, interviews, there was a subdued feeling of mutual discontent between the king and his prime minister. Baldwin assured Edward that 'the *Daily Mail* is the worst judge in England of what the people are thinking', which was that they 'attached most tremendous importance to the integrity and position of the Crown' and that if Edward was to abdicate, he might find some personal sympathy, but also a tidal wave of fury against Wallis, to which the king commented, 'I agree, but it is most unfair.' Baldwin, understandably irritated by the sovereign's detachment, snapped, 'It is unfair, but it is the way of the world.' Edward, he later noted, gave way to 'something like anger' at this, for the sole time in their talks, before remembering himself and asking that the morganatic marriage proposal be formally placed before the Cabinet, and the prime ministers of his various Dominions elsewhere in the world. As Baldwin left, the monarch said, with ostensible guilelessness, that he would be consulting some of his own friends about the best course of action, not least Lord Beaverbrook.

As before, the king had proved himself the master of the parting shot. Yet it was a dearly won little victory; as he later recounted, 'As the door closed behind him I realised that with that simple request I had gone a long way towards sealing my own fate. For in asking [Baldwin] to find out the sentiments of the British and Dominion Governments, I had automatically bound myself to submit unquestioningly to their "advice".'[24]

Beaverbrook had left England for New York on 14 November, intending to head on to a clinic in Arizona for a rest cure for his asthma, but received a telegram from Monckton four days later informing him that 'Mutual friend feels situation now urgent and would welcome your immediate return.' An intrigued Beaverbrook responded, 'Can you tell me by way of preparation for my job why crisis is upon us now?' Monckton responded, 'Friend has now declared to authorities definite decision as soon as absolute coast is clear. They are now considering next steps and you will appreciate situation which may arise.'[25] Beaverbrook had received similar telegrams from Edward. The magnate wrote that 'in effect, [the King] asked me what was to be done' and 'I was told . . . that my presence was required for advice . . . I asked at once if the advice expected from me would be limited to the newspapers. I was told "No", it was to go beyond that, and if I wanted further information I might have it.'[26]

Realising that he was involved in something altogether unprecedented, Beaverbrook returned immediately. As recently as October, it had become common knowledge that he had little respect for Edward. Nicolson had been informed by the loyal courtier Ulick Alexander that Beaverbrook's dislike of the king stemmed from jealousy, and that he 'hates anything which he feels he cannot destroy'.[27] The monarchy itself, however, now became a target. Beaverbrook wrote with faux-innocence that 'This immense volume of pressure, coming from so many quarters, confused me . . . It led me to think that I might have a considerable status when I returned and so might be an important factor in the situation.'[28]

He headed straight to Fort Belvedere, arriving on 26 November. Edward's first words when the two of them met, delivered as he was 'grasping his hand', were 'You have done a fine thing for me, and I shall always remember it.'[29] Beaverbrook wrote, in an unpublished passage from his memoir, that 'He actually met me at the door, in this way showing his anxiety.' It was unprecedented that the King of England would present himself as a suppliant to a newspaper baron, but this was a time in which the expected order had been overturned. Quite literally anything could happen.

Over lunch – Beaverbrook had a special menu prepared, as he was on a diet – Edward briefly outlined the situation, indicating who was on his side and who was opposed to him and Wallis.

Duff Cooper, Lord Rothermere and Churchill were all considered 'solid'; Baldwin, Samuel Hoare and much of the Cabinet, less so. However, he believed that Clement Attlee, leader of the Labour Party, would potentially support the morganatic marriage, which would have been crucial. With Attlee behind him, Edward could allow Baldwin's government to collapse, a state of affairs that he might even have preferred. If Churchill were to assume the role of leader of the opposition, and Attlee became prime minister, there would no longer be any majority in Parliament against the proposed marriage.* Edward now believed, or so Beaverbrook maintained, that he had found a feasible solution to his dilemma.

The magnate disagreed with him. He later wrote of 'a certain failure of candour' on Edward's part in his previous discussions with Baldwin about his intentions, and of how he emerged with 'discredit'[30] in essentially lying about his plans towards Wallis. Therefore, Beaverbrook attempted to change the direction of the narrative, as if he was placing pressure on one of his editors to alter a story. His advice to the king, emphatically delivered, was to abandon any idea of a morganatic marriage, as Baldwin and the government would reject it and it would reduce Edward to the status of a helpless pawn. Yet as he pointed out, there was no need for this. He remained the ruler of Great Britain, and it was unprecedented for the executive to remove the sovereign because they disagreed with a course of action he was taking. The only comparable example was the case of Charles I, and nobody wished to see another Cromwell in charge, especially at a time of looming international crisis.

Beaverbrook was also a master of realpolitik. He suggested that Baldwin and the Cabinet would rather agree to the king marrying Wallis than allow the government to fall, and, before too long, the dynamic of power would be reversed; all it required was patience

---

* Edward was incorrect in this assumption. Attlee wrote in his autobiography that none of the Labour Party would have supported him, save for a few intellectuals 'who can be trusted to take the wrong view on any subject'.

and an unwillingness to fold. He left Edward with the apt advice to find an ally within government – presumably Duff Cooper, as his friend and the most apparently sympathetic figure in the Cabinet – and to continue trusting in the counsel of Walter Monckton. In the latter regard, at least, he was offering sincerely useful counsel. What he did not indicate was the extent of his own agenda. As he wrote, 'The King must prevail and Baldwin must be destroyed.'[31]

The animosity between Baldwin and Beaverbrook was legendary. Ever since Baldwin had chosen to make an implacable enemy of him with his incendiary attack on 'power without responsibility', the furious proprietor had lost no opportunity in instructing his papers to oppose him, and did everything he could to undermine and harass him throughout his prime ministership. As Beaverbrook wrote, by 1936 'it appeared to me his end was in sight. He was politically distrusted. He would shortly go down in disgrace.'[32] Baldwin, for his part, retained a more English reserve, but said to Harold Nicolson earlier in the year that 'I hate no one, my dear fellow, but there are a few people whom I despise.'[33]

The abdication crisis became the perfect battleground for this antagonism between the two men, with Edward and Wallis as pawns in the centre. As Helen Hardinge put it, 'Lord Beaverbrook turned King Edward's attitude into a completely irrational but pervading bitterness . . . [He] used the latter as an unwitting tool in his own war against Baldwin.'[34] Perhaps the best indication of Beaverbrook's motivation was a comment, reported by Churchill's son Randolph, when the magnate was asked why he – hardly a devoted monarchist – had committed so much time and effort to supporting Edward when few others would have done so. His reply was pithy and vicious: 'To bugger Baldwin.'[35]

After Beaverbrook left Fort Belvedere, he visited Monckton for a candid discussion of the situation. The lawyer 'fell in with my views in a way that struck me as more convincing than the agreement the King had already expressed'.[36] Monckton had no great faith in the morganatic marriage idea, but promised to give some thought to how the situation might be ameliorated. Beaverbrook also canvassed opinion from Churchill, whose attitude towards the whole situation was summed up by 'let the King have his cutie', and who leaned towards the morganatic solution as the best available option; and then met Samuel Hoare, who he believed might be 'the King's man' within Cabinet.

Although Hoare had previously been dismissive of the idea of Edward marrying Wallis under any circumstances, Beaverbrook believed that he had a crucial advantage. For years, the First Lord of the Admiralty had been taking money from him in exchange for leaking information from Cabinet meetings. Therefore he went to see Hoare less as a courtesy and more with a view to obtaining some return on his considerable investment.

Compromised though he may have been, Hoare held firm against the idea, even as Beaverbrook argued that all he was asking was that Edward be offered advocacy, rather than personal support. The only concession that Hoare allowed was that he would continue to feed his employer information from the Cabinet meetings, without committing to any personal involvement. Beaverbrook then considered turning to Lord Hewart, the Lord Chief Justice, which Edward initially agreed with. And then matters shifted.

The king was delighted at his alliance with the newspaperman. As he wrote, 'Where before I had stood alone, now I had a powerful champion.'[37] Yet he also realised that Beaverbrook was neither straightforward nor wholly reliable. He was struck by the reluctant realisation that 'However carefully I walked, [my actions] would involve me in a long course of seeming dissimulation for which I had neither the talent nor the appetite.'[38] Therefore, he telephoned his supporter at two in the morning the next day. Beaverbrook recounted that this had 'greatly embarrassed me', due to Edward speaking 'with such freedom that I was positively alarmed, and he, in turn, was impatient of the guarded nature of my replies'.[39] One reason for Beaverbrook's reticence was his increasing belief that Edward's telephone was being bugged. This, as it later transpired, was an accurate assumption.* The king, acting under the instructions of Wallis, told Beaverbrook that she had no interest in becoming queen, and would prefer to be his wife in a morganatic marriage.

The irritated and exhausted proprietor then 'knew that the agreement between us was null and void', and that 'the fatal weaknesses of the King's position were rapidly becoming apparent'.[40] Beaverbrook trusted in Edward's popularity with the public, and Baldwin's relative lack of appeal, and believed that, given time, there would have been a widespread acceptance of Wallis as his wife, to say nothing of his nemesis's ignominious defeat. Yet the sovereign was no tactician. Preoccupied with matters immediately at hand, he was unable, or unwilling, to bide his time and wait to see how public opinion went.

One of these matters was the increasing unhappiness of Mrs Simpson. She had received a series of threatening letters at Cumberland Terrace, and wrote, 'I began to feel like a hunted animal.'[41] She had confided in Sibyl Colefax that she was caught between people's entreaties to leave the country, and her lover's fixation with her. 'They do not understand that if I [left], the King would come after me regardless of anything. They would then get their scandal in a far worse form than they are getting it now.'[42] Although she attempted to keep the details from Edward, he was informed of a suspected plot to blow up her house, and so removed her and her Aunt Bessie, who was visiting, to Fort Belvedere on 27 November. It would be the last time Wallis saw London in years. Once at the Fort, she felt no less of a prisoner. As she put it, 'This was no longer the enchanted Fort; it was the Fort beleaguered.' The only mercy, and a petty one at that, was that the press, unbelievably in retrospect, kept their silence.

Yet even as Edward attempted to assure her that 'I still think something can be worked out', Wallis began to toy with a new idea: remove herself from England, possibly for ever, and damn

---

* See Chapter Ten.

the consequences. She wrote to Sibyl that 'I am planning quite by myself to go away for a while. I think everybody here would like that – except one person perhaps – but I am planning a clever means of escape.' She was intelligent enough to realise what she was up against. 'After a while, my name will be forgotten by the people and only two people will suffer instead of a mass of people who aren't interested anyway in individual feelings but only the workings of a system . . . It is an uncomfortable feeling to remain stopping in a house where the hostess has tired of you as a guest.'[43]

As a miserable Wallis underwent something of a breakdown, Baldwin convened a meeting of the Cabinet to discuss the proposal of the morganatic marriage, as he had promised. It was the first occasion that the affair was discussed openly, and despite the weeks of intrigue and rumour that had preceded it, many of the ministers were staggered at the news. The prime minister offered the morganatic suggestion as impartially as he could, but stressed both how recalcitrant Edward was being and how he seemed to be in thrall to the likes of Beaverbrook and Harmsworth. He concluded by saying, 'It seems that the King has been encouraged to believe that Winston Churchill would in these circumstances be prepared to form an alternative Government. If this were true, there would be a grave risk for the country being divided into two camps – for and against the King. This clearly would be fraught with danger of the most formidable kind.'[44]

The idea of a 'King's Party' – a shadow government emerging without accountability or a mandate – was enough to shock the Cabinet into rejecting the proposal of a morganatic marriage immediately. Simon wrote that 'There was no dissent from the view of Mr Baldwin . . . that it was impossible to contemplate special legislation to impose inferior status on the future wife of the King.'[45] Even Hoare, mindful of the views of his peers, did not offer any advocacy of Edward's position. Only Duff Cooper dissented, and that was to weakly plead that the king be given more time; Baldwin put him down with the statement: 'The situation has gone too far to admit of any postponement.'[46]

Nicolson wrote in his diary that Ramsay MacDonald said, 'in deep sorrow', that '[Edward] has done more harm to his country than any man in history', and mused that although the Cabinet and the Privy Council were set on his abdication, the king retained an unshakeable belief that the country, the so-called 'great warm heart of the people', supported him. Nicolson believed that this was untrue: 'The upper classes mind [Wallis] being an American rather more than they mind her being divorced . . . The lower classes do not mind her being an American but loathe the idea that she has had two husbands already.' He concluded that, despite he himself liking Wallis well enough and having some sympathy for her, she had lied to Sibyl in maintaining that she had no intention of marrying Edward, and 'I cannot feel that she ought to be anything better than a fool or a minx.'[47]

Without Cabinet support, it was inevitable that the Dominions would not be amenable to the idea of a morganatic marriage, especially as Baldwin was able to use his influence to achieve the desired result. Although Anthony Eden spoke of the 'scrupulous impartiality' with which the telegram of enquiry was worded, the observation of the Dominions Secretary, Malcolm MacDonald, was more revealing: 'It is vital that the [Dominion leaders] should reach quickly, spontaneously and unanimously the same conclusion about the constitutional solution.'[48] The telegram simply read, 'Do you recommend the King's marrying morganatically? Or, if the King insists upon marrying, do you recommend abdication?'[49] There was no longer the possibility of allowing Edward to remain as sovereign provided that Wallis was either dispensed with altogether or kept locked up in the Fort. Instead, it had been decided that the troublesome king had caused enough trouble for one nation. Better that he was forced out quickly, and his responsible, selfless and above all compliant brother take his place.

Although Hoare did not act for Edward at the Cabinet meeting, he met Beaverbrook for lunch immediately afterwards to tell him how badly things had gone for the king. Even as his irritated paymaster believed that the situation was 'difficult but by no means impossible',[50] the appeal to the Dominions made matters considerably harder. Beaverbrook, a pressman through and through, understood that a brutal economy of language was the best way of persuading someone to do as their questioner wanted, and that the initiative in this case lay with whoever was allowed to frame the question: in this case, Baldwin and the Cabinet.

He headed to Buckingham Palace to meet the king in an agitated state, and obliquely referred to his similarly unfortunate royal forebear by saying, 'Sir, you have put your head on the execution block. All that Baldwin has to do now is to swing the axe.'[51] As he stressed the essential social conservatism of the Dominions – 'I am a Canadian . . . Their answer will be a swift and emphatic no'[52] – and argued that Edward had the right to send out his own, considerably different, telegram framing the question in more favourable terms, he found little support from the king, who swung between disinterest and fatalism. As Beaverbrook put it, 'He followed a policy of total drift which carried him inevitably to disaster.'[53] Harold Nicolson found much the same, as he criticised Edward's 'deplorable levity, which at moments amounts to infantilism'.[54]

Others were less content to fiddle while the institution of the monarchy threatened to burn. The Duke of York, gradually accepting the inevitability of what was coming, wrote to Godfrey Thomas and grimly promised, 'If the worst happens, and I have to take over, you can be assured that I will do my best to clear up the inevitable mess, if the whole fabric does not crumble under the shock and strain of it all.'[55] Although he had initially responded with 'consternation and incredulity'[56] to Hardinge's suggestion that abdication was likely, Bertie had written to his brother on 22 November, after a difficult interview, to say, 'When you told me of your decision to marry Wallis the other evening, I do hope you did not think that I was unsympathetic about it. Since then I have been thinking a great deal about you, as I do so long for you to be happy with the one person you adore . . . I do realise all your great difficulties and feel sure that whatever you decide to do will be in the best interests of this country & Empire . . . I feel I must send you this note, because when we were talking the other evening, I am afraid I could not say what I really felt, as your news came as a great surprise to me.'[57]

Monckton, acknowledging that his monarch and friend would need counsel and assistance, gave up his practice and was either by Edward's side or in his service throughout December. Beaverbrook, meanwhile, devoted himself to frantic scheming and intrigue. A lunch here with Samuel Hoare; another meeting there at Buckingham Palace, all for the same purpose: to buy time in the hope that the government would fall, and that its replacement would look more kindly on Edward's predicament. Even as the king grandly stated that 'Mrs Simpson will not be abandoned', it had become increasingly clear that the crisis would soon lurch into its final act.

Nonetheless, few could have foreseen the event that would lead to its eventual precipitation.

Chapter Nine

'Make Britain Great Again'

Had it not been for a single speech that he made on 1 December 1936, it is likely that the name Alfred Blunt would have disappeared into obscurity. Born in Brittany in 1879, he had spent decades in distinguished ecclesiastical service that had resulted in his becoming Bishop of Bradford in 1931. His mental health was not always robust, and he suffered a series of breakdowns, but he was a popular figure, who inclined towards Anglo-Catholicism and admitted to 'a liking for a certain amount of [the] ceremonial'.[1]

A socialist and a 'good mixer', he was as likely to be found making sandwiches and doing the washing-up at parish functions as he was to be delivering theologically bold sermons. One canon at Bradford Cathedral praised his 'true scholar's essential humbleness of mind', which translated itself into an enquiring wish to deal with the ills of society. In 1933, he wrote that 'Human society is organised on wrong principles; its guiding motives are self-seeking individualism and the dominance of money. God is a side issue in the life of very many.'[2] Although he did not, on that occasion, mention of whom he was thinking, it became increasingly clear that a man who possessed these wrong principles in abundance was Edward, then Prince of Wales.

As 1936 wore on, Bishop Blunt found himself concerned by the apparent lack of godliness that the king – and defender of the faith – was exhibiting. Although Blunt was not a priggish or sanctimonious man, he believed that the Coronation, which was planned for the spring of 1937, was a serious ritual, steeped in religious observance, and one that should be regarded with considerable gravity. At the diocesan conference at the beginning of December, he felt that he should discuss the service, and the king's apparently lackadaisical attitude towards it.* What he did not realise was that his carefully chosen and thoughtful words would license the press to end their increasingly restrictive policy of silence.

Blunt spoke of the king's 'avowedly representative position', and, while allowing that 'his personal views and opinions are his own, and as an individual he has the right of us all to be the keeper of his own private conscience', he stated that 'in his public capacity at his Coronation, he stands for the English people's idea of kingship'. He drew on his erudition to maintain that 'It has for long centuries been, and I hope still is, an essential part of that idea that the King needs the grace of God for his office . . . Whatever it may mean, much or little, to the individual who is crowned, to the people as a whole it means their dedication of the English monarchy to the care of God.'

The part that led a hundred hacks to believe that the news of 'the king's problem' could now be brought into public knowledge was when Blunt talked of 'the faith, prayer, and self-dedication of the King himself; and on that it would be improper for me to say anything except to commend him to God's grace, which he will so abundantly need, as we all need it – for the King is a man like ourselves – if he is to do his duty faithfully. We hope that he is aware of his need. Some of us wish that he gave more positive signs of such awareness.'

A journalist on the Bradford *Telegraph and Argus*, Ronald Harker, took notes of Blunt's speech, and believed that it was a clear – if necessarily coded – allusion to events taking place in London, particularly the king's relationship with Wallis. As a result, he filed his story to the Press Association, which duly wired the account of Blunt's speech to every newspaper office in England, along with

---

* John Simon wrote sorrowfully that 'unfortunately, Edward VIII did not even go to church on Sundays'.

Wallis Simpson, 1936. Although she pronounced herself 'nothing much to look at', Mrs Simpson enraptured Edward VIII sufficiently to come close to bringing down the monarchy. She divorced her second husband Ernest in a scandalous case in October that year, but rumours of collusion nearly derailed the entire thing.

Fort Belvedere, 1936. Edward's private residence in Windsor Great Park, 'the Fort', was a zealously cherished hideaway for the King, his friends and, of course, Wallis.

George V and Queen Mary. Neither the previous King nor the Queen Mother had faith in their son's regal abilities; George commented that 'after I am dead, that boy will ruin himself in twelve months'.

Cosmo Lang (with Edward). The Archbishop of Canterbury loathed the King, but overreached himself with a coruscating sermon he preached after the abdication.

George McMahon, July 1936. The would-be assassin of Edward VIII was sentenced to a year in prison, but both the attempt itself and the subsequent trial were shrouded in murky secrecy and intrigue.

Edward and Wallis on holiday, August 1936. Edward and Wallis's cruise on board the *Nahlin* was both a public relations triumph and the start of international awareness of their liaison.

Alec Hardinge. The King's private secretary loathed his master, who he believed was morally unfit to rule, and eventually set the abdication in motion by conveying his candid thoughts to him in a devastating letter.

Duff and Diana Cooper. The Secretary of State for War and his wife were loyal, although not uncritical, friends to Edward before and during his brief reign.

Wallis and Edward at Balmoral, September 1936. Their sole Scottish trip together was a public relations disaster, as it was felt that Edward had snubbed more deserving subjects for his mistress.

Joachim von Ribbentrop, 1936. The German ambassador to Britain in late 1936, 'Herr Brickendrop' was a pompous and unpopular functionary who endeared himself to Hitler by claiming to have Edward's ear.

Lord Beaverbrook and Winston Churchill. The newspaper magnate and the politician formed an alliance with the aim of defending Edward's right to remain on the throne, even if this meant founding a so-called 'King's Party'.

Walter Monckton. The so-called 'architect of the abdication' was a brilliant lawyer whose intellect, patience and charm proved vital in bringing about a satisfactory resolution to the crisis.

Edward visits Abertillery, Wales, November 1936. When the King announced that 'something must be done' after seeing the plight of impoverished coal miners, he inadvertently triggered a political storm.

Daily Express

TODAY'S WEATHER: MILDER
RADIO PROGRAMMES: PAGE 23.

NO. 11,409   TUESDAY, DECEMBER 8, 1936   ONE PENNY

Mrs. Simpson Authorises
Dramatic Statement From Cannes

I AM WILLING TO WITHDRAW

If Such Action Would Solve The Problem

LATEST NEWS
Telephone: Central 8000

LORD BROWNLOW
READS SIGNED
DOCUMENT

'A Situation Which Has Become
Both Unhappy And Untenable'.

Daily Express Staff Reporter

CANNES, Monday Night.

Mrs. Simpson is "willing, if such action would solve the problem, to withdraw forthwith from a situation that has been rendered both unhappy and untenable."

Her offer is made in a statement signed by Mrs. Simpson herself which Lord Brownlow, Lord-in-Waiting to and close friend of the King, read to a Press Conference in the Hotel Majestic, Cannes, tonight. The statement said:—

"Mrs. Simpson, throughout the last few weeks, has invariably wished to avoid any

Mrs. Simpson

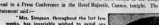

Daily Express, December 1936. An overwhelmed Wallis offered to leave Edward and England and to frustrate the abdication, but by then her actions were too late.

Stanley Baldwin, December 1936. 'Honest Stan', the Prime Minister, dealt with the crisis with a mixture of straightforwardness and occasional frustration, which climaxed in a make-or-break speech to the House of Commons.

Edward VIII abdicates, 11 December 1936. Edward made a live broadcast from Windsor Castle to explain his decision to abdicate, which was generally received extremely well by its listeners.

George VI, 'Bertie', December 1936. Edward's younger brother became King after his abdication. The prospect terrified him, but his understanding of duty was much greater than Edward's.

Abdication protest, December 1936. The revelation that Edward was about to abdicate polarised opinion, leading to everything from public displays of support - as here - to death threats being sent to Buckingham Palace.

Instrument of abdication, December 1936. Edward's abdication was the most remarkable event in the history of the monarchy since the execution of Charles I in 1649.

INSTRUMENT OF ABDICATION

I, Edward the Eighth, of Great Britain, Ireland, and the British Dominions beyond the Seas, King, Emperor of India, do hereby declare My irrevocable determination to renounce the Throne for Myself and for My descendants, and My desire that effect should be given to this Instrument of Abdication immediately.

In token whereof I have hereunto set My hand this tenth day of December, nineteen hundred and thirty six, in the presence of the witnesses whose signatures are subscribed.

SIGNED AT
FORT BELVEDERE
IN THE PRESENCE
OF

'The King leaves Britain', December 1936. It was believed impossible for a former monarch and his consort to live in their former country as private citizens, and apart from a few brief visits, neither Edward nor Wallis ever spent any significant time in England again.

Edward and Wallis, June 1937. Edward and Wallis eventually married, but relations between him and his family had deteriorated to such an extent that the wedding had virtually no guests.

Edward and Wallis with Adolf Hitler, 1937. Edward's Nazi sympathies have been much debated, but it is undoubtedly true that Hitler believed that the former King was 'a kind of English National Socialist'.

an editorial written by the editor of the *Yorkshire Post*, John Mann, which explicitly stated, 'Dr Blunt must have had good reason for so pointed a remark. Most people, by this time, are aware that a great deal of rumour regarding the King has been published of late in the more sensational American newspapers . . . Certain statements . . . cannot be treated with quite so much indifference: they are too circumstantial and have plainly a foundation in fact.'

Mann, who knew the effect that his words would have on national opinion, came close to preaching himself when he stated, 'An increasing number of responsible people . . . fear . . . the King may not yet have perceived how complete . . . must be that self-dedication of which Dr Blunt spoke if the Coronation is to bring a blessing to all the peoples of the Empire, and is not, on the contrary, to prove a stumbling block.'[3]

There has been some ambiguity as to whether Blunt himself knew of Edward's liaison with Wallis. It would be easy to portray him as a learned but unworldly man whose carefully considered speech achieved an entirely unexpected end, thanks to his unintentional and apparent allusion to the ongoing scandal, and he himself issued a statement denying any knowledge of the affair. However, he had attended a meeting at Lambeth Palace a fortnight before, at which Cosmo Lang had talked scathingly about 'a twice-divorced American lady whom the American press openly called the Queen-designate of England', and declared that 'the British newspapers were responsible but could not be silent for ever'.[4] The Bishop of Wakefield's wife wrote a witty limerick about the affair:

He did not set out for a stunt
Or wanted to come to the front
But despite his desire
Set the heathen on fire
His name, like his language, was Blunt.[5]

Beaverbrook even maintained that Lang had directly put Blunt up to the speech, although there is no evidence to support this supposition. Yet whether or not it was a coded reference, the idea that Edward's royal authority was now so diminished that a bishop might make a public attack on his spiritual credentials was unprecedented. Duff Cooper summed it up when he wrote, 'I suppose it was the first time in the century that the sovereign of Great Britain had been publicly rebuked.'[6]

Initially, as Beaverbrook promised Edward in a telephone conversation, the stories in the papers would be essentially neutral in character, a reporting of Blunt's speech and Mann's editorial commentary. Yet many newspaper editors, especially Dawson of *The Times*, were restless. He had written an editorial on 30 November that referred to the 'steadiness and balance' of Parliament and contained an allusion to 'any crisis that may arise, whether foreign or domestic',[7] which virtually any well-informed reader would have recognised as a barely veiled reference to the news that was not yet being printed. Now that the so-called 'gentlemen's agreement' was at an end, reaction would be swift and total. Dawson wrote in his diary of 1 December that 'I decided in the end to print the speech in full, but to refrain from my own comment . . . anything else would look like collusion.'[8] Even Beaverbrook's own papers were obliged to cover the story, although, as he told Edward, 'The *Express* will, with the other newspapers, report the facts. It is our duty to do so.'[9]

The newspapers' silence had been unprecedented. As John Simon put it, 'It was indeed a most extraordinary fact that in a country where there is no censorship of news, where rival journals compete strenuously for circulation, and where any attempt by governments to control topics of discussion would have been fiercely resisted and everywhere disregarded, the British Press by a voluntary ordinance . . . had maintained complete silence for six months on a subject which would otherwise have been eagerly canvassed in every household in the land.'[10] Through a mixture of coercion and tact, the saga had been kept away from the front pages, but this was now, inevitably, at an end. As Hardinge put it, 'The publicity which came like a thunderclap on December 2nd completely altered the situation.'[11]

Beaverbrook, of course, had his own ideas on the best way to control the situation. He knew how the narrative was likely to progress. The first editorial stories would appear in the papers most sympathetic to the government, and would be correspondingly hostile to Edward. There was then the necessity to, as the publisher put it, 'counter hard, and at once'. As he spoke with his 'natural belligerence', the magnate made it clear to the king that the only way in which he would be able to marry and remain on the throne would be by becoming the victor in a hard-fought propaganda war. His belief, which 'many others hold with me [is] that there is nothing wrong in the King's marrying a woman who has divorced her husband. A strong case can be made.'[12]

His personal loyalty to his monarch was not in doubt. When Hoare, purportedly acting on behalf of Baldwin, approached him to suggest that his papers' support for Edward was damaging the 'united front' that otherwise existed, Beaverbrook responded steadfastly that 'I have taken the King's shilling. I am a King's man.' Yet he was frustrated by Edward's unwillingness to join him in the battle royal that he so desperately wished for. The king said to him on the evening of 2 December that 'I mean to retire into private life.' Beaverbrook, who still believed that he should not abdicate, and did not want to abdicate, was irritated by what he saw as an unwillingness to fight, and perhaps even win, the conflict that was upon him. Had he known of the reason for Edward's disinterest, he might have been more sympathetic.

While she was at the Fort, Wallis began to discuss with Edward an idea that, had it been executed, could have been a significant factor in the crisis. She, like other Americans, knew of the impact that the president's so-called 'fireside chats' had on popular opinion, and she also recognised that the Christmas broadcasts George V had delivered in previous years were a successful means of communicating with one's people in a more intimate and personal fashion than any newspaper article or similar public proclamation could be. Thus she proposed that Edward should do the same, explaining the situation to his people and asking for their support and understanding. His initial reaction was a favourable one. He showed 'a flash of his normal enthusiasm' and said, 'Darling, it may be grasping at a straw, but I'm going to try it. It's a damn good thing. But I'll have to get the Cabinet's permission, and that will take some doing.'[13]

Before he could attempt to deliver his speech, however, Baldwin informed him on 2 December that the Dominions would not accept the idea of a morganatic marriage. The prime minister did not report that this unanimous rejection was the result of careful diplomacy, with the result that the Dominions were able to say that they would support the decision of the British government. Ignoring Edward's petulant objection that 'Parliament has not been consulted . . . the issue has never been presented',[14] Baldwin carefully stated what Edward's options were. The first, and his preferred solution, was that the king abandon the idea of marrying Wallis altogether. The second was that he could marry, contrary to the Cabinet's advice, and bring down the government, thereby triggering an election where his marriage would be the dominant question. Or, of course, he could abdicate. The prime minister was already exhausted; Dawson reported that 'he was getting worn out and sat with his head in his hand, propped up by the table'.[15] But he was not to be beaten at this time of national crisis. As Dawson wrote, '[He] was quite clear about his course.'[16]

Edward was reported to have said, when told that he could not contract a morganatic marriage, 'I have known that all along', but insisted, 'I can't do my job without her. I am going to marry her, and I will *go*.'[17] He repeated, as if mesmerised, 'Wallis is the most wonderful woman in the world', and the prime minister, taking pity on him, replied, 'Well, sir, I hope that you may find her so. Whatever happens, I hope you will be happy.'[18] Edward ended the interview by telling Baldwin to forbid *The Times* to publish an attack on Mrs Simpson the next day; the prime minister tried, and failed, to explain that it was not in his, or anyone's, power to tell the press what to do.

In fact, Wallis would be the first to go. That evening, she realised that her continued presence was hugely unhelpful to them both, and said, 'I'm going to leave. I've already stayed too long. I should have gone when you showed me the Hardinge letter. But now nothing you can say will hold me here any longer.'[19] Bricks had been thrown through her window; abuse had been screamed at her in the street. Those who were incensed by the situation but were unwilling, or afraid, to attack the king directly took solace in pouring out vitriol towards his consort. This time, he realised that it would be foolhardy to stop her departure. He replied, 'It will be hard for me to have you go, but it would be harder still to have you stay.'[20] He asked his lord-in-waiting, Peregrine 'Perry' Cust, Lord Brownlow, to accompany her; before Brownlow left, he asked the king point-blank whether he intended to abdicate. 'Oh no,' Edward replied, something that Brownlow later called 'the first and last important lie of our friendship'.[21]

Wallis left for her friends' villa in Cannes along with Brownlow in the early hours of the morning, under the alias of 'Mr and Mrs Harris', convinced that she would never see her lover or England again. Their parting was, she wrote, 'infinitely sad and forlorn', although not everyone regarded it as such. Hardinge, who had seen the 'as charming as ever' Edward for the last time on 2 December, sneered that her departure was accomplished 'in humiliating haste and at the dead of night',[22] and a footman irreverently remarked to the butler, 'Well, that's the end of that'; when counselled, 'Don't be so sure', he replied, 'We'll keep our fingers crossed.'[23]

The coverage in the papers on 3 December was much as could be expected, although one minor comfort was that the dreaded full-frontal attack in *The Times* was, as Nicolson described it, 'a confused and muddled jumble', as Dawson had written it himself. The editor's over-excitement at being able, at last, to attack the king openly had led to 'an amalgam of tortuous and pompous nothings',[24] which concentrated more on the constitutional implications than the relationship itself. The other papers wrote, in Nicolson's words, 'more in sorrow than in anger'. The exception was Beaverbrook's *Express*, which ignored the story altogether. The harsher criticisms would come the next day. Even so, Bertie, passing through Euston station that day, was 'both surprised and horrified to see that the posters of the *Daily Press* had the following as their headlines in block letters: THE KING'S MARRIAGE'.

The Duke of York hastened to see Queen Mary to tell her of his surprise that the matter had been made so public, and saw his brother, together with Walter Monckton. He described Edward as 'in a great state of excitement . . . [He] said he would leave the country as King after making a broadcast to his subjects & leave it to them to decide what should be done. The Prime Minister went to see him . . . and David said to Queen Mary that he could not live alone as King & must marry Mrs S.'[25] Bertie's despondency at this 'dreadful announcement', exacerbated by his brother's mania, can only be imagined.

Edward seemed not to understand the consequences of his actions. A few days before, he had written to his mother to say, 'I feel so happy and relieved to have at last been able to tell you my wonderful secret; a dream which I have for so long been praying might one day come true. Now that Wallis will be free to marry me in April it only remains for me to decide the best action I take for our future happiness and for the good of all concerned.' Ignoring her justified fears, he concluded, 'God bless you darling Mama for all your sweetness to and understanding of your always very loving and devoted David.'[26] This was a typical example of Edward only hearing what he wished to hear. As Queen Mary later informed Wigram, with justifiable weariness, 'I cannot think why my eldest son speaks of my "sweetness" to him during that awful time, because I thought I was extremely outspoken and tried to express my displeasure, but I suppose he never listened to what I said.'[27]

At this stage, it was Edward, rather than the now-absent Wallis, who took the brunt of public disaffection, although a gang of boys was observed walking down the King's Road in Chelsea singing

'Hark, the herald angels sing/Mrs Simpson's pinched our King!'[28] Nicolson reported that the general mood in Parliament was one of depression, citing the king's 'passionate selfishness', and the fact that 'in eight months, he has destroyed the great structure of popularity which he had raised . . . I do find a deep and enraged fury against the King himself.' He concluded that abdication was now inevitable, and that 'we are all staggered with shame and distress . . . I never dreamt it would come to this.'[29]

This was echoed by Godfrey Thomas, who wrote despairingly to Queen Mary that 'Words fail me to express what I feel on the subject, and the implications of the contemplated action do not bear thinking about. (The word "abdication" alone is so entirely and horribly foreign to English history.)' Mindful of his recipient, he blamed Wallis – 'One hardly ventures to blame the King because, as regards that side of his life, he seems completely bewitched – but what the lady has to answer for, no tongue can tell' – and concluded that 'the tragedy of the present outcome has broken my heart . . . Now that . . . a real crisis . . . has come, no-one has been allowed to help.'[30]

A few remained ostensibly loyal to Edward, at this darkest of hours. The Liberal politician Walter Peacock affirmed that 'We have all observed with admiration the way in which your Majesty has brought common sense to bear in carrying out all your duties and has disregarded tradition where tradition is out of date & your steadfast championing of the cause of the underdog.'[31] The ambiguity as to who the underdog was – Wallis, perhaps, or Edward himself – was left open.

Lionel Halsey, whose pension the king had tried to stop, also offered his respects: 'May I write one line of sincere and heartfelt sympathy in the awful tragedy which has come to pass . . . I do feel more deeply than I can express the awful days you are going through . . . Since the first day I was asked by you to go to Canada in 1919 until today, I have had the very greatest admiration, love and respect for you . . . I still believe that your Majesty is the only person who can lead this country through the difficult days ahead and keep our Empire intact.'[32] Nonetheless, Halsey also informed Queen Mary of his opinions the following day: 'I feel perfectly miserable about the whole thing, and only wish I could have been more successful [in averting it]. It is indeed a real tragedy, and more especially when one knows that, if it was not for the fact of the influence of bad friends, His Majesty by his own personality and ability could and would have even increased that wonderful prestige and heritage which King George left for the Empire.'[33]

Churchill, of course, remained steadfast. His enthusiasm for a morganatic marriage had led him to write to his wife, '[Beaverbrook] rang me up to say that he had seen the gent . . . [he] was definitely up for it. It now turns on what the Cabinet will say.'[34] Although Baldwin, and others, believed that the exiled politician was using the crisis as a means of re-entering front-line politics, whether as leader of the so-called 'King's Party' or as head of a new Conservative administration, Churchill genuinely liked Edward and wished to help. He told the trade unionist Walter Citrine, who had informed him that the unions would always back the government over the king, that 'I will defend him. I think it is my duty.'[35] His major errors were to underestimate the relationship between the king and Wallis – 'His present attachment will follow the course of all the others', he confidently and incorrectly informed Marie Belloc Lowndes – and to believe that he was the wise counsellor Edward would listen to. Lascelles later sighed that 'Winston's sentimental loyalty to the D of W was based on a tragic false premise – viz. that he really *knew* the D of W – which he never did.'[36] It is doubtful that anyone, save Wallis and Monckton, managed to penetrate the royal carapace.

Churchill, along with Beaverbrook and the king's solicitor, George Allen, favoured the idea of Edward making the broadcast that he had discussed with Wallis. Accordingly, the king began writing a speech on 3 December that would play to his greatest strengths, aided by Monckton, Churchill and others. He would present himself as a servant of the people, 'that same man whom you had known so well as the Prince of Wales'. He wrote of how his motto of '*Ich dien*', or 'I serve', was the guiding principle of his life, and praised the 'open-hearted welcome' of the Dominions and the 'courtesy and consideration' of the British newspapers, before speaking of how 'I could not go on bearing the heavy burdens that constantly rest on me unless I could be strengthened in the task by a happy married life and so I am finally resolved to marry the woman I love when she is free to marry me.' He struck an explicitly personal note – 'You know me well enough to understand that I could never have contemplated a marriage of convenience . . . I have been a very lonely man' – and, after stating that Wallis would never become queen and had no wish to be so, concluded by saying, 'I feel it is best for me to go away for a while so that you will have time to reflect calmly and quietly but without undue delay on what I have said . . . I shall always have a deep affection for my country and for all of you.'[37]

Had the Cabinet given Edward permission to broadcast the speech, events would have happened with speed. Godfrey Thomas asked Sir John Reith how quickly the broadcast could be put out, to which Reith suggested that, if the prime minister assented, it could be done from Windsor Castle on the evening of 4 December. Both men believed the broadcast was likely to take place, as long as Baldwin gave his agreement. This would then allow the king to head to Europe for a few days, or weeks, and remove himself from the intolerable strain he was under. Should public opinion, managed by Beaverbrook and Harmsworth, appear to be on his side, he could then return, and the idea of marriage, morganatic or otherwise, could be discussed once more. If the broadcast went badly, he could reunite with Wallis and remove himself from the stress and misery of the situation in another country. He was said to be 'in a great state of excitement', as the Duke of York put it; like Wallis, he was undergoing some kind of breakdown, with only a carefully honed degree of self-restraint keeping him from collapsing altogether.

Once again, Baldwin, like a portly harbinger of bad tidings, appeared at Buckingham Palace, this time at the late hour of nine.

The prime minister, too, was agitated and tired, not least because his car had been involved in a collision with another vehicle a couple of hours before. He had told an unsurprised Archbishop of Canterbury of the latest developments that day, and had batted back Churchill's innuendo at Prime Minister's Questions earlier on, announcing that the situation was too fluid for him to be able to discuss it publicly in any detail. Wilson had suggested that Edward was likely to propose a broadcast, so it was no great surprise to Baldwin when the king put it forward; his brisk response was that it would be unconstitutional. An aggrieved Edward replied, 'You want me to go, don't you? And before I go, I think it is right, for her sake and mine, that I should speak.'[38] Baldwin answered, with justifiable exhaustion, 'What I want, sir, is what you told me you wanted: to go with dignity, not dividing the country, and making things as smooth as possible for your successor. To broadcast would be to go over the heads of your ministers ... You may, by speaking, divide opinion; but you will certainly harden it.'[39]

It was then that Baldwin, who had made the running consistently since the beginning of the crisis, made two tactical errors that, in their own fashion, prolonged the events for several more days. The first was relatively minor: he allowed the king to believe that there was still a chance he would be permitted to make his broadcast, regardless of his own feelings, by telling him he would discuss it with the Cabinet the next day. Had he simply told him that it was impossible, it would have hastened matters. The second, which he regretted almost immediately,* was to concede to the king's apparently innocent wish to see 'an old friend with whom I can talk freely'.[40] This 'old friend' was Churchill, whom Baldwin had hitherto forbidden to be in direct contact with Edward, fearing collusion between the two. Now, there was nothing stopping

---

* Duff Cooper described him saying at Cabinet the next day, regarding this permission, that 'I made a bloomer last night. I am very sorry for it. I realized it afterwards. I suppose I was tired at the time.'

the principal members of the 'King's Party' from assembling and scheming openly.

The king, exhausted from what he called a 'terrible day', then held a tense and awkward interview with his mother at Marlborough House – his first in ten days – at which his protestation that 'I have no desire to bring you and the family into all this. It is something I must handle alone' did not produce any sympathy or understanding, only continued disappointment that he would not change his mind. Helen Hardinge wrote that Queen Mary sent a note to her husband the following day in which 'her feelings about HM's treatment of his family were fully expressed', to wit that 'the King was . . . doing his best to pretend that the Royal Family did not exist'.[41] Osbert Sitwell later reported that Mary told him their disappointment was especially great because they believed that the Prince of Wales would become a remarkable king; as she put it, 'He had seemed to have proved himself a master technician of his rare and difficult trade.'[42] Instead, he exhibited his frustration with his unbending mother by adopting an attitude of coldness, leavened with open rudeness, that she believed was a result of Wallis's influence, and for which she never forgave him.

After this unsatisfying meeting, Edward then returned to the Palace, to find that neither Beaverbrook nor Churchill believed he would be allowed to deliver his broadcast, nor that he should leave the country and allow an effective coup to take place in his absence. Exhausted, lonely and despondent, he felt, as he stood outside Buckingham Palace, the same 'powerful resurgence of the intense dislike for the building I had always felt'. As if accepting that he was never destined to be king, he mused, 'Did I really belong in there at all? The answer came immediately – certainly not alone.'[43] It would be the last time he entered the much-loathed Palace as King of England. With the loyal and equally exhausted Monckton by his side, he prepared to head to the Fort, but as he left the gates, a crowd of onlookers, well-wishers and gawpers, attracted by reports of his presence, let out a loud cheer.

Pleased, Monckton said, 'Ah, that's better!', but Edward

momentarily toyed with the idea of getting out of the car and delivering a version of his broadcast there and then; as he wrote, 'The
spotlights playing on the façade, the lonely figure of the King pleading his cause – the scene could have been extremely effective.'[44]
But, perhaps under Monckton's guidance, no such unprecedented
display of royal humility took place. The two headed on to the
Fort, where Monckton would remain by Edward's side until the
end of the crisis. This decision was made out of sympathy as much
as necessity, as the lawyer knew that his friend was undertaking
'an unutterably lonely battle'.[45]

Fort Belvedere, which today is leased to a Canadian retail magnate and his wife, is a curious place. Located in Windsor Great
Park, close to the town of Sunningdale, it was initially built in the
eighteenth century by the architect Henry Flitcroft in the Pallad-
ian style, as a folly. In 1828, it was extended and rebuilt by Jeffry
Wyatville, who had also redesigned Windsor Castle, and was given
to Edward by his father, when he was Prince of Wales, in 1929.
Monckton called it a 'curious castellated country house, [which]
sometimes reminded me of a child's battle game, for outside the
house itself surrounding the nearest lawn was a little castellated
wall through which peeped small guns or cannon, trophies from
wars of long ago'.[46]

George V purportedly said, 'What could you possibly want that
queer old place for? Those damn weekends I suppose.' The 'queer
old place' became the closest thing his son would have to a private
home. He later wrote of it that 'I came to love the Fort as I loved
no other material thing – perhaps because it was so much my own
creation.' It was not a place that allowed privacy; it was so shaped
that if a voice was raised on the ground floor, it could be heard
distinctly throughout the rest of the house. But it was his sanc-
tuary, a place that he associated with Wallis and, in Monckton's
words, with 'quiet and simple seclusion'. Now, in the final days of
his reign, it became his fortress; he considered that its militaristic
trappings made it 'a most appropriate place for a King making his
last stand'.[47]

*

On Friday 4 December, a groundswell of popular opinion in favour of Edward began making itself known, to Beaverbrook and Churchill's delight. The stock exchange, which had been suffering since the beginning of the crisis on Wednesday, stabilised. Massed ranks of people throughout the country spontaneously sang 'For He's a Jolly Good Fellow', and held placards saying 'God Save the King . . . from Baldwin'. A group of elderly women outside Buckingham Palace were heard to shout, 'Flog Baldwin! Down with the bishops!' As they were led away, they sang a chorus of 'God Save the King' in protest.

The popular press came out in support of the king, but so did the eclectic likes of the *New Statesman* and the *Catholic Times*. Sitwell described the scene vividly, writing that 'The deep-seated and smouldering appeal of monarchy was evinced in the most unlikely places. Large mobs of inquisitive, worried but deeply moved subjects gathered round every building in which the person of the sovereign might be present, and peripatetic crowds wandered like herds . . . There were no divisions of class . . . Poor and rich exhibited in this sudden eruption of feeling the same degree of violence, whether compassionate or angry or just puzzled.'[48]

Some of this support was unexpected, and possibly unwelcome. The British Union of Fascists, led by Oswald Mosley, marched to Victoria Park Square in east London, where Mosley announced to cheering crowds – as many as 50,000 people, by the exaggerated and partisan estimation* of the BUF's specially produced newspaper, *Crisis* – 'Let the people speak . . . The King should not be forced to abdicate by a junta of politicians who have no mandate from the people. The Government was elected to do something which it has not done and now it is trying to do something which it was never elected to do and something which the people of Britain would never elect it to do. Therefore, I demand that this question be put

---

* The *Daily Express*, itself no impartial title, estimated that around a tenth of that were present.

before the people of this country.' In his peroration, he declared, 'Let us sweep away by the vote of the people the interfering old women at Westminster, and give us a Government that will use the power of action to make Britain great again.'[49]

It is likely that Mosley, an opportunist as much as he was an orator, took Edward's side with essentially cynical motives, as many others did. It was the king who was supported, rather than Wallis; as a barmaid put it, when interviewed by the Associated Press, 'What's she got that I ain't?' Backed by the likes of William Joyce, the so-called 'Lord Haw-Haw',* who argued that 'on this issue, as on many others, Socialists and Conservatives will combine', and referred to Mosley as 'the first King's man in the nation',[50] the more intelligent of the fascist movement understood that, with Baldwin's authority weakened by Beaverbrook's attacks, the possibility had arisen that the government would fall, thereby creating a vacuum in which a populist movement might flourish. Had this taken place, Ribbentrop, far from being a figure of ridicule, might even have achieved the English alliance that he had promised Hitler, with Mosley as prime minister and Edward happily married to Queen Wallis and prepared to look the other way as Germany achieved its territorial aims.

None of this occurred to Beaverbrook, who simply thought that 'with a favourable public supporting him, the King could re-declare his intentions in his own good time and season'.[51] He believed that momentum had been regained, thanks to the support of the *Mail*, the *News Chronicle* – which chose to attack its usual patron, Baldwin, who felt that he had been 'wounded in the house of a friend',[52] as Dawson described it as 'particularly mischievous' in its pressing for a 'morganatic' compromise'– and, inevitably, the *Express*. As Beaverbrook wrote, 'If public opinion could be brought round to the King's side, and if Mrs Simpson would agree to offer a withdrawal from the marriage, Baldwin would find that his seemingly impregnable position had been overturned. The future was

---

* And who was executed for treason in 1946.

bright with promise. Victory seemed to be within our grasp.'[53]

Up to a point, Lord Copper.* For every public display of loyalty, there was another assertion of horror and disapproval at what had happened. Letters began to pour in from 'concerned citizens' to Sir Thomas Barnes, the King's Proctor, begging him to look into the unusual and hurried circumstances of Wallis's divorce. A letter from May Lewis, a British citizen living in America, was typical: 'Won't you please intervene in this matter and prevent it from becoming effective in 6 months time? A more flagrant piece of "collusion" and arranging for those concerned would be hard to find ... King Edward has known this notorious and brazen Simpson woman for 10 years . . . [He] should not be asked to abdicate but he should be forced to do so, we can get a better King than he any day, he is a disgrace, and the Simpson woman should have been booted out of the country long ago.' The righteously angered May wound up by calling her king and his consort 'the objects of scorn, contempt and, in some cases, ridicule of almost every decent person one meets'.[54]

Miss Lewis was naturally influenced by the sensational coverage of the American press, which had been unfettered for months, but Barnes was unable simply to ignore such requests, emotive though they were. Had every angry letter-writer known that on the evening of 3 December, Baldwin had suggested to Edward that the King's Proctor might well be asked to intervene before the decree nisi was finalised, they would have doubled or trebled their efforts, the white-hot excitement of potential vindication motivating them to write as many letters as their pens or typewriters would allow them.

It is difficult, by now, to imagine a more dramatic series of incidents in British history. The king withdrawn and half crazed with frustration and bitterness; his lover fleeing, hotly pursued by

---

* The allusion to Evelyn Waugh's *Scoop*, is especially apposite because Beaverbrook himself was the model for Waugh's grandiloquent newspaper proprietor Lord Copper.

every journalist with a notebook and camera; his prime minister attempting to control his Cabinet, his own health and the possibility of a rival political party emerging as if from nowhere; the popular press tearing each other apart in the brief moments when their all-powerful proprietors were not locked in secret conference with royalty or politicians; the people taking the most definite of sides in the greatest social conflict that the country had seen since the Civil War; and the fascists, in Britain and beyond, rubbing their hands at the prospect of an unprecedented crisis bringing the country to its knees.

It was a time for heroism, quiet and understated though it might be. And heroism, in the most unlikely form, was what was about to emerge.

Chapter Ten

'The Best Story Since the Resurrection'

Had a curious member of the public walked past a telephone box by Green Park, opposite Buckingham Palace, in early December 1936, they could well have seen a tall, handsome and assured-looking man holding a suitcase. If this made him look like a travelling salesman, it was a useful piece of misdirection. Inside the telephone box, this man – 'Tar', as he was known – was placing what looked like a small wire on the junction box, with the aid of a telephone engineer to help him decipher which was the correct one.

The resourceful bugger needed this in order to be able to listen in to telephone conversations of the utmost national importance. These were not merely being made by the Duke of York, who lived nearby at 145 Piccadilly, but also by the king himself. Although he was now permanently resident at Fort Belvedere, he continued to make a series of calls to London, and beyond. Tar's aim was to gather the greatest amount of information that he could about the monarch's mental and political state, and feed it back to his superiors at MI5, who had arranged this most clandestine – and entirely legal – of operations.

The letter of 5 December authorising this action struck an oddly hesitant and embarrassed note. There were numerous corrections in pencil, as if to play down the gravity of what it was asking for, and it was not written by either of the main actors in the case, John Simon or Horace Wilson, instead being deputed to a subordinate. No typed copy exists, and it is a surprise that this highly incriminating page was not disposed of by its recipient, Thomas Gardiner, the head of the GPO. It is little surprise that the letter is entitled 'Most Secret', as what it was asking Gardiner to do was entirely unheard-of, even at a time of constitutional crisis such as this. After the usual preliminaries ('The Home Secretary asks me to confirm the instruction conveyed to you orally, with his authority, by Sir Horace Wilson'), the request is stated bluntly: 'You will arrange for the interception of telephone conversations between Fort Belvedere and Buckingham Palace on one hand and the Continent of Europe on the other.'[1]

Although his name is nowhere mentioned, the instruction would have inevitably come directly from Baldwin, who felt that the situation was one of sufficient gravity that Sir Vernon Kell, the creator and first director of MI5, was essentially asked to commit treason. Kell was no patsy, being a much-decorated war hero and proud possessor of an entry in *Who's Who* that described him as 'Commandant, War Department Constabulary'. His organisation, which had been created in 1909, had never been asked to perform a similar task before, and so sensitive was the work undertaken that the files relating to it were kept closed in the National Archives until recently.

Kell needed to be convinced of the justification for the request, and so its absolute necessity was made clear to him. Edward was felt to be personally unstable, with or without Wallis; there were unsubstantiated rumours, spread by the likes of the Archbishop of Canterbury, that he was drinking heavily and taking drugs in order to cope with the situation, and behaving erratically in consequence.* Lang, who was becoming his most persistent nemesis, had written to Geoffrey Dawson on 6 December to state, after a

---

* Monckton specifically denied Edward's drinking heavily in his abdication account, and the king himself later wrote in his own memoir that 'I have seldom taken a sleeping-pill in my life and have an instinctive abhorrence of even the mildest form of narcotic.' This is corroborated by Ziegler. Beaverbrook, however, wrote of how 'he smoked continuously, sometimes cigarettes, often a pipe . . . there was plenty to drink. Always whisky with water and a piece of ice.'

conversation with Clive Wigram, that 'HM is mentally ill, and that his obsession [with Wallis] is due not to mere obstinacy but a deranged mind.' Lang, admittedly in an account coloured by personal dislike of the king, also stated that 'more than once in the past he's shown symptoms of persecution-mania' and threatened 'recurring quarrels with his ministers' should he be allowed to remain on the throne.[2] Therefore, spying on Edward was portrayed as public service rather than personal betrayal.

There were other, equally compelling reasons why Kell agreed to act. The king was felt to be susceptible to undue influence, through both the support of Mosley and his fascists and his rumoured sympathy towards the Nazi regime in Germany. It was even believed that, *in extremis*, he might call upon one or both organisations to support him in the event of a King's Party being formed. This explains the particular reference in the letter to 'the Continent of Europe', which covered both communication with Wallis, unhappily sequestered in Cannes, and any possibility, engineered by the ever-eager Ribbentrop, of an unprecedented situation arising whereby the ruler of one nation could essentially ask the dictator of another for assistance in overthrowing a stubborn and troublesome government. The possibility of national unrest – even full-blown civil disobedience – swung his decision in the desired direction.

Once persuaded, Kell needed his best agent to accomplish the espionage, and turned to his right-hand man, Tar, or Thomas Argyll Robertson. Tar would go on to considerable distinction during World War II as the director of the so-called 'Double-Cross' or 'XX' campaign of spreading disinformation against the Germans, in which he managed to successfully convince Nazi intelligence that the D-Day landings would take place at Calais, not Normandy. Now, he was being asked to accomplish something less momentous, although equally unprecedented, and he carried out his work by means of a relatively straightforward method, which has only grown in notoriety over the decades since: phone tapping.

Kell and Tar were aided in this subterfuge by information being fed back to Special Branch by Edward's bodyguards, in whom he had wrongly placed complete trust, and also by the intelligence gathered on Wallis before and during – and indeed after – the abdication crisis. Those members of her security staff who had been asked to make her house at 16 Cumberland Terrace secure had had ample opportunity to place surveillance equipment within it, unbeknownst to her, and took full advantage of their privileged position. It was undeniably a betrayal, but by this stage it also seemed a necessity.

The bugging took place at a time when England seemed to be on the brink of disaster. The army officer and MP Edward Spears called the general misery that existed 'indescribable', and likened the national situation to that of a desperate man who, having finally regained his professional career after many struggles, was informed that his daughter was pregnant by his chauffeur. As all seemed on the verge of collapse, Spears's friend Bob Boothby remarked on 3 December that, if the crisis continued, the monarchy was in severe danger of no longer existing.'

Edward had few friends and allies, but those who were left stayed steadfast throughout the crisis. Beaverbrook had his own motivations for acting the way he did, but Monckton remained by the king's side as a comrade-in-arms as much as a legal adviser. Mountbatten wrote warmly to him to say, 'Do you realise how many loyal supporters of all classes you have? If you want me to help you, to do any service for you or even to feel you have a friend of Wallis' to keep you company, you have only to telephone . . . I hate to feel that there is nothing I can do to help except bite people's heads off who have the temerity to say anything disloyal about their King – and there are practically none who do so – at any rate in my presence.'³ And on the evening of 4 December, Edward was allowed his first formal interview with the man he believed could yet assist him in resolving the situation in a satisfactory and dignified fashion: Winston Churchill.

Churchill had already spoken out on behalf of the king in the

House of Commons earlier that day. Dawson, no admirer of his, wrote that 'Winston, who is out for mischief, looked very glum.'[4] After Baldwin had stated that there was no provision in law for a morganatic marriage except by legislation, and that 'His Majesty's Government do not intend to introduce such legislation', Churchill cut through the cheers by asking pointedly that Parliament be consulted before any executive order was given. The Conservative politician Leo Amery had found him ranting in the corridors that 'I am for the King, and I will not have him strangled in the dark by ministers, and bumped off without the chance of saying a word to Parliament or the country in his defence.'[5] At last he had his chance.

Churchill's own account of his meeting with his ruler at this time plays down the poetic aspects of his advice, but Edward later wrote that 'When Mr Baldwin had talked to me about the monarchy, it seemed a dry and lifeless thing . . . but when Mr Churchill spoke it grew, it became suffused with light . . . I saw him that evening in his true stature.'[6] For the first time in his reign, inspired by the rhetoric of this brilliant man, he began to understand that he was on the verge of throwing away the greatest privilege an Englishman could possess.

It was little wonder that, as Churchill stated later, 'HM was most gay and debonair for the first quarter of an hour . . . [but] it was obvious that the personal strain he had been so long under, and which was now at its climax, had exhausted him to a most painful degree.' The politician intentionally limited the scope of his advice to suggesting that 'If you require time, there is no force in the country which would or could deny it you', and reminded Edward that Baldwin had taken two months' rest earlier that year to recover his health after the stress of Parliament, and that 'your strain was far more intense and prolonged'. Helen Hardinge claimed that Churchill made the further suggestion that, *in extremis*, the king should follow the example of George III and retire to Windsor Castle, stationing royal physicians at each entrance. This eccentric course of action was not followed.

Churchill had outlined a simple and practical plan to Edward, to buy time as much as anything else. He could not offer a solution, but what he did give the king was a brief moment of hope. He instructed him not to leave the country, nor to see Wallis again, but feared that '[Edward] ... completely lost the thread of what he was saying and appeared to me driven to the last extremity of endurance.' With just a touch of steel, he informed the king that 'Mr Baldwin is a fatherly man and nothing could induce him to treat you so harshly in such a matter.'[7] As he left, he said, 'Sir, it is a time for reflection. You must allow time for the battalions to march.'[8] When Edward later repeated this advice to Monckton, he did so in conscious imitation of Churchill, but without any attempt at ridicule. Matters were too grave for that.

In fact, at this time of highs and lows, a particular depth had been plumbed earlier that day when Baldwin, after meeting with his Cabinet, had confirmed their unanimous decision to reject Edward's offer to broadcast to his people.* He wrote that 'There is a fundamental distinction between the position of the King and the position of a private person ... Such a broadcast could only be given on the advice of his Ministers, who would be responsible for every sentence of it. In these circumstances Mr Baldwin cannot advise that the King should broadcast as proposed.'[9] Edward took the news calmly, but responded that Baldwin should make a statement in Parliament the following Monday confirming the king's continued desire to marry Wallis, and the fact that he wished to make a public broadcast. This was seen as antagonistic, to say nothing of constitutionally impossible. As Duff Cooper, hitherto Edward's most prominent supporter in government, put it, 'So long as the King is King, every utterance that he makes must be on

---

* One quirk was that Baldwin's advice only applied as long as Edward was king. It stated, 'If a sovereign takes the formal action which is necessary to renounce the throne, and if he becomes a subject of the reigning sovereign, his claim to broadcast stands on quite a different basis.' In other words, Edward believed that he would be at liberty to make this and similar broadcasts if he were to abdicate.

the advice of his ministers, who take full responsibility for every word. If, therefore, we could now advise him to make this speech, we could not allow him to.'[10]

Cooper had grown weary of the partisan views on both sides. He was no friend of Beaverbrook, and had been irritated by what he termed Churchill's 'oration' on the subject the previous week, but he also found the junior members of the Cabinet, even those who broadly shared his more sympathetic views, alarmist and hysterical, terrified by the prospect of a Churchill-led government emerging if Baldwin's was to collapse. Still, as he wrote, 'The prospects of a General Election on the King's marriage were not agreeable to contemplate. An attempt might even be made to upset the Parliamentary system altogether. It had disappeared in other countries recently: why not in this? Beaverbrook and Rothermere would work with Winston; so would the Fascists; so might some elements of the Left.'[11]

It was now generally believed that Edward or his supporters were up to something, a perception aided by the government chief whip Henry Margesson informing Baldwin that day that around forty MPs would join a King's Party if it existed. This phantasmagorical grouping was something that Edward later described as resembling 'a rocket . . . not a very big rocket, but for a moment it hung brilliantly in the sky',[12] claiming with the benefit of hindsight that he was 'dubious of its motives and apprehensive of its consequences'. He still responded warmly to the public sentiment behind it, which was based on loyalty and affection to the monarch and 'a residue of good will accruing from my services to the Empire'.[13] It did not seem to have occurred to him that most of the sentiment lay with the institution of the Crown rather than the man himself.

There was never a formal discussion between Edward and anyone else about the possibility of founding a political party that would act in his interests, or at least appear to. This was not for want of willingness on his part. In his memoir, he describes, with *Hamlet*-esque introspection, 'a night of soul-searching', after which he decided not to 'encourage the growth of this movement', on the grounds that, despite his self-proclaimed popularity and charisma – 'a multitude of the plain people stood waiting to be rallied to my side' – he could not be responsible for a civil war, even one fought 'in words and not in blood'. He acknowledged that if he was the ruler at the head of a King's Party, he would still be ruler, but 'no longer King by the free and common consent of all', and thus the monarchy would be partial and political, rather than loftily standing above such concerns. It apparently did not occur to him that an unelected party of this nature – with the explicit support of Mosley and the BUF, among others – would have caused a civil war that would likely have involved blood, as well as many harsh words.

His most powerful supporter, meanwhile, fretted at the frustration of his desired victory. Despite what Beaverbrook termed 'the support of so large and influential a section of the Press', nothing was happening as he wished it to. Baldwin remained prime minister, the king was not in charge of an unelected semi-political party, and his papers were not making the necessary difference, despite their vast readership. Ziegler comments that 'It is easy to overrate the importance of the press, both in society and in the mind of the King.'[14] It was probably no coincidence that Monckton had informed Beaverbrook on 3 December that he could no longer see him, ostensibly because he was negotiating with the government about abdication terms and would be unable to meet with other interested parties. As the publisher wrote, 'For the first time, I believed that the King was seriously determined to abdicate.'[15]

Nonetheless, he had no intention of abandoning his intrigue. Like Macbeth, he was 'in blood stepped in so far, that should I wade no more, returning were as tedious as go o'er'. He wrote to Monckton the following day offering sympathy for his predicament and asking whether the 'ban' also applied to telephone communication and 'letters discreetly and properly framed', and if it did, whether 'some other person' might be selected as a go-between.[16]

He was still in touch with Churchill, who remained adamant in his insistence that Edward should not abdicate. When Beaverbrook received him on the evening of 4 December, Churchill believed that the king was prepared to fight for his throne; he was 'once more in the field',[17] or so Beaverbrook hoped. He was, however, even more heartened on what he called 'a day of spectacular ups and downs'[18] by a coded message that came from France. It read, 'WM Janet strongly advising the James Company to postpone purchase of Chester shares to next autumn and to announce decision by verbal methods, thereby increasing popularity, maintaining prestige, but also the right to re-open negotiations by the autumn.'

It would not have taken Bletchley Park's finest to crack this particular code. Wallis was WM Janet, Edward either Mr James or, as here, the James Company, and the 'purchase of Chester shares' was the abdication. Beaverbrook – who was codenamed 'Tornado' in other messages – was thrilled. He wrote, 'Here, it seemed, was a last chance. If the Churchill policy was followed, and if the renunciation was heavily emphasized, there was every hope that the day might yet be won.'[19] This was not merely over-optimistic, but blinkered. For all his power and influence, Beaverbrook possessed a shockingly myopic view of what was really going on at this time. The only area in which he was right – and considerably more knowledgeable than most of his allies and enemies – was in understanding Wallis's increasing desperation for the nightmare to end. He had by now come to the conclusion that she would have to be sacrificed in order for Edward to remain on the throne, or, as he put it, that 'the crisis might yet be solved by an act of renunciation on [her] part'.[20] This, as he saw it, was a price worth paying. He might have been surprised by how readily she would have agreed with him.

Since leaving Fort Belvedere, Wallis had endured an eventful few days. She quickly realised that her travelling companion Lord Brownlow was not merely by her side to offer company, but was one of a group of 'friendly conspirators', including Beaverbrook, Monckton and Harmsworth, who wished her to abandon Edward and thus allow him to remain on the throne. She later recalled that Brownlow initially feared that Edward would attempt to follow her to France, and suggested that she head to Lincolnshire instead; as he said, 'You are the only person who can influence the King. Has it not occurred to you that by leaving him to make up his mind alone, you will almost certainly bring to pass the conclusion that you and all of us are so anxious to avert?'[21] She refused, fearing that greater blame would attach itself to her if she was still in the country during the abdication itself. 'It would be said that I was afraid of losing the King; that, having left him at the Fort, I had lost heart and run back in order to hold him.'[22]

This was probably the wrong decision, something acknowledged subsequently by Wallis herself. Removing her from the Fort and the epicentre of the crisis was a necessary move, but, as she wrote later, 'The instant I started across the Channel, I had ceased to exist, so far as my being able to influence the King's mind was concerned.' As she and Brownlow discussed who might be able to persuade Edward to give up the idea of marrying her, and thus remain on the throne, she also realised that she was about to go from being the most infamous woman in England to the most notorious one in Europe. Brownlow whispered to her as they left the ferry at Dieppe, 'You've been found out . . . it may be difficult to shake off the posse.'[23] This was heroic in its understatement.

The 650-mile journey from Dieppe to Cannes was bedevilled by incident. Wallis's bodyguard, Inspector Evans, was jittery and nervous, at one point knocking a camera out of a young girl's hands for fear that it contained a gun. ('King's orders.') As Wallis made brief, tense phone calls to Edward, where the poor reception led to her raising her voice out of frustration and fear, she wildly suggested those who might offer counsel, including Cooper, Lord Derby and none other than the Aga Khan. The king was unable to hear, or heed, her advice. As they miserably shuttled from one grand hotel to another ('The Duc de Guise slept in this room the night before he was murdered', Brownlow noted 'with unexpected cheerfulness'[24] at one stop in the Loire), they were pursued by dozens of reporters and photographers, whose numbers swelled to the hundreds by the time they arrived in Cannes.

Wallis later described her flight as an 'agonizing experience', leavened with moments of bleak humour. Brownlow's dignity was somewhat compromised by his having smuggled a bottle of whisky upon his person, which had then broken on the journey. As they travelled in the car, Wallis, to her distress, became aware of a strong odour of alcohol, and insisted that they drive with the windows open, even as Brownlow morosely sniffed his whisky-sodden coat.

They passed through Lyons in some agitation, accompanied by cries of 'Voilà la dame!', and at one point Wallis found herself escaping through the bathroom window of a restaurant where they had just lunched, closely followed by Brownlow. ('Too bad Stanley Baldwin missed that little scene', he remarked.) She eventually arrived at the Cannes villa of her friends Herman and Katherine Rogers in the early hours of 6 December, crouched in the back of a car with a rug over her head, although not before Brownlow, unable to make himself understood in a telephone call announcing their arrival, all but broke down in public, vigorously punching the telephone box in frustration and loudly cursing the French communications system.

The farcical aspects of Wallis's flight did not obscure the misery that she faced. Unable to communicate easily with Edward, she began to consider her options. She could not return to England without running the gauntlet of a suspicious and unsympathetic press, and her presence would only place additional, and intolerable, pressure upon the king. Unchecked fascination awaited her in America, where the satirist H. L. Mencken, in the Baltimore Sun of 4 December, had called the royal romance 'the best story since the Resurrection . . . the biggest Cinderella story you could imagine'. As one of the best-known faces in the world, there was no chance of her beginning her life afresh. She had all the pitfalls of enormous fame, and only a few of its compensations. It seemed, yet again, as if she would have to break with Edward, and so it was with steely resolution that she began to write: 'Darling, I am sending this by air as I think it important you have it before . . . '[25]

*

Back in England, the games continued. Those opposed to the policy of immediate abdication had begun to marshal themselves into 'hard' and 'soft' camps. The 'soft' camp, which included the likes of Cooper and Margesson, felt that Edward needed to be given more time, and consequently allowed to separate from Wallis of his own accord, especially if she ended the relationship herself. This would then allow him to remain on the throne, at a time of enormous international discord, and avoid further ructions. The public had shown itself to be in the king's favour, and no government would want to oppose a popular ruler.

The 'hard' camp, which was led by Beaverbrook and Harmsworth, was less interested in nuance. They sought to bring down the government, replace it with a King's Party led by Churchill, and allow Edward to marry Wallis, even to make her queen if he so wished. They also took note of the public support, and believed that it could yet be marshalled in a more intervention-ist direction if needed. Churchill himself did not explicitly support either of these groups, yet he was widely believed to be, as it were, the kingmaker. When the Conservative politician Lord Salisbury wrote to him to say, 'I am watching your attitude now with great anxiety', he spoke for many of his parliamentary colleagues.

As the factions formed, the king began to unravel. He said to Baldwin, as if hurt, 'I have never let you down, have I?'[26] This com-ment indicated his weariness with participating in any intrigue or politicking, as well as some naïvety. Baldwin told his son that Edward 'was like a child of sixteen'.[27] From a philosophical per-spective, he began to believe that there was no longer any meaning in his reign. As he later recounted, 'I had been raised under the great imperative that the Crown must remain above politics. If adherence to this doctrine should cost me the Crown, I had no choice but to subscribe.'[28] He also tried to protect the absent Wallis. He refused to allow Beaverbrook to obtain an exclusive interview with her - or, as the magnate slithered, to 'present her attitude and her position in a fair and true light' - because it would only represent further intrusion and upset for her; as Edward described it, 'a martyrdom that was contrary to her nature'.[29]

By the morning of 5 December, the king had decided that he was no longer willing to participate in the soul-destroying circus as either reluctant ringmaster or chief clown. He summoned Monckton, who had been taking care to remain in contact with as many parties as he could. He was the most sympathetic of go-betweens, but he was now to be asked to bring matters to a close. Edward brusquely informed him that 'I want you to go to London immediately and warn the Prime Minister that when he comes to the Fort this afternoon I shall notify him formally that I have decided to abdicate.'[30]

Had he looked at Monckton at that moment to see how he took the news, he might have noted that his friend's usually open and amiable face was clouded over with concern. Edward had, until that point, simply assumed that, as sovereign, he retained the autonomous right to dictate what happened, and that the consequences would be to his benefit; he had airily believed that an Act of Parliament would tidy everything up and he would then be free to marry Wallis.

Monckton tactfully explained that this was impossible. Wallis's decree would not be finally granted until late April, and there was still the likelihood that various parties would approach the King's Proctor before that time with claims that an adulterous relationship had taken place between her and Edward before she had petitioned for divorce. If Edward abdicated, there was every chance that the decree would fail altogether, or, as Monckton put it, they would be 'subjected to the inconveniences that beset anyone caught in so sensational an incident'.[31] Even if it did not fail, the king, whether still on the throne or not, would be unable to be reunited with Wallis until the divorce became final, which he described as 'a monstrous strain upon two people who had already been through the fire'. In desperation, Edward asked, 'Is there anything that can be done?'

Monckton returned his gaze. When he had served as an officer in the hell of Ypres in 1917 and 1918, he had seen a world entirely separate from what he had understood as reality, a time in which hideous, violent death became as commonplace as the mud and the rats that made the life of every soldier an endless misery. Yet not only had he retained his humanity and humour in such dire circumstances, he had also managed to bring a glimpse of compassion into his men's lives, whether it was making sure at 5 a.m. that they had been given their cigarette ration, or simply talking to them and cheering them. One friend of his remarked of him that 'He obviously has a something, a peace which carried him through everything . . . [He is] a most strong and helpful person.'[32]

So it was with this calm assurance, a lifetime in the acquisition, that Monckton could look at his friend the king and reply, 'Yes. I think there is.'

Chapter Eleven

'This Is a Bugger'

Late in *Henry IV, Part II*, there is an affecting scene between Henry IV and the king-in-waiting, Prince Hal. The old monarch lies dying, and his son visits him on his deathbed, but not before trying on the crown, which he quickly realises is 'so troublesome a bedfellow'. Upbraided by his waking father, he swiftly swears fealty, declaring of the crown itself that 'The care on thee depending hath fed upon the body of my father; therefore thou best of gold art worst of gold.' Henry, moved by his son's anguish and remorse, offers him some regal advice in his final hours. Dismissing the 'troublesome' crown as nothing more than 'an honour snatched with boisterous hand', and one obtained through 'by-paths and indirect crooked ways', he fervently hopes that Hal will restore the honour that is due to it with 'better opinion [and] better confirmation', ending his paternal homily with his hopes that 'action, hence borne out, may waste the memory of the former days' and that '[God] grant it may with thee in true peace live.'

Edward, although not the most widely read of monarchs, knew from his own strained relationship with George V that the act of passing over the crown was one rich in ritual and significance. Not only did it denote the end of one reign and the beginning of another, but it represented a chance for the people to come to terms with what kingship, or queenship, represented. A good ruler was a universally beloved figure, and earned the sobriquet of 'father or mother to the nation', while a poor sovereign was tolerated through precedent but disliked and distrusted. Edward realised, long before he abdicated, that posterity would place him in the second category. He had never wanted to rule, but it was his fate. Had he never encountered Wallis, he would probably have remained king until his death, just like his father and grandfather.

There had been weak, venal and wicked rulers before him, and the period of stability and prosperity that came about after his reign – apocalyptic war notwithstanding – cannot solely be credited to his brother and niece. Never before, however, had a king simply abdicated his throne, along with all responsibility to the office of the Crown and his people, of his own free will. As John Simon acidly noted, those rulers who had previously been compelled to abandon the crown (Edward II, Richard II) tended to meet with violent ends shortly afterwards. Edward VIII regarded the situation that he was in with irritation – 'Kingship is perhaps the last remaining occupation from which it is impossible to resign in good grace, with the confidence that one's motives will be understood',[1] he huffed – but he was all too aware that he would lose the love and support of his nation as soon as he gave up the crown. As he entrusted the arrangements to Monckton, it was with the vain hope that some dignity could yet be salvaged, and that he would not simply be plunged into darkness.

His counsellor, meanwhile, saw the difficulties that his friend faced. He also had a clearer idea of the ways in which public opinion worked. He later wrote that 'Between Thursday 3rd December and Sunday 6th, there was a great wave of sympathy for the King and a desire in many quarters to retain him at all costs.' He was also able to communicate easily and on equal terms with all involved in the crisis; quite literally, he walked with the king and yet did not lose the common touch. Tact was his greatest weapon. He persuaded a vacillating Baldwin that, rather than regarding Churchill's visits to Edward as a strategic error, permitting them was a piece of wise statesmanship. As he put it, 'The King felt that, though there was no conflict between him and his Ministers, their interests were potentially necessarily divergent.'[2]

Still, there was the growing necessity of finding a solution to the crisis that would satisfy Parliament and legal opinion alike. Monckton arranged a lunch with Horace Wilson, along with the king's solicitor Thomas Allen and Baldwin's private secretary Tommy Dugdale, on 5 December, in order to propose his potential idea, which he had already discussed with Edward earlier that day. The king had reacted to it with enormous gratitude, describing it as a 'lifeline thrown across a crevasse',[3] and Monckton hoped for similar approval from his influential dining companions. Swing them, he thought, and Baldwin and the Cabinet would follow; after that, parliamentary approval should be easily obtained. He was helped by the knowledge, confided to him by Wilson, that Parliament would expect an answer of some kind on Monday 7 December, especially as the House of Lords had been specially summoned that day.

Therefore, Monckton dealt with the situation in as sequential and legalistic a fashion as he could. The incontrovertible evidence was that Edward would not be shaken in his intention to marry Wallis. The king had requested the possibility of her decree nisi being made absolute immediately, which could have been referred to the High Court, but as Monckton and Wilson agreed, this smacked of the government attempting to influence the course of justice in order to expedite an agreed abdication. Monckton then proposed a second option: that two parliamentary bills be drawn up, one allowing for Edward to renounce the throne, and the other putting forward legislation that the decree nisi should be granted simultaneously.

This was a game of dangerously high stakes, but it offered the possibility of tying up the whole matter neatly and finally, with the assent of Parliament. As Monckton put it, 'This would finally have cleared up a grave constitutional position affecting the whole world and have left no ragged ends or possibilities for further scandal.'[4] Wilson agreed that they did not want a disaffected Edward 'knocking about Europe for four months with all the consequential possibilities for mischief-making'; as he put it, with heroic restraint,

'There [is] a mess and the English way of dealing with it [is] to clear it up thoroughly at the earliest possible moment.'[5]

As Monckton could claim the scheme as his own, there was no chance that any member of the Cabinet or royal household could be embarrassed should it fail to be adopted. On a personal level, it resolved his fear of a worst-case scenario, that of Edward abdicating his throne and still being unable to marry Wallis should the decree fail and she remain married to Simpson. His personal attitude was closer to Baldwin's than Edward knew – 'There is little doubt that due provision would have been made for an income and title if he had expressed his willingness to go at once'[6] – but this stemmed less from a desire for the whole charade to be over and more from an honest wish that his friend be spared further humiliation and intrusion.

Wilson, Allen and Dugdale all agreed that, in the face of the Hobson's choice they were confronted by, this was the most elegant means of bringing about the abdication. Set against it was the chance that, by involving Parliament in the decision, it offered the opportunity to bring down the government. Monckton reported Baldwin, who supported the so-called Divorce Bill, saying that 'he would resign if he could not carry his colleagues'.[7] This was a risk that had to be taken.

With lunch concluded, Wilson returned to Downing Street to canvass opinion. It was surprisingly favourable. Simon, after initially rejecting the idea, was persuaded of its viability by the attorney general stating that a direct approach to the divorce court was impossible, and the feeling began to be that 'If it were done when 'tis done, then 'twere well it were done quickly.' It was especially desirable that there would not be a period of several months that would be an effective interregnum, when, as Wilson put it, 'the Throne, through its late occupant, would once more be the subject of press comment and public notice generally'.[8] It was agreed that Baldwin would meet his Cabinet colleagues, especially the potentially awkward ones, on Sunday 6 December, and see what could be done. Monckton, naturally, would be present. It seemed, at last, as if a deal was at hand.

*

The message from Beaverbrook to Churchill, delivered on Saturday morning in the latter's Morpeth Mansions flat, was simple and negative: 'Our cock won't fight.'[9] The politician was surprised. Just the previous night, he had sent Edward an upbeat note, announcing 'news from all fronts', including the glad tidings that 'No pistol to be held at the King's head . . . his request for time will be granted . . . No final decision or Bill till after Christmas – probably February or March.'* Using military metaphors – 'good advances on all fronts giving prospects of . . . assembling large forces behind the King', he had suggested a brief return (presumably a conjugal visit of some sort) for Mrs Simpson, stressed the loyalty of the Northern Irish prime minister Sir James Craig and described Beaverbrook with admiration as 'a tiger to fight . . . a <u>devoted</u> tiger – very scarce breed'.[10] Now this particular big cat was before him, and doing anything but purring.

Beaverbrook despaired of Edward doing anything that would enable him to remain King of England. He had been a great proponent of Wallis leaving the country, and believed that he would be able to break Edward's resolve without her present: a misreading of the situation. (The typescript of his memoirs deletes the word 'exploiting' in relation to Mrs Simpson's departure, and replaces it with 'delaying'.) He had what he termed 'a divergence of views' with Churchill over the issue before them. Beaverbrook, realising that the government was not about to collapse, urged agreement with it, but, as he wrote, 'Churchill was prepared to stand up against the executive.'[11] After he told the politician, 'You're bound to be beaten in any quarrel with the government, and, even if you win, the victory will be useless', there then followed what he

---

* He also drew Edward's attention to a piece in that day's *Evening Standard* by George Bernard Shaw, 'another fictitious dialogue', entitled *The King, The Constitution and the Lady*. Despite touches of wit – 'If I were superstitious', the Archbishop of Canterbury says, 'I should be tempted to believe that the devil was putting all these arguments into his Majesty's head' – its partisan nature makes it more a diatribe than a dialogue.

euphemistically termed 'a clash of viewpoint and of policies'. The magnate wanted Mrs Simpson to withdraw from the marriage, and to preserve Edward upon the throne, with a view to tackling Baldwin on a later occasion; Churchill wished to buy time, and for Edward and Wallis to be united.

There was no agreement between them. When Churchill read Beaverbrook a press statement he had prepared, full of emotive rhetoric and passion – 'I plead for time and patience . . . If an abdication were to be hastily extorted the outrage so committed would cast its shadow forward across many chapters of the history of the British Empire' – the publisher found himself unmoved, despite Churchill's disingenuous* suggestion in it that the marriage 'may conceivably, for various reasons, never be accomplished at all'.[12] Beaverbrook left Morpeth Mansions 'making it plain that we were taking different paths and that I was not a party to the attempt to stand against the Government'.[13] So much for his self-proclaimed status as a king's man. His parting words, delivered with a verbal shrug, were 'No dice.' As he later sighed, 'I considered myself out of it. It was all over so far as I was concerned.'[14] He spent the remainder of the abdication crisis 'depressed and disappointed',[15] planting trees in the garden of his Surrey mansion.

His dream of a King's Party was over. He accepted no blame for this. He later wrote in his memoirs that 'the weaknesses of character and the defects in conduct of the King must be taken into account . . . He was completely under the influence of Mrs Simpson and subject to her approval or rejection of each and every project',[16] and then, equivocating, deleted the passages, which can still be found in manuscript in his private papers.

Churchill sent his statement to both Baldwin and the press anyway. Edward later praised it as 'a masterly and objective exposition [which] stated the case with power and dignity', and declared

---

* Some of Churchill's biographers gave him a greater benefit of the doubt in this issue, arguing that rather than lying, he simply had no idea of Edward's devotion to Wallis.

that 'Under different circumstances, the effect of Mr Churchill's magnificent plea on my behalf would almost certainly have been profound ... but through no fault of Mr Churchill it came too late.'[17] Yet while Beaverbrook had proved that he would walk away once it looked as if his objective had been thwarted, Churchill remained a foul-weather friend to the king to the last, despite the advice of those around him not to jeopardise his career. It nearly cost him everything.

Meanwhile, Churchill and Beaverbrook's nemesis was beginning to feel uneasy. Baldwin had been imprudent to stake his premiership on persuading his colleagues to back the Divorce Bill; as Edward later wrote of this naturally cautious man, 'I never understood what persuaded him to make this handsome but rash promise.'[18] Many members of the Cabinet were implacably opposed to divorce on religious grounds, and it seemed as if Baldwin had over-committed himself to an offer he had no easy means of executing. Monckton, however, was not so convinced that Baldwin had made a promise, saying, 'Certainly, neither I nor the King attached any importance to it *at that time*.'[19] This ambiguity would prove a lifeline.

Both Churchill and Baldwin visited the Fort on the evening of Saturday 5 December. Edward's conversation with the former consisted mainly of discussing the press statement that would be published in the papers the following day. Churchill believed that his closing lines were especially vital; in them he openly argued against the constitutional basis on which Edward's future was being discussed, and implied that a stitch-up had taken place. As he had written, 'There is no question of any conflict between King and Parliament. Parliament has not been consulted in any way, nor allowed to express an opinion. The question is whether the King is to abdicate upon the advice of his Ministers of the day. No such advice has ever been tendered to a sovereign in Parliamentary times.'[20] Edward was affected, but his course would not alter. And, like death and taxes, the inevitability of the prime minister's appearance continued the evening's shenanigans.

The meeting between the king, Baldwin and the ubiquitous Monckton, tense though it was, produced a mutually agreeable outcome. According to the prime minister, Edward had never been 'more cool, clear minded, understanding every point and arguing the different issues . . . No man could have done this better.'[21] This was in contrast to Churchill and Beaverbrook's belief that the king was virtually a nervous wreck; when this was delicately mentioned to Edward, he was annoyed at what he saw as Churchill's duplicity. At last, to Baldwin's relief, the king announced that he was prepared to agree to the abdication, as long as Parliament passed a Simpson Divorce Bill along with the Abdication Bill. The prime minister concurred. As he announced to the extraordinary Cabinet meeting that he convened the following day, 'The King was making a tremendous sacrifice in the interests of his country. Ever since he had become Prince of Wales he had been doing his duty to the people with great assiduity, and he thought he was entitled to ask that the people should free him in the present case.'

It was a more emotional encounter than either man later acknowledged. Baldwin's son Oliver told Harold Nicolson that the two had walked in the silent grounds of the Fort together, and that when they returned and sat in the library, the prime minister felt sufficiently miserable at the situation to ask for a whisky and soda. When it arrived, he, 'with awkward ungainliness', proposed a toast to his monarch, saying, 'Well, Your Majesty, whatever happens my Mrs and I wish you the most complete happiness.'[22] The simplicity and apparent kindliness that this paternal figure presented was too much for Edward, who broke down in tears, leading Baldwin to weep in solidarity with his king. They sat together for a while, crying and drinking, until Baldwin collected himself, finished his whisky and returned to London. Work had to be done.

Edward's fear was, as Wilson had suggested at lunch that day, of becoming a rootless and stateless former monarch. It was taken as read that an abdicated king could not continue to reside in the country that he had once ruled, and he saw a dreadful scenario becoming possible in which he lost his crown, his lover and his status, being left to drift around Europe for months, if not years. Baldwin promised that he would do his best to smooth over 'the possibly awkward ones', and, perhaps for the first time in the crisis, the three men all believed themselves to be on the same side. Even an alarm later that night, as Neville Chamberlain heard intelligence that two aeroplanes had been chartered in Edward's name for immediate departure to Zurich, and warned Baldwin that the king was contemplating flight, was swiftly resolved: the aeroplanes were cancelled. It remains unclear whether Edward had actually ordered them in a moment of panic, or if it was simply a rumour put about by some frightened courtier,* but it seemed grimly appropriate that anything – even the sudden disappearance of the monarch overseas – could be contemplated.

The following morning, Baldwin convened the promised Cabinet meeting. He began by reminding those present –around half the normal Cabinet – that the meeting was 'one of the greatest importance', and then outlined the case, which he had privately suggested he was sure would be carried through. He noted that 'The King believed that his own honour was involved in this marriage and that nothing would turn him from it', assured them that Edward did not want division in the country and that he would depart of his own free will, as long as the bills were passed. Simon and Chamberlain both spoke in support of this, arguing that it was a transactional arrangement in which all parties received something they desired.

Baldwin delivered his summary, and then left for a meeting with Queen Mary to update her on the situation, during which she reputedly said, 'I see the world around me being shattered – the world which took me so long to build up.'[23] Bertie had written to

---

* Duff Cooper wrote in his diary that '[Beaverbrook] told me that it had been touch and go one or two nights before as to whether the King would not suddenly leave England and have done with it. His private aeroplane had apparently been under orders to fly at a moment's notice.' Whether this is true or merely troublemaking by Beaverbrook – or Cooper – it seems in keeping with the paranoid atmosphere that had developed by this point.

her the previous day to share his own horror, saying, 'It has been awful for all of us, but much more so for you, when David has been trained for the great position he holds, and now wants to chuck away. I am feeling very overwrought as to what may befall me, but with your help I know I shall be able to carry on. Times I feel are going to be very difficult for everybody at least for a week or two, until the shock is passed. I really cannot believe that David is going.'[24] Mary shared his disbelief, but it was leavened with anger.

On his way out of Downing Street, Baldwin, seemingly in good spirits, passed Monckton and told him that he would inform him of his colleagues' decision later. Unfortunately, upon his return, it became clear that the room had taken against the proposal. In what Oliver Baldwin later called 'an extraordinarily tortured discussion', it was decided that the bill was neither legal nor moral, as it smacked of backstairs dealing cooked up between a few interested parties, rather than something agreed upon by Parliament. In this regard, at least, the Cabinet agreed with Churchill. Ramsay MacDonald was especially hostile, later describing it as 'a sordid story', and noting with moral certainty that 'ministers discussed the proposal and the more they thought of it the more they opposed'.[25] Reluctantly, Baldwin agreed that the bill should be abandoned, leaving him without an obvious next option. The well-informed Beaverbrook – kept in the loop by Samuel Hoare* – sneered that 'Sunday was a dreadful day for the "self-interested manipulator"', and wondered how the 'extremely agile Prime Minister' would wriggle out of this situation.[26]

After the meeting, Monckton himself was summoned into the Cabinet Room by Chamberlain, who had changed his mind over the course of the morning. If he was embarrassed by his duplicity,

---

* Hoare later wrote to Beaverbrook, on 10 December, that 'I am glad and grateful that another crisis brought us together again. It is almost a year to the day since my resignation. The first friendly word from the outside came from you. I never forget these things nor shall I forget our talks of the last fortnight, and your manifest wish to help me in my career.' He neglected to offer his thanks for the large sums of money Beaverbrook paid him for his information.

he showed no signs of it, as he announced that the Simpson Divorce Bill was unacceptable as '[it] smacked of a bargain where there should be none; that the second Bill would affront the moral sense of the nation and that it would be resisted and debated, and that during the course of the debate unpleasant suggestions would be made'.[27] He also suggested that the continuing uncertainty was causing the country financial hardship. He provocatively asked Monckton what the king's reaction would be to this news, but the lawyer played a straight bat, responding, 'I cannot possibly answer this, but I expect that his Majesty will ask for time and to be allowed to consult others because he would feel that a divergence of view had arisen.' He also stressed that 'he would be, as indeed he was, gravely disappointed', and that the half-Cabinet's decision meant that the king would linger for weeks, rather than days, despite Baldwin's stated hopes that the matter would be resolved by Christmas.

As he left the room, Monckton's true feelings about the matter could be seen when he confided to Horace Wilson, 'The situation reminded me of the story of two soldiers in Passchendaele who were going back from the line on leave. They were machine-gunned, they were shelled, they fell into waterlogged shell-holes and finally they lost their way. Thereupon one said to the other, "Bill, I've often said as 'ow it was a bugger, when it wasn't a bugger, but this is a bugger."' Monckton wearily concluded, 'I believe that this story seemed appropriate to the Prime Minister and to those of his colleagues to whom he passed it on.'[28]

If Monckton and Baldwin had hoped for a more supportive response that evening at a full meeting of the Cabinet, they were to be disappointed. Even Duff Cooper, who had offered conditional support for Edward throughout the crisis, was appalled by Baldwin's suggestion. As he stated, 'This was a disastrous proposal . . . [It would] introduce legislation which, according to existing law, would legalise adultery, in order to expedite his departure', as well as depriving Ernest Simpson of his rights. (Cooper presumably was unaware of the financial deal that had been agreed upon, whereby all of Simpson's costs, so publicly awarded against him, were later secretly refunded.) An exhausted Baldwin responded, not without irony, that 'The King will be disappointed. He was looking forward to being married on New Year's Day.' Cooper wrote of his irritation with Baldwin treating the matter 'rather lightly', and regarding abdication as an inevitability to be hurried through, instead of a dreadful last step. That the prime minister was attempting to orchestrate an unprecedented matter of hideous complexity did not occur to him. As Cooper left Downing Street after the Simpson Divorce Bill was formally abandoned, he heard, with some trepidation, a cry that had become commonplace throughout England: 'We want King Edward! Down with the politicians!'[29]

When Edward heard the news from Monckton, who did not hide his irritation at the outcome, he was furious, although he later described himself as 'philosophical'. He did not, however, deny 'that my disappointment was profound'. He blamed Baldwin – who was now expected to address the House of Commons on Monday 7 December to update it on matters – asserting that, despite the prime minister's denials that he had exerted any influence on him to abdicate, 'pressure of a kind was certainly applied – the static yet implacable grip of a vice which, having fastened around an object, never relaxes'. He railed against the 'constitutional rhetoric which preserves the fiction of kingly authority', and concluded, 'How lonely is a monarch in a struggle with a shrewd Prime Minister backed by all the apparatus of the modern state.'[30] That Baldwin might have been doing his best to help rather than hinder his desires seems not to have occurred to the king.*

Monckton dined with Alec Hardinge on Sunday evening to discuss what could be salvaged from the wreckage of the day. Hardinge, who occupied himself with plotting against his employer, was unperturbed by the failure of the Simpson Divorce Bill.

---

* Although a contemporary account by the king's financial adviser, Sir Edward Peacock, noted that the monarch 'spoke with gratitude of SB's kindness and help', suggesting that his ill-will towards Baldwin developed subsequently.

His wife wrote that the bill could have been looked at in two ways: 'as a simple humanitarian gesture to a man who had already suffered much; or as one which made the reward for abandoning the throne, the nation and the Empire, marriage in highly privileged circumstances'. If Hardinge's feelings were ambiguous from this summation, then Helen's summing-up was a clear insight into his beliefs. 'The basis of King Edward's case throughout had been, of course, that he was asking only for the same right as that enjoyed by his subjects; however, he eagerly supported this plea for special treatment.'[31]

Both men agreed that Edward would abdicate, and that it was important that his decision should seem reasonable, dignified and made for the country's good rather than that of the individual. Helen wrote that 'By this time it was also apparent that only thus could the individual man be saved from complete personal collapse.' For the first time, money was mentioned. Hardinge suggested that an allowance of £25,000 a year would be adequate recompense for a former king. As a point of comparison, Edward had been giving Wallis a 'very handsome income'[32] of £6,000 annually in June 1935, and it was suggested that he had given her jewellery worth over £100,000 around Christmas and New Year in 1934. The government vetoed the allowance as 'quite unacceptable', but the price of Edward departing quietly and without rancour had, for the first time, been suggested.

The only person who still attempted to keep Edward upon the throne, even as the king himself lost interest in it, was Churchill. On Sunday, he conferred with his friends Archibald Sinclair and Boothby, and it was agreed that the king could no longer resist the advice of Baldwin and the Cabinet. They decided that, if he was to make a public statement agreeing to abide by the Cabinet's advice as to his marriage to Wallis, he would be granted at least another four months' breathing space until her divorce was finalised, and possibly the indefinite postponement of such a decision. Governments fell; public opinion changed. Churchill wrote to Edward, stating explicitly, 'The only possibility of your Majesty remaining on the throne is if you could subscribe to some such declaration as the following - "the King will not enter into any contract of marriage contrary to the advice of His Ministers".' He ended the letter: 'I cannot claim any authority behind this suggestion except my own belief. But I earnestly hope it may be considered.'[33]

Edward was moved by his friend's loyalty, but rejected the basis on which the appeal was made. As his decision was to marry Wallis at all costs, 'his fundamental resolve was unchanged, and, as he declared, unchangeable'.[34] Although Churchill mused whether a personal appeal could have made any difference, he also acknowledged that 'no human effort could have altered the course of events'.[35] This did not stop him the following day from doing something that he believed to be brave, loyal and principled, regardless of the personal cost.

After the disappointments of his defeat over the Simpson Divorce Bill, Baldwin had rallied by Monday, helped by some warm statements of confidence he had received. In a conversation with Lang that morning, he described himself as 'like a dog in a sheep-dog trial who has to induce a single sheep into a narrow gate'.[36] The backbencher Harold Macmillan, who had resigned the government whip, offered 'my deep admiration of your handling of the present constitutional crisis', along with his support, and asserted that 'the slightest weakness now would be a shattering blow to the whole basis of Christian morality, already gravely injured during recent years'. Lady Violet Bonham-Carter, daughter of Lord Asquith, wrote to commend Baldwin's actions, promising that 'all the forces of decency are with you in solid loyalty', and continuing, '[I] thank Heaven for [my father's] sake that he didn't have your task to perform. But I also thank Heaven that you are there to do it.'*[37]

He was also heartened by the realisation that any nascent 'King's

---

* She also wrote to Dawson on 9 December to praise his paper - 'how good *The Times* has been in these days . . . thank heaven the forces of decency have routed Beaverbrook, Rothermere [and Oswald] Mosley' - and bemoaned Churchill's involvement, calling it 'tragic and to me quite inexplicable'.

Party' was without widespread public support. Despite the likes of the Conservative MP Sir Reginald Blaker vowing at the weekend that many from his party would keep Edward on the throne, and the *Daily Mail* featuring an open letter from Lord Rothermere trumpeting the king's 'superlatively splendid' qualities, such statements were isolated firecrackers and squibs, and not the destructive conflagration that he had feared. Voters, especially the working classes, did not like the idea of a twice-divorced woman – and an American, to boot – becoming their queen; as MacDonald noted, public opinion was rich in 'common sense and outraged feeling'.[38] Leo Amery wrote in his diary on 7 December that 'The country as a whole was getting progressively more shocked at the idea that the King could hesitate between his duty to the Throne and his affection for a second-rate woman.'[39]

Although there had been times, especially after the defeat of the bill he had proposed, when Baldwin believed that his resignation would be the inevitable by-product of the crisis, he now considered that the two-day break had been his salvation. When his friend G. M. Young said, 'I believe you were the only man on Friday who knew what the House of Commons would be thinking on Monday', Baldwin replied, 'I have always believed in the weekend. But how [the politicians] do it, I don't know. I suppose they talk to the station-master.'[40]

The prime minister was thus in a more upbeat mood than he could have considered likely when he answered a pre-arranged question from Attlee about the state of the king's affairs.* He responded that, while the government did not wish to hurry Edward, the monarch was inevitably aware of the damage that any vacillation would cause. He also assured the House that 'with the exception of the question of morganatic marriage, no advice has been tendered by the Government to His Majesty, with whom

---

* Attlee, that most pragmatic of politicians, backed Baldwin throughout the crisis. He wrote in his memoirs that 'I suppose that few Prime Ministers had a more difficult task than that which faced Baldwin, and, in my view, the country owed him a debt of gratitude for the way in which he handled it.'

all my conversations have been strictly personal and informal . . . [His Majesty] first informed me [some weeks ago] of his intention to marry Mrs Simpson whenever she should be free.'[41] He ended by expressing the House's 'deep and respectful sympathy with His Majesty at this time'.[42]

He sat down to cheers of approval, and an irritable Churchill stood up to ask a question. He had barely listened to Baldwin, had ignored his statement of sympathy, and so was roundly humiliated. His neighbour had tried to discourage him from speaking, but Churchill retorted, 'I am not afraid of this House. When I see my duty, I speak out clearly.'[43] For the third time in four days, he attempted to ensure that 'no irrevocable step will be taken before the House has received a full statement', but he was unable to complete his question because of the anger and hostility he faced. He was besieged with cries of 'No! No!' 'Drop it!' and 'Twister!', and, unusually, was entirely lost for words, until he barked, 'If the House resists my claim it will only add the more importance to any words that I may want to use.'[44] He stood alone, attempting to make himself heard, but the cacophony grew too great, and the Speaker announced that he could not finish his statement. It was then that Churchill, exhausted and disappointed by what he saw as the inflexible nature of everyone involved in the crisis, and angered by his reception, lost his temper irrevocably, and shouted at Baldwin, 'You won't be satisfied until you've broken him, will you?'[45]

He left the chamber in a state of fury, but swiftly realised that his less-than-statesmanlike behaviour had had a disastrous effect on both his advocacy for the king and his own career, which, as he remarked to J. C. C. Davidson moments later, he now considered finished. *The Times*, admittedly a paper not disposed warmly towards him, described the events of the day as 'the most striking rebuff of modern parliamentary history'.[46] Churchill's friends turned against him with remarkable speed. Boothby roared that 'You have delivered a blow to the King, both in the House and in the country, far harder than any that Baldwin ever conceived of . . . *and you have done it without any consultation with your best friends and supporters* ... What happened this afternoon makes me feel that it is almost impossible for those who are most devoted to you personally to follow you blindly ... because they cannot be sure where the hell they are going to be landed next.'[47]

Churchill stumbled away a virtual pariah, but Baldwin's standing, so precarious over the previous days, months and years, was now at the highest it had ever been in his premiership. Dawson wrote that '[His speech] was an amazing demonstration of his strength and a complete obliteration of Winston.'[48] George Lambert, a former chairman of the Liberals, showed the new-found enthusiasm that the Commons felt for him by asking, 'Does the Prime Minister realise the deep sympathy for him which is felt in all sections of the House?' His words elicited hearty applause, as Baldwin recognised the gratitude and respect his colleagues felt for him, even if their reaction might have been summarised as 'rather him than me'. His position was assured. There was even a moment of levity when Willie Gallacher, Britain's only Communist MP, stood up and asked whether the cause of the crisis was not, in fact, the economy.

The king saw the situation differently. He summoned up the image of Churchill, 'undaunted, and quite alone', standing up for what he believed to be right, even as 'the hostility smote him like a great wave'. He later mused that 'I always regretted that incident, and would give much for the power to erase it from the records of that ancient assembly that owes him so much', even as he expressed his pride that 'of all Englishmen it was Mr Churchill who spoke up to the last for the King, his friend'.[49] He knew that it was his moral duty to offer Churchill his sympathy. Yet his attention was distracted by what he darkly called 'the conspiracy'. It represented the final, desperate attempt by his friends and opponents alike to resolve the crisis in definite fashion. And to his dismay, it was his beloved Wallis who was at the heart of it.

Chapter Twelve

'Wherever You Go, I Will Follow You'

When sorrows come, they come not single spies, but in battalions.

As Edward retreated into seclusion and a single-minded determination to abdicate, whatever the cost, Wallis was reduced to a pitiful state of fear and uncertainty. He was still king, whatever his enemies might wish; she was merely his consort, and an increasingly unpopular one at that. As she cowered in the Rogers' Cannes mansion, her only direct conversation with Edward came through largely incomprehensible telephone calls, in which she had to shout in growing frustration. Even as she struggled to remember the code that had been devised for these calls, she believed that 'He had turned remote and unreachable . . . his inner defences had gone up in a manner that I had observed in other, less fateful circumstances.'[1] She bitterly regretted not having taken Brownlow's advice to remain in England. As it was, she felt deeply alone and impotent; in her parlance, 'eanum'.

Her situation was not helped by concerns about her safety. One of the reasons the government had given for not allowing Edward to broadcast to the nation was that 'it would ensure that individuals would seek to intervene in the divorce proceedings and might even lead to some attempt on the lady's person'.[2] There was never an attempted plot to assassinate Wallis,* although she was disturbed by a series of anonymous letters by an Australian who claimed he

---

* Chips Channon's wife, Honor Guinness, expressed a desire on 6 December for someone to 'get at' Wallis, and thus save the king.

was heading to her French hideaway to kill her, which led Herman
Rogers to keep a loaded pistol by his bed. There was, however, a
great deal of public interest in the circumstances of her divorce,
and its suspected illegality. A bill making the decree nisi legal immediately would have ended this speculation, but its failure meant
that, with several months to go before Wallis and Ernest were divorced, it was possible for anyone to approach the King's Proctor
and offer their objections to the separation.

On Sunday 6 December, Brownlow laid out the situation as it
stood. 'As I see it now, there is only one possible way of stopping
this dreadful drift. It is for you to renounce the King.' This did not
come as a surprise to Wallis, who had reached the same conclusion
herself. As she put it, 'Since he would not give me up, I would have
to give him up, and in a way that would leave him no choice but
to accept this decision.' She knew that he would be devastated, but
felt she had no alternative: 'Apart from the moral considerations
affecting his kingly position, my own self-respect was at stake.' She
had seen, over the previous weeks and months, the way in which
she had become an object first of international curiosity, then of
hostility. If she became the woman for whom the King of England
abdicated, she would be notorious for ever. Her only hope was
to make Edward understand that 'the price of marriage would not
just be the forfeiture of the throne . . . [It] would include as well
the destruction of my reputation.'[3] Great foreboding Wagnerian
chords seemed to echo, each one spelling the inevitable doom that
awaited her.

Aided by Brownlow and Rogers, she drafted a statement to be
released to the press. It was short and unfortunately ambiguous
in its wording. It stated that 'Mrs Simpson throughout the last
few weeks has invariably wished to avoid any action or proposal
which would hurt or damage His Majesty or the throne. Today
her action is unchanged, and she is willing, if such action would
solve the problem, to withdraw from a situation that has been rendered both unhappy and untenable.'[4] Brownlow believed that the
statement needed to go further and insist that Wallis would not

marry Edward under any circumstances, but she, mindful of the king's increasingly precarious emotional and mental state, would not plunge the knife in with the fatal precision it required.

In any event, Edward had received a letter from her, either late on Sunday 6 December or early on Monday, that had attempted to explain her intentions: 'I am so anxious for you not to *abdicate* and I think that the fact you do [want to] is going to put me in the wrong light to the entire world because they will say that I could have prevented it.' Her solution, offered hurriedly and without the careful consideration it needed, was that the king postpone any plan to leave the throne until at least October 1937, and that they should remain separated from one another. ('We can arrange to [meet] secretly through our friends.') She stressed how 'terrified' she felt at what would happen to her if Edward persisted in his planned abdication, and implored him, 'Isn't it better in the long run not to be hasty or selfish but back up your people and make an eight-month sacrifice for them.' Baldwin was cast as the panto-mime villain, for having misled Parliament by claiming that Wallis wanted to be queen,* and she concluded that 'We would have no happiness and I think the world would turn against me, when now we have their sympathy.'5

Edward did not reply to this letter, and the next contact the two had was when she read him her press statement in a telephone call on Monday afternoon. Over a 'noisy and uncertain' connection – the symbolism was irresistible – Edward took it badly. 'At first he was unbelieving, then hurt and angry', Wallis wrote, before, after a long silence, he slowly said, 'Go ahead, if you wish; it won't make any difference.' She disagreed, and for a few hours, it seemed as if she had achieved something; Brownlow believed that the state-ment had either ended the crisis altogether, or at least checked matters. It is hard not to feel sympathy for Wallis, who wrote that

---

* This was debatable. Baldwin had stated in Parliament on 4 December that 'The lady who [the King] marries . . . necessarily becomes Queen . . . and her children will be in direct succession to the throne.' This was more an account of the status quo than an emotive attack.

'a terrible weight lifted from my mind. That night, for the first time since leaving the Fort five days before, I slept soundly.'[6] Easy lies the head unencumbered by the crown.

The king, meanwhile, saw this as 'an unexpected development which for a short but terrifying interval threatened me with the loss of the marriage for which I had already in spirit relinquished my throne'.[7] He ascribed the 'conspiracy', as he termed it, to an eclectic mixture of men that included Baldwin, Beaverbrook, Wilson, Brownlow, Wallis's solicitor Theodore Goddard, Monckton, and his own solicitor George Allen. The latter two had acted not out of treachery, he believed, but out of an excess of loyalty, which 'prompted them to leave no avenue unexplored, however unpromising its turnings, that held out the remotest possibility of keeping me on the throne'. And he acknowledged the ambiguity of Beaverbrook's motives, but also that 'it was not his intention to destroy my happiness'. As for Baldwin, Wilson and Goddard, however, they were traitors and opportunists all, fit only for withering contempt and scorn.

Wilson, who was not very interested in Edward's or anyone else's opinion of him, attempted to ascertain from Monckton whether Wallis was sincere about abandoning the king, or whether she intended to return to England. Monckton replied that her coming back seemed unlikely, but also that it was worth sending Goddard out to Cannes to, as he expressed it, 'put before her considerations which would induce her to stay away'.[8] These 'considerations' undoubtedly included the front pages of several national newspapers, which had turned against her with the venom she had expected they would.

Wilson knew that Goddard was not well disposed towards his client, on the grounds that he believed he had been misled by Wallis assuring him that, after the divorce trial, 'she would take steps gradually to fade out'. He had conveyed this intelligence to the government and then, humiliatingly, had had to withdraw it. He was also not deaf to the rumours that he was hearing about intervention and collusion in the divorce case, and, along with Wilson, wished for a definite conclusion to an embarrassing and painful episode. It was unlikely to come for free. As he put it to Wilson, 'What price could be paid to Mrs Simpson for clearing out?'[9]

Wilson, who described this as 'rather a facer', placed the onus on Goddard to find out what Wallis wanted, and 'to say anything that he thought proper to her as to the reasonableness or otherwise of what she thought might be done'. It is a wonder he did not add 'Pounds or guineas?' to his instructions to the solicitor. On Monday 7 December, Goddard then saw Edward, who, fearful of an intervention, expressly forbade him to go to Wallis. Wilson and Baldwin met the solicitor afterwards, and, with a mixture of charm and steel, invited him to choose between his loyalty to his soon-to-be-former monarch and his professional reputation, especially having acted in an infamous and potentially illegal divorce that could soon crumble. As Wilson put it, 'I want you to go to Cannes and find out what is really behind this. Immediately. Tonight.'[10] It was not for nothing that the civil servant was described as occupying 'a more powerful position in Britain than almost anyone since Cardinal Wolsey'.[11]

The solicitor would be paid five hundred guineas as a fee: a considerable sum, but a hard-earned one. As Wilson wrote, 'Mr Goddard said that he was satisfied that intervention [in the divorce] had been determined upon and might be imminent, and, so far as could be judged, would be successful. This strengthened Mr Goddard in his view that he ought to go. The Prime Minister shared that view.' There is satisfaction, as of a hard-won victory, in Wilson's report that 'Mr Goddard, with two companions, left for Cannes by air on Tuesday morning, 8 December.'[12] The identity of these companions would soon cause further speculation and difficulty.

Wilson's and Goddard's fears that an approach to Sir Thomas Barnes in his role as the King's Proctor was inevitable were soon justified. Baldwin had already warned Edward on 3 December that Barnes's involvement seemed unavoidable, and so it proved.

Various members of the public had already submitted letters, but as these were based purely on hearsay and rumour, they could not be taken seriously. It was only a matter of time, however, before someone better informed would come forward, with their treacherous motivation based either on idealism or money. Wilson himself had said to Goddard that he had his own information as to the 'rumours and statements' about intervention in the divorce suit, although he qualified this by stating, 'It was all rather general in form and so far as I knew no attempt had been made to check it or follow it up.'[13]

In fact, an anonymous man had already telephoned Barnes at his house on the evening of Sunday 6 December, not only making very specific allegations about the king's association with Wallis, but also claiming to be able to produce definite evidence. Barnes dismissed his would-be informant, telling him that he could not regard a telephone conversation as the basis for taking action, but the next day, he informed Wilson that, in his capacity as King's Proctor, he had received a number of letters from the public, and these had increased enormously over the previous few days as the news about Wallis became general knowledge. As with the unknown caller of the previous night, he could ignore unspecific and vague claims of information, but he now told Wilson that 'I have received a formal request for intervention from a reputable firm of solicitors, who set out in their letter in detail the grounds upon which they requested my intervention in the suit.' These grounds were firstly the adulterous association between the king and Mrs Simpson, and secondly the existence of collusion between Mr and Mrs Simpson as to the divorce proceedings.

Although it was extremely rare for the King's Proctor to intervene in divorce cases, mainly because his resources were so limited that he could only act when his information was scrupulously reliable, the occasions when he did usually resulted in the divorce being rescinded. This occurred in twenty-one out of twenty-three cases in 1935 and twenty-five out of twenty-six in 1936.[14] There seemed every chance that Wallis's divorce would become one of these instances. As Baldwin's private secretary Tommy Dugdale expressed it, 'During the morning of the 8th December, it became apparent from certain additional information . . . that it was very doubtful whether Mrs Simpson would in fact be able, when the time came, to obtain a decree absolute.' Barnes took on a quasi-judicial role in deciding whether to refer the divorce to the court, but in order for it to proceed any further there needed to be a member of the public, preferably of a respectable and sane disposition, who was prepared to testify to Edward's adultery. For the time being, at least, nobody came forward.

It was briefly felt on the evening of Monday 7 December, when Wallis's statement was broadcast from Cannes, that the crisis might be either postponed or ended altogether. The *Express* and *Mail* declared that this was a breakthrough, and Duff Cooper wrote of being at a dinner party where 'the women were all in a state of wild excitement and happiness',[15] but Monckton, although he acknowledged that 'this when published was looked upon as being perhaps the end of the crisis', recognised that 'We at the Fort knew that the King knew of the statement before its publication and that his intention was quite unchanged.'[16] All now rested on the results of Goddard's interview with Wallis in Cannes.

The solicitor arrived in France at two in the morning of Wednesday 9 December, in a private plane lent to him for the occasion by the government. He had never flown before, and as bad luck would have it, it was an appalling flight, necessitating a landing at Marseilles to deal with a faulty engine. As Goddard suffered from a weak heart,* he was accompanied by a physician, Dr Kirkwood,

---

* Egerton believed that this was untrue – 'we had never heard in the office, or seen any sign, of such a condition and we were a little sceptical of the need for a doctor in attendance.' He speculated that Kirkwood's presence was down to Goddard's determination to get 'every ounce of publicity out of the case' and that a doctor 'would guarantee the attention of the press and emphasise the importance of the business on which he was engaged and the sacrifice he was prepared to make in the service of his client'. He succeeded: rather too well.

and one of his legal clerks. This innocuous group of people, however, found themselves the subject of controversy, thanks to an
erroneous belief that Kirkwood was a famous gynaecologist. The
clerk, inevitably, was described as an anaesthetist, which gave rise
to fantastic rumours, eagerly seized upon by the waiting journalists, that Wallis was pregnant.* When they arrived at Cannes, and
telephoned the villa to ask to see her, Brownlow was furious at the
fuss. He had already told Wallis, with some anger, that 'Herman
and I have done everything in our power to protect your dignity,
your good name and peace of mind, and the prestige of the King.
This is the last straw.'

Edward had already telephoned Wallis the previous day, informing her of Goddard's imminent arrival. Angry at having had
his orders ignored, he adopted a tone that he later conceded was
'rather imperious'. He told Wallis, 'You must not listen to this man.
Do not be influenced by anything he says', but she replied, 'Of
course I have to receive him. He has come a long way, at some risk
to himself, and courtesy requires that I listen to what he has to say.'
She did promise that she would do nothing without consulting
the king, but this did little to reassure him. As he put it, in regally
proprietorial language, 'Deprived of my moral support, she was
no longer so sure of herself, and the violence of the storm raging
about us both terrified her.'[17]

In fact, Wallis was not at all terrified or uncertain. She knew
what she wanted, and that was to make a permanent break with
Edward. As she wrote a few days later to Sibyl Colefax, when the
crisis had finally come to an end, 'I knew him so well, I wanted
them to take my advice. But no, driving on they went, headed for
this tragedy. If only they had said, let's drop the idea now and in the
autumn we'll discuss it again . . . In the autumn, I would have been

---

* Some biographers, including Frances Donaldson, state that Goddard's true
reason for heading to Cannes in such haste was to retrieve royal jewels that
Wallis had been improperly given. Egerton wrote 'it was assumed in the office
that [Goddard's] flight was in this connection', although Wallis's (undeniably
self-serving) account suggests otherwise.

so very far away. I had already escaped.' She regarded her adopted home with contempt – 'I saw England turn on a man that couldn't defend himself and had never been anything but straight with his country'[18] – but her abiding desire was to extricate herself from this dreadful situation and flee. Where, she barely knew. America was out because of the press; China, distant though it was, seemed like the only realistic option. Yet a return to the sing-song houses was not a likely, or desirable, prospect. It was instead time to face a different kind of music.

Brownlow, in his self-appointed role as Wallis's protector, was initially reluctant to admit Goddard to the house. Only when the hapless lawyer disclosed the medical reason for Kirkwood's presence was he even partially mollified, and even then he only allowed Goddard into Wallis's presence under strict conditions. He was to enter alone, without a briefcase or anything remotely resembling a doctor's bag, and – in a touch of sadism – Brownlow insisted that his taxi could not come closer than a hundred yards of the Rogers' house, meaning that he had to run the gauntlet of the increasingly ravenous press in order to enter. No wonder Wallis reported him as being 'chastened' when he finally entered the drawing room.

Still, this was as nothing to how his client was feeling. Goddard later described her to Dugdale as being 'in a most terrified state of nerves', and desiring 'complete capitulation [and] willingness to do anything'.[19] He attempted to persuade her to withdraw the divorce action, which would immediately resolve the crisis, as it would mean that Edward could no longer marry her. Wallis was surprisingly keen to help. She told him that 'I will do anything within my power to keep the King on the throne', to which a relieved Goddard replied, 'That is what I was sure you would say, and so informed Mr Baldwin.' Wallis later considered that 'His expression was that of a man conscious of playing a crucial and successful role in a historical situation.' It helped his case that he tactfully pointed out the weight of public opinion against her, and, in Wilson's words, 'a number of other disadvantages attendant upon pursuing the other courses open to her if she rejected his advice'.[20]

One salient fact that may have assisted her desire to stop Edward from abdicating was that, as Wilson silkily described it, 'Perhaps it had not been made sufficiently plain to the King and to Mrs Simpson that, if the King were to affront public opinion by abdicating, it was very doubtful whether Parliament would be prepared to grant money to the King after he had gone. It was thought that a hint of this position ought to be conveyed to the King and Mrs Simpson.'[21] The last thing the financially conscious Wallis wanted was to be in thrall to a penniless, bitter former monarch.

Brownlow was summoned for his advice, and played devil's advocate. He doubted whether there was time to stop the king from abdicating, nor if he would accept Wallis's decision. As he argued, 'For you to scrap your divorce will produce a hopeless anti-climax and an all-round tragedy.'[22] Yet Wallis felt it was incumbent on her to attempt to avert disaster. Brownlow thus composed a short, tragic note saying, 'With the deepest personal sorrow, Mrs Simpson wishes to announce that she has abandoned any intention of marrying His Majesty',[23] which she then signed.

It was time to call Edward, and tell him of her intentions. The line, as usual, was dreadful. With Goddard by her side, Wallis informed her lover that she was about to begin proceedings to withdraw her divorce petition, and that this was her heartfelt wish. Edward replied, calmly, 'It's too late. The abdication documents are already being drawn up. The Cabinet is meeting this very moment to act upon them. I have given them my final word. I will be gone from England within forty-eight hours.' His next words told Wallis, if she did not already know, the manner of man she was dealing with, and would find herself associated with for the rest of her life. 'Of course, you can do whatever you wish. You can go wherever you want – to China, Labrador, or the South Seas. But wherever you go, I will follow you.'[24]

*

As Goddard made his troublesome and ultimately unsuccessful*
journey to see Wallis, Edward did his best to regain control. On
Monday 7 December, he saw the Duke of York for the first time
since 17 November, when he had informed his brother that he
intended to marry Mrs Simpson. Their reunion was an awkward
one. Edward wished to talk business; he wanted to talk about the
physical process of abdication, and, as he put it, 'the disposition of
family property, heirlooms and so forth'. Bertie, however, was in
a state of trepidation. He had written to his mother as far back as
6 November that 'It is all so worrying & I feel we all live a life of
conjecture; never knowing what will happen tomorrow, & then
the unexpected comes.'[25] He may have assured Godfrey Thomas
that he would take over the throne if he needed to, but a truer
expression of his feelings came when he told his private secretary,
Sir Eric Miéville, on 29 November, 'I feel like the proverbial sheep
being led to the slaughter.'[26]

When the brothers met at last, what Bertie called 'the awful &
ghastly suspense of waiting' was over. Pacing up and down the
room, Edward declared that he would abdicate, and that his mind
was made up. The two also discussed the vexed issue of Wallis, and
it is likely that Edward hinted that he would leave without causing
any trouble as long as no problems were created with her divorce.
While it was not in Bertie's power to make such a guarantee, any
more than it would have been within Edward's while he ruled, he
was able to assure his brother that he would do what he could to
facilitate their reunion before too long. While the king may have
felt a growing sense of relief that his decision was made and that he
was soon to be relieved of his responsibilities, his younger brother
felt the opposite. Nonetheless, he possessed a sense of duty that
the king did not, and so, after dinner at the Royal Lodge in Windsor, he returned to the Fort once again. As he wrote in his account

---

* Egerton noted that the abdication, and his role within it, cost Goddard his
anticipated knighthood – 'I am afraid the point was noted with some glee in the
office' – and mused: 'by and large, people get the solicitor they deserve.'

of the abdication, 'I felt having once got there I was not going to leave. As he is my eldest brother I had to be there to try & help him in his hour of need.'²⁷

The following day, the Duke of Kent appeared at the Fort. Edward presented this in his memoirs as a show of brotherly affection, with much emphasis on George arriving 'uninvited and unannounced', and then declaring, 'Whether you want to see me or not, I have come.'²⁸ In fact, he was there in a desperate attempt to persuade the king not to abdicate, knowing that it would place an impossible burden on Bertie's shoulders. Neither of the brothers was positively inclined towards Wallis. Lucy Baldwin described them as 'furious against the lady', and George and Tommy Dugdale later had a heart-to-heart during which the duke 'was very like King George V in his outspoken language'.²⁹ Yet Edward was not to be moved. When George begged him to change his mind, he was informed, with true regal hauteur, 'I made it up long ago. Why should I change it now?'³⁰

Edward's fraternal discussions were interrupted by the arrival of Baldwin, by now a familiar presence at the Fort. He had been buoyed by his warm reception in the Commons the previous day, and felt that there might, after all, be some chance that the king could reconsider his decision. He packed his overnight bag, and remarked to Wilson, 'He must wrestle with himself now in a way he has never done before, and if he will let me I will help him. We may even have to see the night through together.'³¹ The image of the two men, pyjama-clad and desperately clasped together in prayer, is a diverting one, but Baldwin was not called upon to do nocturnal service for his sovereign. He travelled down with Monckton and Tommy Dugdale, remarking that he would like to be with the king as a friend should he wish it, but the gravity of his mission hung heavily upon him. He was a nervous passenger, polluting the car's confined space with pipe smoke and demanding that they drive slowly. Monckton wrote, 'I was praying for the journey to end . . . I knew that the King must be more tired than ever and might hate the prospect of the Prime Minister staying the night.'³²

He was correct. The king ('even more tired than I had thought, and . . . worn out')[33] noticed the appearance of Baldwin's suitcase with horror, describing it as 'just too much'. Despite his more emotional moments with the prime minister in previous days, he had had enough of him. As he scathingly put it, 'His part in my life was over, and I did not propose to have him on my hands that night, snapping his fingers, storing up little homely touches for his report to Parliament.'[34]

There then followed 'a last fruitless talk', before Baldwin, knowing that his work was done, suggested that he leave.* Edward, perhaps enjoying his premier's discomfort, replied, 'I could not do that. The prime minister has been so kind as to come here to help me, I could not let him leave without giving him dinner.'[35] His mood was also lifted by a conversation with Wallis on the telephone. According to Lucy Baldwin, he entered the room 'gesticulating, with his arms above his head . . . He seemed transported with joy and transfigured.' He announced, yet again, 'She is the most wonderful woman, I have the most wonderful woman in the world behind me in this, she does not mind, it will simply draw us nearer together. I mean to go & leave the way clear for my brother.'[36]

And so the last supper began, in the Fort's drawing room. The major difference was that there were nine at table, rather than thirteen, and more than one of the guests present, to Edward's knowledge or otherwise, had betrayed him. The company consisted of the king, the Duke of York, the Duke of Kent, Baldwin, Monckton, Tommy Dugdale, Sir Edward Peacock, the receiver general of the Duchy of Cornwall, George Allen and Ulick Alexander. Peacock, fearing for Edward's health, suggested to Monckton that the king should have a rest during the meal, but Edward refused, saying, 'I will carry it through.'[37] This would be his last hurrah; do this in remembrance of him.

---

* Monckton believed that Baldwin, 'with renewed vigour . . . put the position even better than before' on this occasion, but Edward 'wearily said that his mind was made up and he asked to be spared any more advice on the subject'.

It was tacitly recognised by the company that there would be no mention of the abdication, and so the atmosphere that night was an odd mixture of the sombre and the joyful. While Bertie described the other guests as 'very sad', knowing as they did of the 'final and irrevocable decision' that had been made, and the meal as 'a dinner I am never likely to forget',[38] the king, as host, kept the talk going and remained in jovial spirits, especially after Baldwin departed at half past nine. Bertie called Edward 'the life & soul of the party, telling the PM things I am sure he had never heard before about unemployed centres etc. . . . I whispered to WM "This is the man we are going to lose." Nobody could believe it.'[39]

Baldwin's parting words to his monarch were 'Can I take it for certain, sir, that if the Archangel Gabriel came down from Heaven and asked you to change your mind, it would have no effect on you?' When Edward agreed that it would not, Baldwin, speaking for himself and Lucy, said, 'There are no two people among your subjects who are more grieved at what has happened than we are, but you must also remember that there are no two people who hope more sincerely that you may find happiness where you believe it may be found.'[40] When the exhausted Baldwin returned home to his wife, his words were less measured: 'I feel as though I have been in Bedlam* . . . He doesn't seem to grasp the gravity of the whole affair.' The two men never met again.

Edward noted of Baldwin that 'his heavy face seemed pasty and lifeless . . . The strain, I realised, had also taken a toll on him.'[41] His own gaiety, in contrast, may have been a conscious effort to be light-hearted and entertaining – the character he was aiming for was that of 'an unbowed, unresentful, if somewhat whimsical sovereign' – but it was worth it. He wrote with satisfaction that Baldwin remarked at Cabinet the next day, 'more puzzled than disapproving', that 'the King appeared happy and gay, as if he were looking forward to his honeymoon'.[42]

---

* Hardinge used the same word to describe the atmosphere of Fort Belvedere throughout the crisis.

The most vivid description of the evening was Monckton's. He called it Edward's 'tour de force', and wrote how 'in that quiet pan-elled room, he sat at the head of his table, with his boyish face and smile, with a good fresh colour while the rest of us were pale as sheets, rippling over with bright conversation and a careful eye to see that his guests were being looked after . . . I was next to [Bertie] and as the dinner went on the Duke turned to me and said "Look at him. We simply cannot let him go." But we both knew that there was nothing we could say or do to stop him.'[43]

It was a fine, bravura performance that proved that Edward, when he made the effort, had a charisma and assurance about him few others could approach. At the conclusion of the dinner, he turned to Peacock in the drawing room with an air of triumph and said, like an actor after his applause, 'How was that?' Peacock was able to reassure him of his 'amazing effort'. It would be in the same drawing room, in two days' time, that he would sign the document confirming his abdication.

Chapter Thirteen

Failing Tragically

'The House is dead, numbed by expectancy.' So Harold Nicolson wrote in his diary on Wednesday 9 December. It now seemed inevitable that Edward would abdicate, an outcome equally dreaded and accepted by all. Goddard's mission to Cannes was not generally known, but it was too little, too late. For the first time in English history, the monarch would voluntarily relinquish his crown, choosing the woman he was obsessed by over his nation. It was an act of supreme selfishness, driven by mania and a fixation upon the unfortunate Wallis. Her efforts to abandon him, although fruitless, were to her credit; less so was the conversation, reported by Dugdale, between her and the king the previous night, during which, after Edward suggested that he might not leave his throne the multimillionaire he had expected to be, 'a harsh voiced twang of rich American invective from Cannes'[1] duly followed.

The question of money was one that preoccupied both Edward and Wallis, during and after his reign. Peacock met with the king on Wednesday morning at 9 a.m., and the monarch stated, somewhat unbelievably, that he had had 'a good night'. Peacock impressed upon him the importance of not doing anything to endanger Mrs Simpson's divorce. Events that day would prove his advice sagacious. He also had the disagreeable task, in his official capacity, of talking to Edward about his finances. At the time of the abdication, the king was reputedly worth just over £1 million, with his fortune coming from a mixture of cash and investments. For virtually anyone else in England, this would have been enough to live a luxurious lifestyle for ever, and keep one's intimates in the highest standards of comfort as well. Yet Edward believed he was being hard done by, just as he felt that he had failed to inherit enough when his father died. Like many wealthy people, he decided that he was in fact poor, and made it clear that one of the conditions of his leaving the country quietly was a settlement fit for a man of his stature: quite literally, a king's ransom.

When Peacock met Baldwin, Simon and others that morning, he told them that Edward was still intent upon going, causing the Cabinet, led by Beaverbrook's man Hoare, to issue a formal declaration of regret at the king's decision – 'Ministers are reluctant to believe that Your Majesty's resolve is irrevocable' – and to ask him one last time to reconsider. Baldwin was still mystified by Edward's whimsical behaviour of the previous evening, and Hoare believed that the prime minister's final, futile request for the king to change his mind was dictated by his own moral beliefs, saying of Baldwin that 'SB would have destroyed himself if the Cabinet had not sent this last request for reconsideration.'[2] Then the talk turned to money. Where there was muck, there was brass.

The general feeling amongst the politicians, as Peacock reported it, was that 'If His Majesty went to Mrs S or did anything to emphasise that side of things before the Civil List Bill was passed, he would not get a penny, because Parliament would refuse to pass it.'[3] Simon's view was that if Wallis was made aware that there might be no money – as well as no divorce – she might be induced to vanish, and the king to retract his abdication plans. Yet it was too late. Hardinge's earlier suggestion of £25,000 per annum hung in the air, and had indeed been included in the abdication settlement, but Baldwin also knew that the chances of Parliament agreeing to the sum being paid out of public money, in perpetuity, were slim. The idea of Wallis being somehow subsidised by the taxpayer seemed incredible. Tommy Dugdale's wife Nancy captured the mood when she wrote that 'Public money should not be voted for the ex King in the Civil List . . . The Royal family . . . should give their brother enough to live on.'[4]

It was with this in mind that Monckton and Peacock went to visit Bertie at 145 Piccadilly on Wednesday morning, with the aim of securing as much for Edward as they could. The Duke of York assented to his brother retaining royal rank and to his continuing to have use of Fort Belvedere if he returned to England, and he agreed to discuss financial matters with Edward further the next day. Monckton and Peacock congratulated themselves on their diplomacy and tact. Had they known what was going on at the High Court of Justice at exactly that moment, they might have been less complacent.

Francis Stephenson, an elderly solicitor's clerk from Ilford in Essex, was an unlikely figure to have been responsible for bringing about a formal investigation into Edward and Wallis's affairs. Yet on 9 December, he filed a suit at the High Court asking that the decree nisi granted in Ipswich on 27 October should be rendered void, on the grounds that it was obtained by collusion. Naming Wallis as the petitioner and Ernest as the respondent, Stephenson's suit stated that 'The said decree was obtained contrary to the justice of the case by reason of the following material facts not having been brought to the notice of this Honourable Court', and went on to openly claim that she had committed adultery with the king at No. 5 Bryanston Court and at Fort Belvedere, as well as on the *Nahlin* and at her address at No. 1 Cumberland Terrace. There was particular scorn aimed at the (admittedly unconventional) fashion in which the divorce had been heard at the Ipswich Assize Court, as well as at Wallis's short-lived residence in Felixstowe.

With what one imagines was a weary sigh, the King's Proctor began his investigation. Although Stephenson was basing his claims on nothing more than hearsay and rumours heard from friends, it was nonetheless now necessary to look into the circumstances of Wallis's divorce and to take evidence from all the innumerable servants, maids and yacht crew, which would be a long and protracted process.

It would not be completed before March 1937,* leaving Edward and Wallis in a state of limbo. Although the various staff interviewed were discreet and loyal, it was symptomatic of the abdication and the lives of those involved within it that its consequences stretched on for years, if not decades. As Wallis wrote, 'David's legal advisers and mine had, of course, been put on notice and were worried. They were worried not at all by the possibility of there being any authentic legal basis for challenging the divorce – there could be none – but rather by the possibility that this strange action was symptomatic of a vengeful desire to prevent David's marriage to me as a final reprisal.'[5]

Popular opinion was entirely against Wallis by this stage, and people were increasingly bewildered by Edward's actions. Lloyd George's private secretary, Joseph Davies, wrote to him on 9 December to say that 'Except for a few like myself who sympathise with any man who has found the one woman he cares for, all classes here were against Mrs Simpson.' Although Davies allowed that 'when they found that marriage might mean abdication there was a tremendous revulsion of feeling in letting him have his way rather than lose him', he placed blame equally on both Edward and Wallis, stating that 'The trouble with the King is that he changes his mind from day to day and the PM doesn't know where he stands', and that 'There are all kinds of vulgar explanations for his infatuation – some say it is all sex and others that it is some kind of mesmerism which has nothing to do with sex at all.' Davies concluded that 'Unless there is some satisfactory solution soon, I fear that the people in distressed areas and others who like to make mischief will call upon the Cabinet to get on with their jobs, in which case quite a dangerous situation might arise.'[6]

The question of sex as regarded Edward was one that had also

---

* Barnes pronounced himself satisfied that there was nothing to indicate 'cohabitation', rather than adultery. Egerton speculated that 'the word was carefully chosen', and that, had Barnes wished to investigate the existence of collusion between Ernest and Wallis in the divorce case, it would have been provable and the divorce would not have been granted.

preoccupied Baldwin, who had not previously given the matter much thought. On 6 December, he had received a letter from a sexual psychologist, Dr Bernard Armitage, which attempted to explain Edward and Wallis's relationship in medical terms. Establishing that the king had 'overcompensated' for sexual inadequacy as a younger man, Armitage wrote that 'Once [Edward] did find a woman who would in all regards satisfy him, he would prove to be singularly and persistently obstinate in attaching himself to her – all the more emphatically because he would think . . . that he was turning himself away from being what would be regarded as an unsatisfactory man into being a thoroughly satisfactory man, acceptable to the general opinion of the nation.' He concluded, accurately, that 'the stage was set for disaster'.[7]

As Nicolson noted of Parliament, there was a strange inertia that had now settled on the public consciousness. The stock market had been volatile for days, with a particular blip on Monday. Beaverbrook's account of the market stated that it had been 'extremely nervous' at the start of the week, with a particular vulnerability in gilt-edged stocks and industrials, and a weak sterling, although it had recovered slightly when Wallis's Cannes statement was broadcast the previous day. Nor was this unease confined to Britain. Sir Ronald Lindsay, British ambassador to the United States, wrote to Robert Vansittart on 8 December that 'The question of the King's marriage has monopolised all written and oral speculation to an extent quite unparalleled in my experience', and that 'The great majority of [American] editors take broadly the view that where the King's wishes conflict with those of his people at home or in his Dominions, it is the King who must give way.'

Lindsay was scathing about Hearst and his empire of newspapers, which had largely supported Edward and Wallis – 'Hearst habitually appeals to the lower strata of people who have no inhibitions' – and called Bernard Shaw's sympathetic skit 'a revolting and stupid piece of writing'. He concluded by sniffing, 'I fear that the effect of this affair is very deplorable. When King George died, I wrote an official despatch suggesting that while the political relations between Great Britain and America were the affair of governments, the psychological and emotional relations between the two peoples were of immense importance and that in this field, the personality of the late King had forged new and very powerful bonds. These bonds have been severed and the loss thereby incurred to Anglo-American relations is very severe.' Although he allowed that 'they may well be built up again', it was his belief that 'loss of prestige does count for something'. It would not be long until Anglo-American relations would be tested once again, in entirely different circumstances, and at least Lindsay's valedictory statement that 'I do not think that the friendly feeling for Great Britain which is now widely prevalent here will be affected'[8] proved accurate.

Even Churchill could do little. He wrote to Dawson on 9 December, mournfully declaring that 'a great deal that you have written lately has caused me pain', and stating that 'nothing can deprive the sovereign of the right of laying down his burden if at any time he finds it unbearable or for any other reason', but he knew it was all over now, concluding his musings on the possibility of Edward being able to marry whom he wished by saying, 'It may well be that all will have been settled one way or another before you get this.'[9]

Baldwin and his Cabinet did not have long to wait before Edward replied to their request that he rethink his abdication. The response was predictably curt, stating, 'The King has received the Prime Minister's letter of the 9th December, informing him of the view of the Cabinet. His Majesty has given the matter his further consideration, but regrets he is unable to alter his decision.' This was greeted with disapproval, and Simon and Chamberlain stated that Edward did not deserve any sort of financial provision. After all, they argued, it had been his decision to abdicate, and to cause a national crisis; why should he then be rewarded for the rashness of his actions? It did not help that Wallis was regarded with contempt. A typical comment was that of the politician Sir Edward

Cadogan, who wrote in his diary that 'Am told HM has squandered all on Mrs S, who's a real gold-digger!' Her extravagance did not endear her to the Cabinet, and in turn the king's reputation suffered a further blow.

Edward himself remained oddly calm and cheerful, as if believing that the worst was now behind him. Despite Hardinge thoughtfully – or maliciously – ensuring a steady flow of letters and information to the Fort detailing the thoughts of his subjects, he took no heed of the feelings of others, keeping Peacock and Monckton constantly occupied. In at least one instance, however, this insouciance may have been shaken. A letter from a former soldier, John Wright, offered an explicit death threat in the event of his marrying Wallis. Wright wrote, 'What do you mean by plunging us all into misery . . . Exactly 100 of us disabled & ex-soldiers who fought for you – some of us you have shook hands with – we have held a private and secret meeting and have decided that should you marry this Mrs Simpson, you will not live long to enjoy your married life. For Your Majesty the following is <u>no idle threat</u> – but a solemn oath taken by every one of us to <u>KILL YOU BOTH . . .</u> We have now subscribed £32 towards expenses to find you where ever you are. We have got 12 revolvers and every thing ready . . . Don't for God's sake disgrace even the working man who at least have married <u>PURE</u> women.'[10]

Edward's equanimity continued, regardless. On the evening of 9 December, he informed the exhausted Monckton that 'I just want a word with you', and Peacock drily noted that 'I learned the next day that the "word" went on until well after three o'clock.'[11] He was amused by the constitutional quirk whereby he was obliged, as monarch, to provide Royal Assent to his own Act of Abdication: an unprecedented situation that nobody had ever believed would be necessary. As he sent Monckton back and forth between the Fort and Downing Street, in thick fog ('I was afraid that he might be delayed on the road, and in consequence keep the Cabinet waiting',[12] Edward mused), there was a final and much-dreaded interview to interrupt his sangfroid. He had to see his mother once more.

Bertie had been in close touch with Queen Mary, seeing her virtually daily throughout the crisis. She had been in a fragile state. As Hardinge noted, with what seems like barely suppressed *Schadenfreude*, 'On more than one occasion Queen Mary sent for me after interviews with King Edward in great distress, because the latter's speech and manner was anything but what one would expect from a son to a mother, especially a mother who is still bowed down with the grief of an irreparable bereavement. When Queen Mary was emphasising the obligations of a sovereign to his people as against his own personal inclinations, King Edward repeated over and over again the same remark, "All that matters is our happiness" . . . Such an attitude came as a great shock [and] King Edward was only with difficulty persuaded to say goodbye to his mother before his departure . . . [His] behaviour to his mother gave one more proof of a mind at least temporarily unbalanced. That is the one and only charitable view that can be taken of it.'[13]

On 10 December, the dutiful Bertie arranged for Edward to see his long-suffering mother at his home in Windsor Great Park, Royal Lodge, and met with her and Monckton at Marlborough House. All three agreed that, the decision to abdicate having been irrevocably taken, it was better executed sooner rather than later. Baldwin expressed a preference for its taking place by the end of the week, with Simon ensuring that the notification of abdication should be broadcast throughout the British Empire. Monckton noted admiringly that 'I have seen many staff officers, but none so competent.'[14] Nonetheless, there was an impression of tremendous sadness, most economically conveyed by the Queen Mother when she stated, 'To give up all that for this.'[15] .

She met Edward at three o'clock at the Royal Lodge. The two were together 'for some time', as Bertie noted. The king attempted to justify himself and his actions in the best light, especially as regarded his dealings with Baldwin, but she made it clear that she continued to disapprove of his actions, and that she was bewildered by the circumstances that had led to their execution. Edward claimed later that 'Her heart went out to her hard-pressed son, prompting her to say with tenderness: "And to me, the worst thing is that you won't be able to see her for so long"',[16] but this seems a romantic fabrication, not least because Edward, frustrated and angry, had 'stormed and raged and shouted like a man demented'.[17] A clearer account of the meeting, and others like it, can be found in the letter Mary sent him on 5 July 1938, after he requested that she write 'frankly about my true feelings with regard to you and the current position'. In it she stated that 'You will remember how miserable I was when you informed me of your intended marriage and abdication and how I implored you not to do so for our sake and for the sake of the country. You did not seem able to take in anything . . . or to listen to any advice. I do not think you have ever realised the shock which the attitude you took up caused your family and the whole nation.'[18] Any maternal blessing that Edward had hoped for was firmly withheld.

The king was then besieged throughout the remainder of the afternoon. Bertie attempted to persuade his brother once again, but realised, to his chagrin, that 'nothing I said would alter his decision . . . His mind was made up.' Realising that Edward was in the grip of paranoia ('[he] had been very suspicious previous to my talk to him'), Bertie took Monckton into his confidence on a journey to London to see his mother, who had returned to Marlborough House. A friendship was forming between the two, in the dire circumstances, that went beyond the usual relationship between a prince and a courtier. Both were intelligent, pragmatic men who were attempting to find a route through the literal and figurative fog they were encumbered by; this friendship would prove of vital importance when Bertie became king himself.

Yet this decent and shy prince was slowly breaking apart. He had no desire to be king, and his wife was driven to write to Edward to warn him, 'I wish that you could realise how hard it has been for him lately . . . I *know* that he is fonder of you than anybody else . . . I am terrified for him.'[19] By Bertie's own account, when he arrived back at Marlborough House, 'I went to see Queen Mary and when I told her what had happened, I broke down and sobbed like a child.'

The queen wrote in her diary, with impressive circumspection, that 'Bertie arrived very late from Fort Belvedere and Mr Walter Monckton brought him and me the paper drawn up for David's ab- dication of the throne of this Empire because he wishes to marry Mrs Simpson!!!!! The whole affair has lasted since 16 November and is very painful. It is a terrible blow to us all and particularly to poor Bertie.'[20]

Her eldest son, meanwhile, was dealing with the absent Wallis. He was irritated by what he described as 'the despairing entreaties of the morning', and asked his solicitor, George Allen, 'Do you mean that I have to go through all that again?' When Allen assured him that 'I am afraid, Sir, that Mrs Simpson is determined', he re- plied, with some anger, 'What can I say to make myself clear? How can I convince her that what she says is utterly impossible?' Allen's solution was clinical in its lawyerly fastidiousness. He wrote the sentence: 'The only conditions on which I can stay here are if I renounce you for all time' on a piece of paper, and handed it to Edward to say to Wallis, which he duly did.

His account of the conversation is a romantic one. He wrote, 'Her answer to me was worthy of the occasion. The void between us disappeared. The truth, of course, is that she tried throughout to make me turn back, and she would have succeeded had I not loved her so desperately and therefore been so determined.'[21] This does not come close to describing Wallis's misery. She wept when the conversation ended, 'conscious only of having failed tragic- ally'. Even as Katherine Rogers assured her that 'You have done everything that could be expected of a woman in this situation . . . No one will blame you', Wallis refused to believe her blandishments. Instead, 'I could not seem to grasp the meaning of what David had done. I found myself whispering as to another self that nothing so incredible, so monstrous, could possibly have happened.'[22]

Wallis had lost. The last hope that she, or anyone else, had of persuading Edward to halt the abdication at the eleventh hour had been extinguished. She sighed that 'We were no longer part of the drama', but the reality was that, ever since her departure to

Cannes, she had not been in a position to influence her lover. WE had proved less an unbreakable union, and more an expression of arrogant masculine power. That the E component of it was king barely mattered; Edward's demonstration of cold disdain for her wishes reflected the patriarchal entitlement of the time. He could do what he liked simply because he was a man, and ignore her with impunity. It would have been better for him if he had listened to her, but he had never listened to anybody in his life. This had proved his downfall, even if he was too obstinate to realise it.

At eight in the evening on the previous day, the Cabinet had assembled in the prime minister's room at the House of Commons. There was some gallows humour; Baldwin remarked to Ramsay MacDonald that he looked glum (Nicolson described MacDonald as being 'like King Lear'), to which he replied, 'My body is here but my soul is elsewhere.' An exhausted Baldwin was still able to quip, 'Well I hope that it's not at Cannes',[23] before he informed the politicians that a draft instrument of abdication had been drawn up, along with a more personal message to the parliaments of the Empire, which were sent back to the Fort with Monckton. The first expressed itself in simple and formal terms:

> I, Edward the Eighth of Great Britain, Ireland and the British Dominions beyond the Seas, King Emperor of India, do hereby declare my irrevocable determination to renounce the Throne for Myself and My descendants, and My desire that effect should be given to this Instrument of Abdication immediately.
>
> In token whereof I have hereunto set My hand this tenth day of December, nineteen hundred and thirty-six, in the presence of the witnesses whose signatures are subscribed.

The other functioned as an early draft of the abdication statement that he later made. Stressing his 'final and irrevocable decision', Edward declared that 'I will not enter now into My private feelings, but I would beg that it should be remembered that the burden which constantly rests upon the shoulders of the Sovereign is so heavy that it can now only be borne in circumstances different from those in which I now find Myself . . . I am conscious that I can no longer discharge this heavy task with efficiency and satisfaction to myself.'[24] Contented with the drafts, he let the exhausted Monckton and Peacock know that he would sign them in front of his brothers the following day. Graceless to the last, he sneered that 'It was a worn and somewhat rumpled barrister who finally materialised out of the fog sometime after midnight, bearing the decisive papers.'[25]

At ten in the morning on Thursday 10 December, in the room in Fort Belvedere where he had held his 'last supper' two days before, Edward calmly signed seven copies of the Instrument of Abdication and eight copies of his parliamentary message. The solemnity was lifted by the tardy arrival of the Duke of Kent, which led to Edward laughing, 'George *would* be late.' The fog that had beset the country for the previous days had lifted, which the king saw as having taken place 'in harmony with the lifting of the almost intolerable pressure of the last few weeks'. According to Edward, 'it was all quite informal', despite the 'dignified dull murmur' of conversation, and its resolution left him with a sense of relief. Despite allowing that he was affected by the occasion, he described himself as feeling 'like a swimmer surfacing from a great depth'.[26] Bertie saw it differently, calling it 'a dreadful moment & one not to be forgotten by those present'; separated from his wife, who was ill with influenza, he was overcome by the 'unbearable tension' of the Fort.

It was the most inauspicious circumstance under which to prepare for kingship, and not helped by the discussion about money that then took place. Edward 'made an impassioned speech, pointing out how badly off he would be' after he abdicated, and told Bertie that he did not have an income of even £5,000 a year, from an estate that he claimed was a mere £90,000. As a result, he hinted that he would retain his interest in Sandringham and Balmoral unless a satisfactory financial solution was arrived at.

Every word that Edward stated with regard to money was a lie. It is possible that, exhausted and jittery, he was acting in a hysterical and frightened fashion, rather than out of calculated deceit, but his intention was to secure the much-desired allowance after his abdication that would provide for both him and Wallis, and if it could only be arrived at by dishonesty, so be it. Philip Ziegler described this as 'the worst mistake of his life', and one that he would suffer the consequences from until the day he died, not least in the breakdown of his relationship with Bertie. The new king later wrote, without rancour, 'You were under great strain and I am not seeking to reproach you or anyone. But the fact remains that I was completely misled.'[27]

At the time, the Duke of York felt a surge of sympathy for his brother, and a solution was arrived upon. He stated that he would underwrite his brother's allowance from the Privy Purse, thus avoiding any public embarrassment if Parliament would not give him a pension from the Civil List. Peacock allowed that the discussion 'tended to become heated, as sentiment and legal fact were getting rather mixed',[28] and brokered a solution. In exchange for his allowance, the king would waive any claim he had to Sandringham and Balmoral, and any royal heirlooms he possessed, on the understanding that his conduct would continue to be of the standard that his country would expect. Bertie later spoke of his relief that the 'terrible' discussion about money ended 'quietly and harmoniously',[29] and praised Peacock for his tact and discretion. Had he known the truth of Edward's situation, such a solution could hardly have been so harmoniously arrived at.

A strange codicil to the saga came that morning, when Edward received a letter from the man he had so publicly cuckolded, Ernest Simpson. Whether out of a genuine desire to ameliorate Wallis's situation, or simply because he believed he had an underappreciated role within the abdication crisis, Simpson attempted to involve himself at the highest level. (Goddard's clerk Robert Egerton wryly observed: 'He maintained, so far as I know for ever, a complete silence concerning his private affairs, and this could be ascribed to either exceptional standards of honourable behaviour or the promise of substantial rewards.'[30] In any case, he never sold his story, even as Egerton speculated: 'Just imagine what he could have made by agreeing to reveal to the press at any time what he knew about the affair!'[31])

He had approached Baldwin twice in order to offer his assistance, much to Lucy Baldwin's mystification, and ministers were formally advised not to have dealings with him, in case there was any difficulty with the divorce. He had also made overtures to Lord Wigram a few days before to say that 'the divorce was entirely a collusion between HM, himself and Mrs S', and that he could 'squash the divorce by turning King's evidence'. Although this may have had the desired effect of derailing Wallis's divorce, Wigram believed that it would also prolong the situation unnecessarily and scandalously, as Edward would simply 'live in sin' with Mrs Simpson. Accordingly, Ernest's offer was refused, so his subsequent letter must be read in that context.

It strikes an oddly over-familiar note, beginning, 'My heart is too full for utterance tonight', and goes on to stress that 'my deepest and most loyal feelings have been with you throughout', as he hoped that Edward 'may find an abundance of happiness in the days that lie before you'. Calling himself 'your devoted subject . . . your loving friend and obedient servant',[32] Simpson may simply have been making a statement of solidarity in difficult times, from one Freemason to another, or perhaps an opaque attempt at extracting money or a much-desired peerage from his ex-wife's lover. In either case, it was unsuccessful. Edward made no reference to it in his memoirs, and Ernest Simpson, the man who had laid down his wife for his king, married twice more. Appropriately, his third wife was Wallis's friend 'Buttercup Kennedy', his partner in staged adultery.

The only indication that Ernest had any especial opinion about his public standing was his hitherto unreported attempt late in 1936 to sue the newspapers for libel. As Egerton observed, 'it was galling enough to be pictured as the complaisant husband, quite content to stand aside while his wife basked in the royal favour, without being accused of doing it for mercenary motives.' Goddard dissuaded him from this course, advising him that a libel suit 'would lead to a scandal of immense proportions and put an end to the King's hopes [of marriage]', not least because Simpson's appearance at court would also have led to a cross-examination about Wallis's relationship with Edward, specifically 'his knowledge of her association with the King, [Simpson's] infidelity with particular reference to his stay at the Hotel de Paris [and] his efforts, or lack of efforts, to save the marriage.' The newspapers were accordingly denied this 'wonderfully informative and priceless material', and Ernest was spared the exposure of his 'immortality or pretended immorality, lying, hypocrisy, misleading the court and general duplicity.'[33]

One recently discovered* and surprising fact about the relationship between Ernest and Wallis is that they remained in touch throughout the abdication crisis, and beyond. Theirs had been an unconventional marriage but one that had featured genuine affection within it. As late as October 1935, she was referring to him as 'angelic'[34] in a letter to Aunt Bessie, although of course this may have been for her aunt's benefit, just as her description of him as 'still the man of my dreams'[35] in another epistle on 31 July mixed admiration with a dutiful wish to live up to Bessie's expectations. She knew that she had to be circumspect with what she told her aunt. She wrote to Ernest at the end of November 1936 that 'I haven't told Aunt B the danger side, simply that my very presence here was hurting the K[ing]', and that she had kept quiet about 'the most alarming letters [that I receive], threatening my life unless I leave'.[36] She reiterated her desire to flee the country, 'perhaps for ever', but knew that her lover was implacable. Even without the resources that kingship conferred upon him, an obsessed Edward could not be escaped.

---

* I am indebted to Anne Sebba for introducing me to the current owner of these letters, who wishes to remain anonymous.

Before the abdication, Wallis's attitude towards Ernest was a contradictory one. Even as she regarded him as a confidant, telling him 'I can never forgive my own country for what they have done to the King and to myself', she was unable to hide her disapproval of the unfortunate 'Buttercup', whom she decried for having 'thrived on the publicity she has got through me and never refuses any of it'.* After insincerely wishing Ernest a happy life, she was driven to muse, 'If I am put on the spot, Ipswich etc. will have been a great waste of time, as far as I am concerned, won't it?'[37]

Despite his own adulteries and lechery, Simpson still harboured affection for Wallis. In October, as he left Bryanston Court, he wrote to her to say, 'I know that somewhere in your heart there is a small flame burning for me. Guard it carefully, my darling, and don't let it go out, if only in memory of the sacred lovely things that have been.'[38] Wallis reciprocated his love, in a fashion that she may never have fully understood herself. While unhappily resident in Felixstowe in October 1936, she had suggested that she was terri- fied of the court, and the divorce, writing, 'I feel small and licked by it all.' Even as she admitted to feeling trapped within 'a mess and awakening emptiness', and referring to her life after England as a 'prison', she was driven to tell Ernest in 1937 that 'I think of us so much though I try not to' and that 'Wherever you are, you can be sure that never a day goes by without some hours' thought of you.'

While some of Wallis's correspondence feels intended for public consumption, the sentiments she expressed within these letters come across as sincere, revealing the depths of her misery

---

* Another reason for her subsequent anger towards Mary Kirk was Mary's rushed publication of a tell-all memoir about Wallis, *Her Name was Wallis Warfield*, which led a 'very sad' Mrs Simpson to write to Ernest calling his inamorata a 'bitch' and moaning, 'charming to make money out of one's friends besides sleeping with their husband'. Mary, for her part, wrote in her diary that 'tho' she loathed and despised having me there, it served her purpose so she could say that E was having an affair with me and she would have to get a divorce'.

and solitude. She knew that her manipulations and games had resulted in her current predicament, and was mired in bitter regret
about them. As she sobbed, 'Oh my very dear, dear Ernest, I can
only cry as I say farewell and press your hand very tightly and
pray to God', it was inevitable that the realisation of how much she
had lost would hang heavy on her, perhaps for the remainder of
her life.[39]

She wrote to him for years after their separation, often in terms
that Edward would have been appalled by; both of them described
him contemptuously as 'Peter Pan'. A letter that Wallis sent him
in February 1937, as Ernest found himself accused of being paid
as much as £200,000 to allow the divorce to take place, commiser-
ated with him about 'all the unjust criticism' and went on to state
that 'It should never have been like it is now ... I am so illogi-
cal and groomed by my pride that – when that is touched nothing will stop what I'm capable of doing and this situation shows
the truth of that remark because if I had told you I would go to
such lengths you wouldn't have believed it humanly possible.'[40]
There was a particular poignancy in the most infamous woman
in the world informing her ex-husband that 'I thought I'd write
a few lines to say I'd love to hear from you if you feel like telling
me a bit.'[41]

What was left unspoken was that, other than statements of affection, she had little to tell him in turn. After all, the events of
her life had been disseminated in every newspaper in the world.
She zealously guarded the few scraps of information that had not
become public knowledge. The cynical might have noted that a
subsequent memoir revealed most, if not quite all, of these, in exchange for a substantial advance. Yet Wallis had few people she
could turn to. Ernest may have been described by Special Branch
as 'of the bounder type', but eventually he proved himself to be a
loyal and discreet correspondent.

Still, as the final reckoning approached in December 1936, a
'pleasant but distant'[42] man whom Wallis had described as 'the
self-appointed embodiment of John Bull'[43] prepared to face the

House of Commons to do battle on her and her lover's behalf. The consequences of his failure, or success, would change the course of English history for ever.

Chapter Fourteen

'Pity and Terror'

He gazed around from his seat on the Treasury Bench in the Chamber. It was quarter to four in the afternoon of Thursday 10 December, and he knew that whatever he said in the next hour would be crucial, not least to the survival of his premiership. Friends, enemies and the curious looked at the tail-coat-clad man before them with anticipation. Only his blue handkerchief gave a touch of colour to his monochrome figure. As he waited for the Speaker to finish reading out the message of abdication to the Commons, he felt a curious sense of calm, far removed from the nerves that he had felt over the past couple of weeks, which had built to a near-frenzy of terror earlier that day. Like an actor waiting for his cue, he knew that he would succeed or fail over the course of the next moments. He remembered the words he had said to Dugdale before he had entered the Chamber: 'This is making history, and I am the only one who can do it.'[1]

Baldwin had asked Monckton that morning to find out from Edward if there were any personal messages that the king would like to have conveyed. The lawyer returned with two notes that Edward had scribbled by hand on small slips of paper. He had been touched by the unexpected request and said, 'That's nice of SB. I appreciate his thoughtfulness.'[2] The first referred to the king's confidence in Bertie as his successor, thus explicitly handing on the baton of royal approval. The second was a more personal one, which stated that 'the other person most intimately concerned' in the matter of the abdication had tried, throughout, to steer Edward away from the course that he had now irrevocably chosen. Baldwin anxiously told Monckton that 'I want to place the King's actions in the best light', and he seemed reluctant to make any reference to Wallis, something that Monckton believed 'was a little hard on Mrs Simpson', but the prime minister knew that Parliament was in an unsettled and uncertain mood. There were those who had sympathy for the king, and even some who felt empathy for Wallis; there were also many who were angered by the whole situation and even blamed Baldwin for allowing it ever to come to this. His speech would have to mollify and placate, as well as inspire.

Although he had had ample opportunity to talk to Edward, and his Cabinet, over the previous days, he had not had the chance to prepare a speech. It was only on the afternoon of Wednesday 9 December, when he had announced that he would make a formal statement the following day, that he committed himself to a public address. He was underprepared and worn out. As a naturally cautious man, he had tried to put together a few notes, based on conversations at Cabinet meetings, and padded out with some thoughts derived from his interviews with Edward. He had had an audience with Queen Mary on the morning of the 10th, when he had told her what would be in his statement, but the meeting did not alleviate his nerves. He barely knew himself what he was about to say. Had the speech been a disastrous one, it could have brought down the government, and reduced him to ignominy. He could be the prime minister who had failed to alleviate, or who had even worsened, the constitutional crisis.

He had lunched at home with his wife and Dugdale. Conversation, such as it was, was stilted, as Baldwin's obvious anxiety was affecting both his appetite and his loquaciousness. It was down to Lucy to attempt to reassure him, by saying, 'Just be yourself, Stan, and you'll be all right.'[3] If this helped at all, his unease was exacerbated by his not being able to find any of the notes that he had made. An increasingly frantic search of Downing Street did not produce them, but he located a few scattered pieces of paper upon which he had jotted down some aides-memoires. It was not enough: nowhere near enough. But under the circumstances, it would have to do. As he was driven to the Commons, a few half-hearted protesters at the Queen Victoria memorial bellowed, 'Down with Baldwin!' He must have wondered if Parliament would do the job for them.

The House was unusually full, and in a state of excited anticipation. Nicolson wrote that day in his diary that '[Parliament] ceases to be an assemblage of mobile beings and becomes something as fixed as a picture of itself; one looks downward for the key-sketch of outlined heads with names and numbers.' Baldwin may have regained his calm, but his sangfroid was soon disturbed by his initial inability to find the key to the red dispatch box that he was carrying with him, containing what remained of his notes, and sheets of paper embossed with the royal monogram. After some frantic rummaging, he found the key lurking in a pocket, and, in Nicolson's words, 'arranged [his] sheets ... carefully, and rather proudly, on the box in front of him'.[4] Farce and tragedy seemed to be jostling one another to see which could claim greater advantage that afternoon, as Hoare, called upon to answer a parliamentary question, placed his file of Admiralty papers on Baldwin's sheets, sending them cascading all over the floor. The image of this tired, heavy man, ageing and half deaf, scrabbling about in an attempt to gather his jottings was somewhere between comic and pitiable. As the Speaker spoke, in a 'quavering voice', Nicolson himself began to feel his sense of nervousness, fearing that 'at any moment, he may break down from emotion'. He noted, not without some self-awareness, that 'I have never known in any assemblage such accumulation of pity and terror.'[5]

The Declaration of Abdication was uncomplicated. It stated that 'After long and anxious consideration, I have determined to renounce the throne to which I succeeded on the death of my father, and I am now communicating this, my final and irrevocable decision.' It recognised 'the gravity of this step', asked for 'the understanding of my peoples in the decision I have taken and the reasons which have led me to take it', and, even as it acknowledged that 'I will not enter now into my private feelings', sought the justification of begging the audience to remember 'that the burden which constantly rests upon the shoulders of a sovereign is so heavy that it can only be borne in circumstances different from those in which I now find myself'.[6] The declaration shrugged that 'I am conscious that I can no longer discharge this heavy task with efficiency or with satisfaction to myself', and so the responsibility was passed to others.

As Baldwin scuttled over to the Speaker to hand him the message to read aloud, expectation grew that a cataclysmic flop was imminent. As Nicolson observed, 'the hear! hears! echoed solemnly like "Amens"'. Baldwin, at that moment, did not seem to have a prayer. Journalists lurking in the press gallery held their pens aloft to report the carnage, moment by painful moment, as the Speaker came to the end of the abdication announcement.

And then the prime minister's speech began.

Today, Baldwin has largely been relegated to the second division of British prime ministers, with his reputation badly damaged by his refusing to take a greater part in rearmament before World War II. He was one of the 'Guilty Men' attacked by 'Cato' (a pseudonym for Michael Foot, the Liberal MP Frank Owen and the Conservative Peter Howard) for their failed foreign policy towards Germany; there was an especial zeal in the attack on Baldwin because all three of the writers were employed by his nemesis Beaverbrook. His ability as a politician, and prime minister, has been debated amongst scholars and historians ever since the events of the abdication. Yet for an hour or so that Thursday afternoon, it seemed to a sceptical Commons that they were in the presence of a speaker temporarily blessed with the rhetorical brilliance of Cicero, the humanity of Shakespeare and the intellectual assurance of Lincoln.

He began by offering his hope that 'His Majesty's most gracious message be now considered', before launching into a virtually extempore account of the meetings between himself and Edward, and the consequences that the abdication would have. He was assisted by the emotion that the reading of the message had engendered;

some politicians could be heard sobbing. He recognised the unique nature of the occasion by saying, 'No more grave message has ever been received by Parliament, and no more difficult – I may almost say repugnant – task has ever been imposed upon a Prime Minister. I would ask the House, which I know will not be without sympathy for me in my position today, to remember that in the last week I have had but little time in which to compose a speech for delivery today, so I must tell what I have to tell truthfully, sincerely and plainly, with no attempt to dress up or adorn.'

Baldwin's open admission of his ambition to address the House in a plain and uncomplicated style looked back as far as Cicero's advice to would-be rhetoricians in *De Oratore* that they should speak '*ut Latine, ut plane, ut ornate, ut . . . apte*', or in a fashion 'correct, lucid, ornate and appropriate'. Either deliberately or as a result of nerves, he spoke in an almost informal manner. Deprived of his notes, he asked Simon, who was sitting next to him, to remind him of dates, as if his feeble memory was constantly in danger of letting him down. He spoke of the integrity and dignity of the king's behaviour throughout the crisis, while taking care to stress the inalienable importance of the Crown itself. It was with this in mind that he read out Edward's message about Bertie, to some effect, saying, 'The Duke of York and the King have always been on the best of terms as brothers, and the King is confident that the Duke deserves and will receive the support of the whole Empire.'[7]

It is likely, as Monckton suspected, that Baldwin omitted Edward's note about Wallis because it would have reminded the House of the woman many blamed for the present situation. It is also possible that he simply forgot, or that he was unable to find the relevant document amongst the mess of his papers. Yet he did manage to bring in an allusion to the agent of the abdication in a way that both acknowledged her existence and continued to praise the king. He stated that 'The King has told us that he cannot carry these almost intolerable burdens of Kingship without a woman at his side, and we know that the crisis, if I may use the word, has arisen now rather than later from that very frankness of His

Majesty's character which is one of his many attractions.' The implicit criticism of Edward, so beautifully understated as to be almost imperceptible, was not lost on many of his audience.

This theme continued when Baldwin went on to describe his audience with the king on 16 November. He portrayed himself as a compassionate and reasonable tribune of the people, telling the stubborn monarch that he did not have the freedom that his subjects had, and that 'in the choice of a Queen the voice of the people must be heard'. Yet he also emphasised his own relationship with Edward, talking of 'a friendship of affection, between man and man', and offered the flourish that 'When we said "goodbye", [this friendship] we both felt . . . bound us more closely together than ever and would last for life.' Although this was not true, and doubtless Baldwin knew this as he spoke, it gave his words an emotional power that played well within the Chamber.

The heightened atmosphere of the day was complemented by his declaiming a few lines from *Hamlet*, which Simon had suggested to him:

His will is not his own;
For he himself is subject to his birth,
He may not, as unvalued persons do,
Carve for himself; for on his choice depends
The safety and the health of the whole state.

Simon, Baldwin and presumably a good number of those present knew that this came from the third scene of the first act, and that the character delivering the lines, Laertes, was attempting to dissuade his sister Ophelia from pursuing a liaison with Hamlet. I tried, was the subtext of Baldwin's suggestion, and nobody could have tried harder than me. But nobody can persuade the king to take action against his will, and that is why I am addressing you today. Like Mark Antony at Caesar's funeral, he declared that he would have 'little or nothing to say in the way of comment or criticism, or of praise and blame'. It was lost on few that the only glorification that would take place that day would be of the prime minister, delivering the speech of his life.

Nicolson's account refers to 'intense silence broken only by the reporters in the gallery scuttling away to telephone the speech paragraph by paragraph'.[8] Journalists who had expected to witness a car crash were instead impressed by the smooth delivery of a masterpiece of political art, which the *Manchester Guardian* praised as delivered with 'infinite daring . . . from notes that always seemed to be in alarming disarray'.[9] Dawson, who was present, described it as 'very effective . . . extraordinarily good',[10] and Helen Hardinge paid tribute to 'the clarity and power of his simple and yet poetic language . . . He was able to rise to the occasion with real nobility.'[11]

Baldwin ended by saying, 'I am convinced that where I have failed no one else could have succeeded. His mind was made up, and those who know His Majesty will know what that means.' He acknowledged the interest with which the world was following events - 'Let us conduct ourselves with that dignity which His Majesty is showing in this hour of his trial' - and asked for calm. He implored the House and, by extension, the watching press, 'Let no word be spoken today that the utterer of that word may regret in days to come, let no word be spoken that causes pain to any soul.' His final peroration stated, 'Let us look forward and remember our country and the trust reposed by our country, in this, the House of Commons, and let us rally behind the new King, stand behind him, and help him; and let us hope that, whatever the country may have suffered by what we are passing through, it may soon be repaired and that we may take what steps we can in trying to make this country a better country for all the people in it.'

As he finished, at 4.33 p.m., he had spoken for just under fifty minutes. There was a moment of silence; long enough, perhaps, for Baldwin to wonder whether his speech had been the dismal failure that he had feared it might be. Then the chorus of 'hear! hear!' began, and he was soon disabused of any notion of failure. His physician, Lord Dawson of Penn, later told him, 'You will pay for this',[12] referring to the strain on his health rather than reputation.

It is likely that the prime minister considered any reckoning well worth the expenditure.

'I suppose that in after centuries, men will read the words of that speech and exclaim "What an opportunity wasted!" They will never know the tragic force of its simplicity. "I said to the King" . . . "the King told me" . . . it was Sophoclean and almost unbearable.' So a reflective Nicolson wrote that day, joining those who realised that something remarkable had occurred in the Commons. Attlee, who was due to respond on behalf of his party, asked the Speaker to suspend the House until six, ostensibly to allow the politicians to consider the matter at length, but in fact because he knew that the heightened emotion in the Chamber meant that normal business was impossible. Nicolson walked out 'conscious that we have heard the best speech that we shall ever hear in our lives. There was no question of applause. It was the silence of Gettysburg.'[13]

On his way out, he saw Baldwin, exhausted but exhilarated, and walked over to him, anxious to compliment his leader on a job done peerlessly well. He 'murmured a few kind words', and the prime minister took his arm. 'You are very kind', he said, 'but what do you really think?' Nicolson 'detected in him that intoxication which comes to a man, even a tired man, after a triumphant success', and was able to answer honestly, 'It was superb.' His only regret, he told Baldwin, was that 'Hitler, Mussolini and Lord Beaverbrook had not been in the Peers Gallery'.* Baldwin, seemingly in an ecstatic daze, told Nicolson that 'It was a success. I know it. It was almost wholly unprepared. I had a success, my dear Nicolson, at the moment I most needed it. <u>Now is the time to go.</u>'

A surprised Nicolson did not reply, as Baldwin, still clinging to his arm, discussed his king with a fervour and candour quite

---

* Queen Mary, however, had been. It is unclear as to whether she had warned Baldwin of her intention to attend, but he had alluded to her in his speech, saying, 'Let us not forget today the revered and beloved figure of Queen Mary, what all this time has meant to her, and think of her when we have to speak, if speak we must, during this debate.'

different to how he had spoken of him a few moments before. 'You see, the man is mad. MAD. He could see nothing but that woman. He did not realise that any other considerations avail. He lacks religion .·. . I do not mean by that his atheism. I suppose that you are an atheist or an agnostic. But you have a religious sense . . . you realise there is something more than the opportune . . . He doesn't realise that there is anything beyond . . . I love the man. But he must go.'

Flushed with triumph, he then turned to his other bête noire, Churchill. 'Do you know, my dear Nicolson', he panted, 'I think Winston is the most suspicious man I know. Just now I said that the King had said "Let this be settled between you and me alone. I do not want outside interference." I meant to indicate by that the reasons why I had not made it a Cabinet question from the start. But Winston thought it was a thrust aimed at him and has been at my Private Secretary in the last five minutes.' He ended with a typical flourish. 'What can one do with a man like that?' Nicolson suggested that Churchill had put himself in a false position, to which Baldwin flung up his hands and said, with some emphasis, 'We are all in false positions!' Nicolson concluded of his leader that 'no man has ever dominated the House as he dominated it tonight. And he knows it.'[14]

Another admirer of the speech was Duff Cooper, who called it 'completely successful . . . [A] complete lack of rhetoric and evident signs of lack of preparation were the qualities which I think most recommended it.' Cooper came across Baldwin in the corridor, and noted the premier's high spirits. As he congratulated him on his efforts, he commented, 'Looking back on it, how right you were to agree to the King seeing Winston.' Baldwin laughed 'very knowingly' and said, 'I never doubted that I was right for a minute. I am only a simple lad, you know, Duff, but there were reasons why I thought it best to put it to the Cabinet the way I did.' Cooper had the tact not to spoil his leader's hour of triumph by reminding him that a week ago, Baldwin had regarded his action as a blunder, rather than a piece of Machiavellian statecraft.

The House reassembled at six. Attlee made what Cooper called 'a short and sensitive speech', again offering his support and sympathy to the king and, by association, Baldwin. Although some radical elements in the Labour Party attacked Attlee for being 'glacially constitutional', and lacking 'push and sting and farsightedness' in this matter, he behaved with statesmanship and empathy, although he was not above joining in a family chorus of 'Hark the herald angels sing/Mrs Simpson's pinched our king' that Christmas.[15] Archie Sinclair, the Liberal leader, spoke in a similar vein, and then it was Churchill's turn. A sense of expectation rippled through a House well disposed towards Baldwin: would Winston make a final speech denouncing the establishment stitch-up that had led to the abdication, or meekly accept it? The House had to vote on the bill still. A barnstorming cry of condemnation might have swung opinion in a different direction.

In the event, Churchill made an intelligent and tactful statement that managed to offer the House a veiled *mea culpa* for his previous statements while slyly continuing to emphasise his earlier points. Leo Amery called it 'an admirably phrased little speech [which] executed a strategical retreat'. Stressing the danger of further 're-crimination or controversy', Churchill emphasised the irrevocable nature of the abdication and his part within it, saying, 'What is done is done. What has been done or left undone belongs to history, and to history, so far as I am concerned, it shall be left.'

He defended Edward both as monarch – 'no sovereign has ever conformed more strictly or more faithfully to the letter and spirit of the constitution than his present Majesty' – and as man, talking of his friendship with the king and praising his 'discerned qualities of courage, of simplicity, of sympathy and, above all, of sincerity rare and precious'. He called it 'the acme of tragedy that those very virtues should in the private sphere have led only to this melancholy and bitter conclusion' and defended his actions by saying, 'I should have been ashamed if, in my independent and unofficial position, I had not cast about for every lawful means, even the most forlorn, to keep him on the throne of his fathers.'

He struck a different, and more prophetic, note in his peroration, reflecting both on what had happened and what was to come. To loud cheers from a House that seemed to have forgiven him, he warned, 'Danger gathers upon our path. We cannot afford – we have no right – to look back. We must look forward; we must obey the exhortation of the Prime Minister to look forward. The stronger the advocate of monarchical principle a man may be, the more zealously must he now endeavour to fortify the throne, and to give to his Majesty's successor that strength which can only come from the love of a united nation and Empire.' Even Dawson, who had stood against Churchill throughout the crisis, wrote to him to say, 'Your speech of yesterday . . . seems to me to present a thoroughly sound, constitutional point of view',[16] as well as stating, 'I should be very sorry that anything I have written in *The Times* should have caused you pain . . . This wretched business is now over.'[17]

That evening, with the abdication now a certainty, those involved in it sat around in clubs or grand houses, drinking Scotch and brooding on what might have been. As Cooper wrote, 'The trouble is that while everyone is tired of the subject, nobody can talk about anything else.'[18] Nicolson spent the evening with the Liberal politician Robert Bernays in the Commons, '[sitting] by the fire and telling sad stories of the death of kings'. That evening, he went to bed 'early, exhausted, sad and tired'.[19] Yet he was torn. In a summary of his feelings that he wrote in his diary later in the year, he allowed that 'I liked Mrs Simpson and thought she did the King good . . . [She] saved him from sulkiness . . . [and] one likes to see a man happy.' Yet he castigated her for her double-dealing ('I am not sure that she was not aiming the whole time at personal advantage') and for her mercenary ways, deciding, 'I still do not believe she is in love with him.' It was Edward who continued to mystify him. Even as Nicolson allowed for his 'immense charm and glamour', he mournfully noted that 'he has never made any woman love him', and concluded that 'There must be something intensely wrong about him.'[20]

Helen Hardinge, whose husband had done so much to make his employer's life difficult, walked home that evening 'shattered by emotion'. She was annoyed to see 'some acquaintances who had had influence with King Edward VIII and had misled him'. She cut them dead – 'the only time in my life that I have wittingly cut anyone' – out of her angry belief that 'This was not just a little frivolous game, but a deeply human drama played on a world stage.'[21] These false comforters were probably those whom Sitwell attacked in *Rat Week* as 'that jolly crew/So new and brave, and free and easy/ . . . that jolly crew/Who must make even Judas queasy'. They included the likes of Emerald Cunard and Johnny McMullen, but Hardinge's contempt may even have been directed towards Cooper or Mountbatten.

She was more generous towards Churchill, albeit much later, allowing that 'He had been mistaken, but he was a great man – great enough to realise that the time had come to explain his position.'[22] The great man himself mused sadly that night at Morpeth Mansions to his friend Wing Commander C. T. Anderson that '[The] poor little lamb [was] treated worse than any air mechanic, and he took it lying down.'[23] As for Beaverbrook, who had hoped to be the king's most trusted counsellor, he saw his enemy triumphant, his monarch on the verge of abdication, and his influence set at naught. He later called it 'silence, total and unbroken . . . The tornado was still raging, but it had passed me by. The abrupt change from the extreme of activity in the very heart of affairs to complete inactivity and isolation had a physical reaction.' Miserably, he recounted that 'my toothache returned'.[24]

Others were more contemplative. Lalla Bill, Edward's nurse as a child, wrote to Queen Mary that day to share her memories of her charge, asking, 'Do you remember, Your Majesty, when he was quite young how he didn't wish to live, and he never wanted to become King – he is a rover by nature then too . . . He is brilliant and he might have felt he was too hemmed in by convention to give scope to his abilities . . . His restless nature wouldn't allow him to settle down quietly . . . I hope the poor boy will be happy now, for no doubt he has led a very unhappy life for years.'[25]

The relationship between the two had once been close. Edward had written to Lalla candidly while a student at Oxford, acknowledging that 'I know I have been an absolute fool, firstly to have overdone the exercise & secondly to have taken such a gloomy view of life & to have had a sort of fit of melancholia. This no doubt was brought on by being a bit below power, & now that you have fed me up, I am much brighter.' He ended by praising her – 'It is merely the expression of thanks of one who is truly grateful for all you have done for him. Best love from your devoted E'[26] – and now, Lalla could only feel frustrated and impotent that her once-beloved prince was making such a momentous decision for, she felt, the wrong reasons.

That evening, Bertie returned home, to see how his ill wife was faring, to find a large crowd outside, cheering the sovereign-to-be. Somewhat overwhelmed at this unlooked-for reception, he asked Peacock and Wigram to dine with him at the Royal Lodge. Peacock described the duke as being 'rather rattled at the prospect of what he had to go through, and what he had just been through . . . He is evidently devoted to his elder brother and has always looked up to him, and this turning away from duty to lady was clearly a sad shock.' It did not help Bertie that the thought of becoming king terrified him. As Peacock noted, 'He drew a most unfavourable picture of his own probably clumsy efforts to carry out the duties which his brother did incomparably better than he thought he could ever hope to do so.' He was in obvious need of a counsellor of his own, and Peacock felt 'a good deal drawn to him because of his modesty and obvious good sense'. The two dined together, and talked frankly of Bertie's fears and doubts. Peacock reported that 'I hope we steadied and cheered him.'[27]

Edward, meanwhile, was putting his house in order for the final time. Earlier that day he had met John Simon and had been informed that, owing to the 'changed circumstances', Wallis would no longer be allowed the detectives who had been protecting her at Cannes, which had led to some distress. Monckton wrote that

'However correct Simon's attitude may have been, I thought he might have spared the King this by taking the risk of criticism himself.'

A tactful word was had, and Simon agreed to keep the detectives at Cannes for the time being 'to relieve the King of anxiety', although it was made clear that this step was not otherwise justifiable.[28] His letter confirming the decision also noted that 'This arrangement should be kept as quiet as possible, for Sir John would not be surprised if questions are addressed to him on the subject in Parliament which he will have to answer candidly . . . Sir John feels that it would be prudent to take advantage of the King's suggestion today that any expense involved would be defrayed by His present Majesty.'[29]

Edward spent his final evening as king with Wallis's Aunt Bessie, and his friends Kitty and George Hunter, without the company of his advisers. The dinner was a miserable one. Kitty confided in Peacock later that night that she and her husband 'wept into their soup and everything else during the meal', in spite of Edward's cheery determination to keep things upbeat. She was also angry with Wallis, exclaiming that she had been fooled by her protestations that she would never marry the king. Clearly she was unaware of Wallis's attempts to extricate herself from the situation. Peacock recounted that, after Edward had finished his nightly call to Wallis, 'We carried on a rather depressing effort to be cheerful, he being the best', before the company went to bed at half one in the morning.

The king was preoccupied with what he was going to say to the nation the following day. He knew that his intention to make the broadcast had met with controversy – 'Some in the government looked coldly upon the idea of my supplying an epilogue to a drama upon which the curtain had already descended' – but he was determined to speak. As he put it, 'I did not propose to leave my country like a fugitive in the night.'[30]

The stage was therefore set for the lead actor to make a final speech before departing as gracefully as could be expected. Once the Commons had consented to the Abdication Bill, he would cease to be king. It would be a long day, and one of the most eventful in British history. Yet for all the unprecedented drama that awaited its participants, 11 December 1936 would not represent the conclusion of this torrid saga so much as the precursor of much of what would happen next. Those actions would shape the nation's destiny, and the lives of those within it.

Chapter Fifteen

'A Far Better Thing I Go To'

If Edward had been in the habit of reading the day's papers, he would not have enjoyed *The Times* editorial on Friday 11 December. Dawson had been a persistent critic of his - whether or not influenced by Baldwin - and the previous day had provocatively suggested that, although 'even a King is entitled to his relaxation and the companionship of his chosen friends . . . what he cannot and will not afford - and what the nation and the Empire cannot afford - is that the influence of the great office which he holds should be weakened if ever private inclination were to come into open conflict with public duty and be allowed to prevail'.[1] The editor had been much buoyed personally by letters of praise he had received, of which one from Viscount Snowden, former Chancellor of the Exchequer, was typical; Snowden congratulated him on 'the magnificent line you have taken in this crisis . . . In its dignity and courage and outspokenness, it has been worthy of the best traditions of *The Times* and a credit to British journalism.'[2]

Now, with the abdication all but inevitable, the leading article tore into Edward, in what an outraged Beaverbrook called 'Dawson's parting and wanton word'. Unlike Baldwin the previous day, Dawson came not to praise the king, but to bury him. Beaverbrook huffed that 'It professed to be an impartial summing-up of the King's character, but it was couched in such terms as might be expected from a magistrate speaking to an incorrigible criminal in the dock . . . Under the veneer of smooth language, it was a biting and blistering piece of invective.'[3] The hardest blow came when the paper repurposed a saying of Tacitus, writing, 'It can hardly have been a better verdict upon the Emperor Galba than it is upon King Edward that all men would have judged him worthy of the Throne if he had never ascended it.'[4]

Dawson was hardly alone. Much of the press coverage was similarly negative, even from previously sympathetic newspapers. The *News Chronicle* sighed that 'When the supreme decision came between personal choice and public duty, he lacked just the requisite fibre to stay the tremendous course',[5] and even the *Daily Mail* shrugged that 'Nothing will assuage the universal disappointment that the King was unable to respond to the entreaties not only of Mr Baldwin but of his subjects.'[6] The Beaverbrook press remained loyal until the end – the *Daily Express* praised Edward, although not without the qualification that 'we have lost a good King, who might have been a great King, one with charm and personality and understanding',[7] and the *Evening Standard* nodded that 'His Majesty emerges from the crisis strong in the respect and affection of his people'[8] – but the final verdict was best summarised by the *Yorkshire Post*, which declared 'The unhappy events of recent weeks have shown in two especially significant matters that King Edward was, in fact, constitutionally ill-adapted for a position which must make such high demands upon its occupant', even as it added the qualification that 'We recall with infinite regret all that his people loved in him as Prince and man.'[9]

It is rare that anyone has a chance to read their effective obituaries while still alive. If Edward did look at the morning's papers, he made no reference in his memoirs to doing so, instead being preoccupied with working on his abdication statement. This was largely crafted by Monckton, with a few lines inserted by Edward at his insistence, such as 'I have found it impossible to carry the heavy burden of responsibility and to discharge my duties as King as I would wish to do without the help and support of the woman I love.'[10] As the monarch continued to bash away at it, Monckton headed over to Piccadilly to see the Duke of York, to discuss what title Edward should have after his abdication. He made the delicate point that the Abdication Act did not remove Edward's right to be called 'His Royal Highness'; that would require another Act of Parliament. As Monckton put it, 'The King . . . was renouncing any right to the Throne but not the Royal Birth which he shared with his brothers.'[11]

Peacock had already talked to Downing Street about this, and the consensus was that Edward would temporarily become 'HRH Prince Edward', until the Duke of York became king and could give him another title. The civil servant Sir Claude Schuster suggested that 'Although the King might have power immediately after his accession to create Prince Edward a Duke, it would be contrary to precedent and custom to exercise his powers until he shall have been sworn in tomorrow.'[12] Nobody wanted to begin the new king's reign – the third of 1936 – with any murmurs of unconstitutionality. There was also the continued uncertainty about the nature of an allowance for Edward, although it was hoped that Bertie would be accommodating. In time, this lack of agreement on the terms of his allowance proved a disastrous mistake, but there was a general understanding that a settlement had been reached in principle and could be finessed later.

Over in Parliament, the final vote on the Abdication Bill had to take place. There was no serious doubt that it would be passed, especially after Baldwin's tour de force the previous day, although there had been some grumbling, which Nicolson described as 'some republican speeches . . . on the line "the spell is broken, why try to weave it afresh"'.[13] James Maxton, chairman of the Independent Labour Party, called the monarchy 'the symbol of a class-ridden society' and hoped that it had received a terminal shock, and his colleague George Buchanan caused a stir by alluding to the idea of collusion in Wallis's still-extant proceedings, saying 'A divorce case was taken when every one of you knows it was a breaking of the law. You are setting aside your laws for a rich and pampered royalty.'[14]

Maxton and Buchanan's protests made no difference. The bill was voted through on its second reading by a majority of 403 to 5, and as it passed its third reading, Baldwin paid Edward tribute, saying, 'We shall always remember with regard and affection the whole-hearted and loyal service that His Majesty has given to the country as Prince of Wales and during the short time he has been on the Throne.' After the bill passed through the House of Lords in a quarter of an hour, the Clerk of the Parliaments, Sir Henry Badeley, read out the Declaration of Abdication. Lord Zetland wrote, 'I do not suppose that many of us who were present will live through a more dramatic moment than we did when Sir H. Badeley turned from the three noble lords seated in front of the throne to the Speaker and members of the House of Commons standing at the Bar and uttered the words *"Le Roy le veult*"*.'[15] Duff Cooper considered that Badeley 'put a special and tragic emphasis into his voice' when he made the pronouncement.[16] At eight minutes to one on 11 December 1936, Edward VIII ceased to be king. He had ruled for 326 days: the shortest reign of any monarch since Lady Jane Grey.

The former monarch was, at the moment when he formally abdicated his throne, having lunch at the Fort with Churchill. The politician had telephoned earlier that day and asked if he could see him, somewhat to Peacock's dismay. The duchy's receiver general wrote simply 'Damn!' in his account of the day, and later included Churchill in his list of 'guilty men' in his description of the abdication, along with Harmsworth, Rothermere and Beaverbrook, stating of them that 'If the story is ever known of [their] activities, it will not be a nice story.'[17] At the time, however, Churchill was a most welcome guest; Monckton commented that 'He vastly improved the form of the proposed broadcast - though he did not alter the substance.'[18] Edward willingly admitted that several of its most memorable lines were suggested by him ('which a practised student of Churchilliana could spot at a glance'), such as how he

---

* Meaning 'The King wills it', this was a phrase that signified that a public bill had received royal assent. Thus, Edward, as monarch, had assented to his own abdication.

was 'bred in the constitutional tradition by my Father' and his describing Bertie as possessing 'one matchless blessing, enjoyed by so many of you and not bestowed on me – a happy home with his wife and children'.[19]

As they sat at their valedictory meal, Edward was demob-happy. Monckton wrote of his 'excellent form', brought on by a mixture of relief and anticipation at being able to escape from England and the stresses of the past months. He felt almost giddy with excitement. Others around him felt more conflicted about his imminent departure. At the end of lunch, Churchill and Monckton prepared to leave for London, shortly after receiving the formal announcement that Edward was no longer king. As the politician stood by the door, he was deeply moved, and began to tap on the floor with his walking stick, before reciting two lines of Andrew Marvell:

> He nothing common did or mean
> Upon that memorable scene.

Monckton immediately recognised the significance of the allusion. The poem that Churchill was quoting was Marvell's 'An Horatian Ode Upon Cromwell's Return from Ireland'. In it, the poet wrote, with notable compassion, about the execution of Charles I. Had Churchill recited the succeeding lines, Edward might have been taken aback by the comparison:

> But with his keener eye
> The axe's edge did try;
> Nor call'd the gods with vulgar spite
> To vindicate his helpless right,
> But bowed his comely head
> Down as upon a bed.

The King was not dead, but there was now a sense of uncertainty as to what should follow. It was initially suggested that Queen Mary should broadcast her own message to the British people, offering them reassurance and an implicit sense of continuity, but Wilson rejected this idea. Instead, a press statement was drawn up, written in her name by Cosmo Lang. Addressed 'to the people of this nation and Empire', it took a personal perspective on the events that had occurred ('I need not speak to you of the distress which fills a Mother's heart when I think that my dear son has deemed it to be his duty to lay down his charge and that the reign which had begun with so much hope and promise has so suddenly ended'), and asked that the nation should keep 'a grateful remembrance of him in your hearts'. There was also some emphasis on her hope that the new king, 'summoned so unexpectedly and in circumstances so painful', should be given the 'same full measure of generous loyalty' that the previous rulers had received. The proclamation concluded, 'It is my earnest prayer that, in spite of, nay through, this present trouble, the loyalty and unity of our land and Empire may by God's blessing be maintained and strengthened.'

Baldwin was happy with the statement, and it was published in the papers the following day. He was also pleased to have received a handwritten letter from Queen Mary thanking him for his 'wonderful speech' and 'the kind way you spoke of the King', as well as telling him that his words '[have] had a quieting effect on people and [have] helped us all very much to face the future with faith and courage'. She ended sympathetically, 'I fear you must be dreadfully tired.'[20] If Baldwin had replied, one imagines that he could have said, 'Yes, me and the entire nation.'

The man most in need of reassurance was the new king. Even as Edward began to feel a sense of ecstatic relief, his brother was in a state of terror. He referred to 11 December as 'that dreadful day', and even as he busied himself with details of his own Accession Council and Edward's title and finances, he was unable to acclimatise himself to his new situation. He noted with amazement in his account of the time that, when he arrived at the Fort that day, 'all D's servants called me His Majesty'. Everyone knew immediately that George VI, as he would be known, would be an entirely different monarch to his brother. The idea of a louche woman such as Emerald Cunard openly referring to him as 'Majesty Divine' seemed impossible, even comical.

The new king and Edward spent a curious final evening together. The prince was in the middle of packing his possessions, prior to leaving the country that night, and as Bertie hesitantly entered his bedroom, space had to be made for him to sit on the sofa. Edward saw that he was in a frightened state; as he later wrote, deploying euphemisms with an obituarist's skill, 'Shy and retiring by nature, he shrank instinctively from the gregarious life I had lived with some zest.' They spoke 'with a frankness recalling the untroubled companionship of our youth', as Bertie tacitly conveyed his terror at the responsibility that his brother's actions had placed upon him. Although Edward understood that 'the situation seemed to cry mutely for a symbolical laying on of hands, a passing of the torch', he instead bluffly told the new king that 'You are not going to find this a difficult job at all. You know the ropes, and you have almost overcome that slight hesitation in your speech which used to make public speaking so hard for you.' It would have been more honest if he had said, 'I've had enough, and it's over to you now. And I wouldn't want to be in your shoes for all the tea in China.'

The now former king may have spent some of his final day looking at the letters of sympathy and regret he received. Read cumulatively, as they today can be on special application to the Royal Archives in Windsor Castle, they become emotionally overwhelming. Correspondents, whether friends, nemeses or sycophants, took one last opportunity to offer him their thoughts. His cousin Alice, Duchess of Gloucester, wrote, 'I want you to know how profoundly I grieve, and how miserable I am for you to have found [yourself] faced with such ghastly alternatives – may your decision lead you at this long last out of all this tragedy to that happiness which you have been seeking . . . You know me too well to pretend that I acquiesce in all this distressing business, but you have ever my loving, if <u>sorrowful</u>, sympathy. Yours is not love, which alters when it alteration finds . . . We shall always be there if you should need us.'[21] The Duchess of York wrote from her sickbed to say, 'I am so miserable that I cannot come down to Royal Lodge . . . as I wanted so much to see you before you go, and say "God bless you" from my heart. We are all overcome with misery and can only pray that you will find happiness in your new life. I often think of the old days, & how you helped Bertie & I in the first years of our marriage – I shall always mention you in my prayers & bless you.'[22]

Time and time again, the messages emphasised Edward's personal decency, his kindness and compassion towards others and the disbelief with which his departure was greeted, diversified by a genuine sense of crushing sorrow, as if something irreplaceable had been ripped away from the very fabric of the country. They act as a valuable counterweight to those who, like Hardinge, refused to believe he was capable of anything other than selfishness, even if the sentiments sometimes feel dictated by duty rather than real affection, as in Helen Hardinge's benediction that 'It is impossible . . . to forget the vast kindnesses we have received at your hands – & I am grateful . . . A London driver . . . speaking of Mrs Simpson said "She must be very wonderful to make him do this." I hope for your sake – sir – that this man was right and that your future will be happy and unclouded.'[23]

More representative was Violet, Duchess of Rutland's deeply personal letter: 'I have been your silent admirer since I first saw you at 2 months old – and all this time our hero prince. I remember you as a boy watching cricket at Lord's with my husband . . . and how remarkable you were in your sympathy and solicitude about a boy who had been hurt – and your wish to know of his betterment. We are all in tears my family and I – and Diana [Cooper] never stops! The tragedy of it all – we think we shall never be happy again. But perhaps you will – it will be bliss – not to <u>have</u> – to work hard anymore.'[24]

Her daughter echoed these sentiments, to hugely moving effect. With the memories of a long acquaintance uppermost in her mind, she wrote, 'I have that faith in you that tells me you have done what you feel & think to be right – what history may show is right

- but I can't choose but weep. I shall miss your grace, your "flare" [*sic*], your unusualness and your great goodness to Duff and me, quite terribly. I shall pray for your happiness, and also for the day when you return to those who love you so, and to the Fort that you so love. Always sir, yours to command, Diana C.'[25] Her husband's message was terser but no less heartfelt. He wrote pithily, 'I hope you will allow me to send you on this unhappy day one word of deep gratitude for the great kindness you have ever showed me. I can assure Your Majesty that when I cease to be your loyal subject I shall ever remain your humble, devoted and grateful servant.'[26]

Diana, especially, had touched upon something that was - and has been - overlooked in accounts of Edward's life and reign. For all his self-regard and immaturity, his flair and unusualness were rare qualities in a monarch, for both good and ill. He had the ability to make people like him, albeit often those who did not have to see his pettiness and inconsistency at close quarters, though sometimes even they remained loyal. One of these was a former girlfriend, Gwendolyn 'Poots' Francis, who was married to his equerry, Major Humphrey Butler. In an emotional letter, she poured out her heart, saying, 'It is physically impossible for me not to say goodbye to you. I wanted so desperately to talk to you or see you for a moment, but felt that our intense despair and sadness could only add to your great distress. May you find happiness and may God bless you darling - Always devotedly, Poots.'[27] It is hard to imagine Wallis writing anything so emotional. But Edward had made his choice, and his imminent departure was to be England's loss.

The final broadcast to the nation was set for ten that evening, after which it was arranged that Edward would head to Portsmouth. From there he would be taken to France on the destroyer HMS *Fury*. It was decided in a slightly hurried fashion what his future title would be - the Duke of Windsor was settled upon, as it paid homage to the adopted family name, and Edward liked the sound of it - and how he would be introduced while he was making the broadcast. Sir John Reith, who was supervising it, had suggested to the new king that his predecessor should be referred to as 'Mr Edward Windsor', but this idea was dismissed immediately. Instead, he would be introduced as 'His Royal Highness, Prince Edward', which offered him the appropriate measure of regal dignity.

Before he addressed the nation, Edward concentrated on the tasks ahead. One of these was to make sure that the text of the broadcast was satisfactory. His mother had counselled against its being made ('Don't you think that as [Baldwin] has said everything that could be said, and has explained all that passed between you and him, it will now not be necessary for you to broadcast this evening, you are very tired after all . . . You might spare yourself that extra strain and emotion – do please take my advice'), but her son, as usual, ignored her. The duke smarted when Monckton let him know that Baldwin would appreciate a favourable reference to his having shown the former king every kindness; 'That's a good one', he commented, having been angered by Baldwin's omission of Wallis in his speech the previous day, which he described as 'an autobiographical triumph disguised as a homily on the errors of a King'. Nonetheless, 'determined not to be petty at the last moment',[28] he acceded to the request.

This explained why the broadcast, somewhat disingenuously, contained the statement 'the Ministers of the Crown, and in particular Mr Baldwin, the Prime Minister, have always treated me with full consideration . . . There has never been any constitutional difference between me and them and between me and Parliament.' Given that his actions had led directly to a constitutional crisis that could have meant either the collapse of the government or, *in extremis*, the creation of an unelected and unaccountable 'King's Party', this massaging of the *actualité* must have led to a few raised eyebrows and spilt brandy-and-sodas throughout Whitehall. Yet it was too late for recriminations, on either side.

Before that, Edward took his leave of the servants at the Fort. In his memoir, he seemed more interested in his pet dog, Slipper, than in those who had faithfully served him, in some cases for decades. This was because it was by no means an uneventful parting.

Fred Smith, who had looked after him since 1908, lost his temper and shouted, 'Your name's mud! M! U! D!' Edward remonstrated mildly, 'Oh, Frederick, please don't say that. We've known each other for so long', but found that Smith's feelings were common amongst his retainers, who felt betrayed by their employer, and made excuses not to accompany him into exile. He later complained to Queen Mary about their 'amazing disloyalty', adding, 'I neither know nor care their reasons but I can never forget how they let me down when I most needed them.'[29]

He also telephoned Wallis, who was in a depressed and emotional state, and had been since the previous day. She had burst into tears upon hearing the summary of Baldwin's speech, realising that her efforts to renounce Edward had been for nothing. He breezily divulged that he would be heading to a hotel in Zurich upon his departure from England, which astonished her. As she wrote later, 'It filled me with fury that the British government could be so indifferent to his new vulnerability, so ungrateful for his splendid services, as to fail to provide him with the privacy and protection he would desperately need in the first months of readjustment.'[30] It did not seem to occur to her that the snub was deliberate. She arranged him more appropriate lodgings at the Austrian castle Schloss Enzesfeld with Baron and Baroness Eugène de Rothschild, and then sat brooding. She later stated, 'That night, I drained the dregs of the cup of my failure and defeat.'[31] These were not the words of someone delighted at the prospect of being reunited with her lover.

Edward left the Fort, bound for the Royal Lodge and then Windsor Castle, where he was to make the broadcast. As he was driven away, he glanced back at his beloved home for the last time. That was when it dawned on him that, along with everything intangible that he had lost, he had, by his own actions, deprived himself of the only place he had ever been happy. As he mused later, 'In that moment, I realised how heavy was the price I had paid: for, along with all the other things I should have to give up the Fort, probably for ever.' The thought caused him 'great sadness', as it had been 'more than a home; it had been a way of life for me . . . It was there that I had passed the happiest days of my life.' The journey to the Royal Lodge was not a long one, but it offered him the opportunity to consider, perhaps for the first time in the crisis, what he was for-feiting. He would never live in the Fort again, and on his fleeting subsequent visits to England, he was saddened by how it had fallen into disrepair. As his friend 'Fruity' Metcalfe reported early the next year, 'It all looked so sad, so empty, that I did not stay long.'[32]

When he arrived at the Royal Lodge, he was joined by his mother and brothers, including the new king. They ate a hurried dinner, which passed 'pleasantly enough under the circumstances', although Edward began to feel nervous about the responsibility that was upon him. He mused, 'I hope I was a good guest, but I rather doubt it.'[33] Then it was time for Monckton to take him to Windsor Castle, where Reith greeted him amicably and led him to the room from which the broadcast was to be delivered. The conversation was determinedly kept on other topics. Monckton recalled, 'Sir John talked to us on Spain and other subjects for a few minutes, and then left the King and me alone.'

Reith himself began the broadcast, with the announcement: 'This is Windsor Castle. His Royal Highness, Prince Edward', and then left the room. Edward, who felt a sense of pressure, shifted his leg around and bashed his shoe against the table, making a loud noise that mystified the millions of people listening. There was a false suggestion that it had been caused by Reith slamming the door in contempt. Monckton felt that the opening of the speech began 'a little nervously', as Edward recycled much of the content of the broadcast that he had not previously been allowed to make, but he warmed up as he went on. There was the same directness ('At long last I am able to say a few words of my own'), praise for his audience ('I have been treated with the greatest kindness by all classes, wherever I have lived or journeyed throughout the Empire . . . for that I am very grateful') and apparent straight talking. He stressed that 'I want you to know that the decision I have made has been mine and mine alone', and that 'the other person most nearly concerned has tried up to the last to persuade me to take a different course'. He ended by pledging loyalty to the new George VI, and said, with 'almost a shout', 'God Save the King.'[34] As he finished, he stood up, placed his arm on Monckton's shoulder, and said, consciously or unconsciously alluding to Dickens, 'Walter, it is a far better thing I go to.'

Edward considered that the broadcast had gone well. Returning to his family, and accompanied by the cheers of the nearby public, 'I had the feeling that what I had said had to some extent eased the tension between us.'[35] Monckton agreed, believing that 'his confidence grew [along with] the strength of his voice . . . I do not know how it sounded to the millions of listeners outside but in the little room itself it was a very moving speech.' Their views were largely shared by the nation. Churchill was in tears as he listened to it at Chartwell, and Beaverbrook pronounced it 'a triumph of natural and sincere eloquence'. Many who listened to it in the pubs and in their front rooms were deeply affected, and there was spontaneous singing of the National Anthem throughout the country.

Those who had been more closely involved in the crisis were less generous, although Dawson allowed that it was 'v. correct and rather moving'.[36] Helen Hardinge, although she herself wept, wrote in her diary that her husband and friends '[thought] it very vulgar'[37] (Alec called it 'deplorable'), and Chips Channon, although allowing that 'it was a manly, sincere farewell' that led him to shed a tear and murmur a prayer, was swift to resume his game of bridge. Wallis, meanwhile, listened to the speech on the radio, lying on a sofa with her hands over her face so that the assembled company could not see her cry. After Edward finished speaking, 'I lay there a long time before I could control myself enough to walk through the house and go upstairs to my room.'[38]

It was time for Edward to depart. Nobody called it exile, but nobody needed to. He took a final leave of his family, which went much as could be expected. Queen Mary was, in Monckton's words, 'mute and immoveable and very royal', as well as 'magnificently brave',[39] and the Duke of Kent gave in to emotion briefly, shouting, 'It isn't possible! It isn't happening!'[40] The others remained calm, talking of everything apart from what had just occurred. When it was time for the new king and the old one to part, they kissed, Edward bowed to George as his monarch and, crucially, 'they parted as Freemasons', indicating a bond between them beyond the ties of family or throne. Whether Edward had followed the Masonic code in any regard for years – if ever – was dubious. George managed to keep his feelings under control, but when he received his brother's bow, he remonstrated briefly. The new Duke of Windsor cheerily dismissed his concerns. 'It's all right old man', he said. 'I must step off with the right foot from the first.'[41]

At half past eleven that evening, Monckton and Edward headed to Portsmouth together, accompanied by the duke's detective David Storrier, and Slipper the dog. There was an eerie sense of calm now, after the drama and occasion of the previous days and weeks. The two men spoke of their common bond, but also of old days at Oxford and people they had known. Monckton wrote that 'He talked quite simply and unaffectedly of old times and associations with the places through which we went, but above all of his mother and how kind she had been to him.'[42]

Eventually, later than expected, they arrived at the docks. Edward, whether out of overexcitement or trepidation, delayed his departure, wandering round the dockyard and taking pleasure in showing Monckton some of the ships, including the *Victory* and the *Courageous*. Neither man remarked upon the irony in the gulf between his situation and their names. Eventually Monckton was rescued from his tour by Sir William Fisher, admiral and commander-in-chief of the Navy, who ushered Edward onto the *Fury*. Fisher, who had ensured that there was medical attention on board in case the duke was in an overactive or troubled state, was relieved to find that, despite his obvious exhaustion, 'His manner betrayed no weariness, his voice had animation and my general feeling was one of relief that he was so normal.'[43] Moved to tears, Fisher bade him farewell, only for Edward to respond, 'Oh, it's not

goodbye.' Monckton, Godfrey Thomas and the others now prepared to see him off. It was a sad occasion, but also a tiring one.
The duke had little care for the concerns of others, and was all but
revelling in the situation.

The ship eventually sailed at two in the morning, but Edward,
who was by now drinking brandy with some vigour, insisted on
sharing tales of the last few weeks with the exhausted sailors, who
ended up taking shifts to listen to their former king. When, at last,
his fund of anecdotes was depleted, he wished to send several
messages of thanks via the wireless, before reflecting on what lay
ahead for him. As he later wrote, 'If it had been hard to give up the
throne, it had been even harder to give up my country. I now knew
that I was irretrievably on my own. The drawbridges were going
up behind me.' He could only take one piece of consolation from
his actions: that 'love had triumphed over the exigencies of politics'.[44] The fact that whatever he felt for Wallis had also fractured
his family, led to his terrified brother being forced into a situation
he had never wanted, and come close to triggering a constitutional
calamity without equal was not mentioned.

Perhaps the most significant letter he wrote that night was to his
mother. As before, he seemed not to have understood the situation
he had placed her in. Thanking her once again for her 'sweetness',
he wrote, 'I loved our last few minutes together and at last being
able to bring dear Papa into our talk. We were different in many
ways and yet you know how devoted I was to him and I cried
when you said he was human.' He acknowledged that his father
would have been horrified by his actions – 'It would have been
hard for him to understand what I have done' – but, incorrectly,
ascribed a greater understanding to Queen Mary, saying, 'You do
so much better and I love you for it and hate to think of the strain
that this last month has been to you.'

A great deal of the letter concerned Wallis ('The only terribly
hard thing for me is that I can't see Wallis until April 27th but she
and I can take that separation with the knowledge of the great love
happiness and companionship which we are so sure we can give

each other'). He appeared not to appreciate the gravity of his actions, blithely dismissing the constitutional crisis he had brought about by saying, 'It was a big thing to do but I know it will be best for all in the end and Bertie will make a fine king and will be able to carry on without any upset and will find that I have left the Crown and the Throne as Papa left it on the same high level it has maintained for so many centuries', and expressing his hope that he might return to England 'as soon as is convenient to Bertie and suitable to the Country for we know there is no other worth living in', although he at least had the grace to acknowledge that 'we will never do so without his asking us'. As he concluded by extolling his 'lovely sacred feelings for Wallis and devotion to you my mother',[45] his lack of tact and comprehension continued to define him, though now as man rather than monarch.

While he wrote his long screed of self-justification, the *Fury* sailed into the night, its once-regal passenger still jabbering and typing away until he no longer had an opportunity to do so. Simon, writing his account of the crisis, felt it appropriate to quote Milton's *Lycidas* as he considered the duke's farewell voyage – 'Comes the blind Fury with the abhorred shears/And slits the thin-spun life.'[46]

Monckton and Thomas returned to London together, on what Monckton called 'a very sad journey'. Thomas, who had served Edward for seventeen years, was especially upset, as he felt he had somehow failed in his duty, and that 'virtually his life's work had been shipwrecked'. Monckton mused that 'We who had been boys together at school [felt] much the same misery as the youngster returning for his second term; and I suspect that each of us was behaving as the youngster would.'[47] The ever-loyal lawyer had a couple of hours' sleep before heading to Fort Belvedere to see if anything indiscreet or private had been left behind. The only items that needed to be removed were a piece of paper with Wallis's telephone number in Cannes, and a biography of Mrs Fitzherbert, the woman to whom Wallis had so gleefully compared herself earlier in the year.

Monckton's feelings about both the man and the matter were

best summarised in a letter that he wrote to Queen Mary the morning after the abdication. Even allowing for his exhaustion, and the necessity to be tactful while dealing with a senior royal, it was remarkable in both its compassion and its perspicacity. After recounting Edward's conversation and how he had praised his mother ('how grand you were and how sweet to him and especially at the last when he wanted it most'), he mused as to what the future held for the man who would not be king: 'There is, and I think there always will be, a greatness and a glory about him. Even his faults and follies are great. And he will, I feel sure, never lend himself to any such dangerous courses as some, not unreasonably, fear. He has shown that he cares for unity: and he felt deeply the unity of the Family with him last night.'[48]

The ever-loyal and ever-decent Monckton was a better friend than Edward deserved. And his hopes that the duke would avoid 'dangerous courses' would, as time went on, prove unfounded. Yet he managed to articulate something of the enduring fascination with Edward, and his relationship with Wallis, that we still hold today. He was a wretched, quixotic ruler, an obsessed and demanding lover and, bar the odd instance of compassion and decency, a selfish and thoughtless man. Ziegler calls him 'the wrong man in the wrong place . . . a pitiful figure'.[49] Yet he brought a glamour and excitement to kingship that made him arguably the most famous and sought-after person in England, if not in Europe. More so than any film star, he had an easy air of intimacy with the common man that led to an inordinate level of popularity and meant that his every action was eagerly and closely scrutinised. He resented this scrutiny, and, Garbo-like, decided that 'I want to be alone', accompanied only by Wallis. This solitude, which he faced for the rest of his life, was a miserable and lonely one, occasionally diversified by scandal and controversy.

Yet as he sailed into the night, he could reflect with pride that he had not shown himself to be an ordinary man, or an ordinary sovereign. He had torn up centuries of protocol and expectation of how a monarch could, or should, behave, replacing it with a defiant expression of individualism. With this, he prefigured a century in which ideas of duty and honour would be increasingly replaced by free will and self-fulfilment. In this regard, he lived up to Emerald Cunard's description of him as 'the most modernistic man alive'.

Wilde once wrote that 'I was a man who stood in symbolic relation to the art and culture of my age.' In a Europe that was preparing for seismic conflict, Edward could have claimed that he was a man, and monarch, whose own symbolic relation was to the personality cult that came to dominate society. He was no longer an Englishman by residence. Instead, he became both citizen of the world and a citizen of nowhere, rootless, stateless and drifting, doomed to scrape by on a mixture of reluctantly offered hand-outs and his former reputation: the Ancient Mariner in Club Class. It was a philosophically fascinating predicament, but a personally unhappy one. And he only had himself to blame for it.

Epilogue

'In the Darkness'

'So ended a reign of which one can only say that it would have been better if it had never been begun', Hardinge concluded in the private memoir he kept of the abdication crisis, echoing the words of his friend Dawson. The former king's private secretary had no affection for his employer, complaining that 'A personality more unfit to fill the reign of a constitutional monarch it would be difficult to find – for what qualities he had were on the surface, and, underneath it, all was sand.' Dismissing the Duke of Windsor's public popularity – 'His undoubted hold on the affection of the least prosperous of his subjects was based on a fallacy for which his superficial personal charm was alone responsible' – Hardinge took pleasure in Edward and Wallis's departure, crowing, 'Tragic was their final disillusionment, and this was the saddest feature of an episode – unparalleled in history and fraught with unprecedented dangers – from which our Empire has emerged with added strength, triumphant in the unity of common ideals.' The king was gone. Long live the king.

Yet with Edward's departure, the question came over the country: what does one do with its former ruler? Churchill believed the answer was relatively straightforward. As he wrote to Boothby on 11 December, 'The only thing now to do is to make it easy for him to live in this country quietly as a private gentleman as soon as possible and to that we must bend our efforts by discouraging noisy controversy and (apart from quasi historical investigation) refusing to take part in it.' He concluded that 'The more firmly the new King is established, the more easy it will be for the old one to come back to his house.'[1] Unfortunately, there were those who did not share Churchill's generous and humane sentiments. One of these was Edward's old adversary Cosmo Lang.

'In the darkness he left these shores.' The broadcast that Lang made to the nation came shortly after he wrote in his diary that 'the reign of King Edward came to a pathetic and inglorious end'.[2] Throughout the abdication crisis, he had lost no opportunity to explore Edward's failings, finding evidence that the king had been both a heavy drinker as a younger man and sexually unconventional. Lang had never liked his monarch on a personal level, noting from an early encounter, 'It was clear that he knows little and, I fear, cares little about the Church and its affairs', even as he allowed that 'He was very pleasant, and *seemed* to be very cordial.'[3] The archbishop attempted to do his Christian duty, but the two did not meet or speak after 21 July 1936, and Lang later wrote, 'As the months passed and his relations with Mrs Simpson became more notorious, the thought of my having to consecrate *him* as King weighed on me as a heavy burden. Indeed, I considered whether I could bring myself to do so.'[4]

Lang associated himself with Hardinge and Dawson and actively pressed for Edward to abdicate and retreat into private life. While he took care never to have any public role in the crisis, he kept in close touch with Baldwin, ensuring that he had every snippet of information and gossip at his fingertips. He made no statement, nor offered any opinion on the crisis, but once it was resolved, he decided that it was time to preach to the nation, and impress them with his considered and impartial views, as a man of God.

It is now widely accepted that what Lang did was a horrendous error. Ziegler calls it 'a curious mistake on his part, which he didn't normally make'.[5] At a time where care was taken to present Edward in as favourable a public light as possible, the archbishop delivered an address that began by comparing his departure to the flight of James II two and a half centuries before,* and then tore into the 'strange and sad' motivation for the abdication, by which 'he should have disappointed hopes so high and abandoned a trust so great'. Wallis was not spared – 'even more strange and sad it is that he should have sought his happiness in a manner inconsistent with the Christian principles of marriage' – but Lang's gravest error was to castigate Edward's counsellors and friends, whom he dismissed as 'a social circle whose standards and ways of life are alien to all the best instincts and traditions of his people'. They were openly criticised – 'today they stand rebuked by the judgement of the Nation' – and Lang justified his attack by saying, 'I have felt compelled [to say these words] for the sake of sincerity and truth.'

Although there was much that was uncontroversial about the address, such as praise for Queen Mary and King George VI, it was the attack on Edward and his circle that became notorious. Inadvertently, Lang had managed to criticise the likes of the Coopers, Lord Mountbatten and Monckton, none of whom were impressed by the virtual libel that had been levelled at them. Although Baldwin wrote the archbishop a supportive letter, praising him for having 'said just what was wanted, and, if I may say so, just what you ought to have said',[6] many others were infuriated. Monckton wrote, with justifiable irritation, to Tommy Dugdale that 'I have not myself enjoyed much the comments which have reached me attributing the Archbishop's rebuke to myself . . . If one speaks deliberately to millions of people and recklessly includes unguarded words intended to attack an ill-defined group, one ought to know that one will wound many whom one would wish to leave untouched.'[7]

Lang received hundreds of letters after the broadcast – 'many highly appreciative, but the majority abusive and even vituperative',[8] as his private secretary recorded. There was a sense amongst the public, disappointed to have lost their glamorous king and still uncertain as to what kind of monarch George would prove to be,

---

* Which, coincidentally, took place on the same day nearly 250 years earlier on 11 December 1688.

that the archbishop had not acted as a soothing and conciliatory presence, but as one who was pursuing his own vindictive and unchristian agenda. Although Lang described the 'difficult task' he had undertaken as one that he had 'fully expected . . . a torrent of abuse'[9] for, even he was shocked when he became the subject of a satirical poem by Gerald Bullett, which stated:

> My Lord Archbishop, what a scold you are
> And when a man's down, how bold you are
> Of Christian charity, how scant you are
> You old Lang swine, how full of Cantuar.

The 'old Lang swine' continued to hold an animus towards Edward, refusing him any formal ceremony for his subsequent wedding to Wallis and continuing to compare him unfavourably to his brother throughout his time as prelate. Yet privately, he also conceded that he had gone too far and had misjudged the mood of the nation. He wrote to Wigram on 23 December to say, 'I realise how much pain recurrent references to poor King Edward personally must be to his mother and family. I thought that what I said had to be said, but hoped that that would be an end to it, and I did not gather that they at all resented the very few words from myself . . . Anyhow, to show all considerateness to the Royal Family . . . I have to-day sent a short note to all the Bishops suggesting that enough has now been said of this kind and that it would be well to refrain from further direct reference to King Edward's conduct or the unhappy circumstances of his abdication.'[10] Even those who disapproved of what the duke had done still believed that there was something fundamentally unsportsmanlike about Lang's public attack on a man unable to defend himself, and the controversy of the broadcast hung over his time as Archbishop of Canterbury until his retirement in 1942.

For others, the end of the abdication crisis was a happier affair, as well as a cathartic relief. As Simon wrote to the Liberal politician

Lady Hilda Currie after its conclusion, 'What a fearful ten days we have been through; it would need an Aeschylus to write the tragedy of what I called in the House of Commons yesterday these inscrutable promptings of a human heart.'[11] Vansittart wrote to Wigram shortly before Christmas in delight that Edward's abdication had ended any suspected connections between the monarchy and Hitler. 'What has happened is regarded in Germany as a blow to the "Fuhrer-prinzip",* which it was considered was going to be promoted by the marriage. There has been consternation in Berlin at the outcome of this matter, and the result is attributed in some high quarters to Bolshevist machinations against the prospect of having a Fuhrer combination here!'

Vansittart, with a mixture of disbelief and relief, concluded that 'It seems almost incredible that serious people should have believed that the projected marriage would result in the establish-ment of the "Fuhrer principle" in England, and in thus ensuring the German hold over our foreign policy. But there it is; and the fact is incontestable – although I should not be surprised if some of the older and more level-headed Germans did not rub their eyes also.'[12] Wigram replied, with commendable understatement, 'I was never very happy about the relations between those parties, even as far back as March last.'[13]

A secret memorandum written shortly after the abdication by the civil servant Orme Sargent, who was troubled by Hitler's rise to power, made the cost of the association between Edward and Ribbentrop clear. Ridiculing Ribbentrop's stated reasons for the former king's departure ('The real reasons for the recent crisis were not those constitutional and moral considerations which had been publicly announced. On the contrary, Mr Baldwin's real motive was a purely political one, namely to defeat those Germanophile forces which had been working through Mrs Simpson and the late King with the object of reversing the present British policy, and

---

* The so-called 'Fuhrer principle' was Hitler's belief that his word was of greater importance than any written or stated law.

bringing about an Anglo-German entente'), he indicated that the German ambassador had, foolishly, 'based the whole of his strategy on the role that Mrs Simpson was expected to play in Anglo-German affairs'.

He now knew that Ribbentrop would be a diminished figure, stating that 'Her disappearance had completely disconcerted him, and he now viewed the future with considerable anxiety, since he feared . . . that the new King would be content to follow the Foreign Office policy.' Hitler, meanwhile, was said to be 'very distressed at the turn that affairs had taken in this country, since he had looked upon the late King as a man after his own heart, and one who understood the Fuhrerprinzip, and was ready to introduce it into this country'.[14] Sargent's sigh of deserved relief at the evaded outcome is almost audible.

It was now business as usual for 'the Firm', as the royal family has been nicknamed. George VI's accession was proclaimed on Saturday 12 December, and he immediately attempted to restore an air of stability and continuity to the country. In a brisk letter that Queen Mary wrote to Edward on 16 December, she allowed that 'That Friday evening was dreadful for us all, grief at parting from you', but expressed relief that 'It was all managed in such a dignified way that things are beginning to settle down after that terrible upheaval, in any other country there would have been riots, thank God people did not lose their heads.' But then it was back to normal life; there was a horse to run at Sandringham, and a new monarch to break in. She concluded, with presumably unintentional irony, 'I hope and think people do not bother you.'[15]

It came as something of a surprise to Hardinge, and his wife, that he was asked to remain as the king's private secretary. He mused to Dawson, while gratefully thanking him for his work during the crisis, that 'In the end, the Empire has, I believe, really profited by this demonstration of unity . . . It is like a haven of rest at [Buckingham Palace] after the bedlam of the last few months.'[16] He also spoke of his 'quite unqualified' relief at Edward's departure.

Although Helen wrote that 'It seemed natural to us that King George VI would want to appoint a member of his own staff . . . to succeed my husband', with both believing that Hardinge would be allowed to retire quietly, he was very happy to remain in post.

Helen did not mention it, but Hardinge's flagrant disloyalty to Edward VIII (whose exile he described as 'tragic, but no more than he deserves')[17] was commonly known, and so a compromise was agreed upon. He would take a three-month leave of absence, and was knighted at the beginning of February 1937. His wife described this as 'a welcome thought from the new sovereign', but couldn't help including a telegram from a friend that may have given away her – and Alec's – truer feelings: 'HEARTIEST CONGRATULATIONS OUGHT TO HAVE BEEN A DUKEDOM.'[18]

Hardinge was conspicuously loyal to George VI until he retired in 1943,* supposedly on the grounds of ill health. He later wrote of him that his greatest qualities were 'courage, modesty and perseverance', and that his strength as king was complemented by his 'happy family circle, such as is dear to the hearts of most Englishmen; for the English like – and indeed expect – to see in their leaders virtues which they themselves are not always prepared to cultivate'. The comparison with his predecessor was implicit, but Helen twisted the knife further, writing as late as 1967 that 'The Duke of Windsor has recently presented himself to the public in a pleasant way, as an ageing avuncular character. We all grow old, and I am sorry for those afflictions that have come to him as the result of age . . . For the man himself it is . . . possible to have sympathy, but not for his writings.'[19] Thirty years of implacable loathing is an impressive record; her husband only managed a quarter-century's worth, as he died in 1960.

There were many other honours granted by the new king, but the most significant was the first, namely the creation of Sir Walter

---

* Although it has transpired that Hardinge found working with Lascelles difficult, and when the latter suggested to George VI that his superior retire early, the king agreed gratefully. He wrote in his diary that 'It was difficult for me, but I knew I should not get this opportunity again'.

Monckton. The lawyer arrived at 145 Piccadilly almost immediately after George's accession, having already agreed to remain attorney general to the Duchy of Cornwall, and was shown to a small room on the first floor. There, the two men chatted for around ten minutes, and George stressed to Monckton that he wished him to be available, as an informal counsellor and friend, just as he had been to Edward. Then, with an absence of regal pageantry and flourish, he pointed to a yellow footstool in the corner of the room, and said, 'We shall be needing that.' With some surprise, Monckton pulled it out, and was asked to kneel, at which the new king produced a ceremonial sword, and tapped him lightly on the shoulder. As Monckton began to stand up, George said, 'No, I haven't done yet', and tapped him on the other. When finished, the king laughed and said, with relieved informality, 'Well, Walter, we didn't manage that very well, but neither of us has done it before.' Monckton later noted that 'Whatever the significance of it, I think I was the only person ever knighted there.'[20]

As the new reign continued, Sir Walter became an invaluable friend to George, especially where financial matters with the Duke of Windsor were concerned. As he wrote, 'I did my best to maintain a bridge between them on this question and eventually after months of anxiety the matter was satisfactorily disposed of.' Ever the diplomat, he kept the horse-trading and general ill-will private, writing in his personal account that 'no useful purpose would be served by recounting the history in detail'.[21]

Peacock wrote, after the crisis had concluded, that 'Monckton . . . was splendid throughout. [He] gave sound advice always . . . [was] indefatigable . . . the King liked [him] very much . . . and [he] spoke to him with great frankness and courage, when necessary.' He did strike a note of caution, however, when he observed that 'Monckton's activities were enough to kill a man', even if he substantiated this by noting that 'he never failed'. Monckton went on to an impressive public career, becoming Minister for Labour and then Minister for Defence, although the post that he coveted, Lord Chief Justice, was never to be his. He served in countless roles with enormous distinction, not least the chairmanship of Midland Bank and the Marylebone Cricket Club. Yet he was worn out and exhausted throughout much of the second half of his life, with the strain of the abdication taking a severe toll upon his health. When he died on 9 January 1965, at the age of seventy-three, his last words, delivered despairingly to his daughter-in-law Marianna, were 'I've had enough.'[22]

Another man whose fragile constitution was substantially weakened by the events of late 1936 was Baldwin. Initially, his reaction to his success was one of pride and gratitude. Even as he good-humouredly complained that he was 'up to the waist in letters'[23] of congratulation from friends and the general public, he revelled in what seemed a happy conclusion to his premiership. Simon commented that 'The rapid clearing up of this mess is a striking tribute to the efficiency of our form of Government, and Baldwin is beyond all praise.'[24] The prime minister was lionised by all, although some considered it a reaction of relief, rather than hard-headed political calculation.

Lloyd George's wife Margaret wrote to a friend that 'Tory, Liberal & Labour [alike] think that Baldwin handled the situation magnificently & as a result his stock, which slumped to rock-bottom after his infamous speech on re-armament, has now soared skyhigh. It has never been higher.' Elsewhere in the letter, she damned the king as surrounded by 'a lot of incompetent fools, & decadents', railed against the 'injudicious & vulgar style' of the Rothermere and Beaverbrook press, and mused as to whether Edward's considerable personal popularity was not checked by the circumstances of his departure. As she put it, 'Baldwin's speech on the Bill itself was "crota*" to the last degree & no one seemed to think it strange that little or nothing should be said about the departing King & the services he gave as P of Wales for 25 years.'[25] Such was the all-encompassing nature of Baldwin's victory that

---

* Slang for 'quota'; her implication was that Baldwin's speech was more perfunctory than his admirers suggested.

he could dispense with memories of Edward without difficulty.

Nonetheless, as Lord Dawson had warned him, 'You will pay for this.' As it became clear that the rise of Hitler and fascism was not to be checked, those around him began to accuse him of self-indulgence and fiddling while Europe prepared to burn. He remained prime minister until after George VI's Coronation, finally resigning on 27 May and making way for Neville Chamberlain. The rest is well known, and responsible for the dip in Baldwin's post-war reputation: a dip that shows no especial sign of coming to a close, although his status as a 'guilty man' has at least been superseded by more balanced accounts of his public career.

His nemesis, Beaverbrook, wrote to the Australian senator R. D. Elliott shortly after the abdication, on 15 December 1936. In his letter, he struck a different tone to the pugnacity that defined many of his previous interactions. Bemoaning that 'I have been on the unpopular and defeated side', he stated his case concisely. 'I believe that King Edward need never have gone. I took - and I still hold - the view that if he had sympathetic handling from the Government, coupled with a determination to delay the issue by every possible means, we stood a good chance of avoiding a marriage fatal to his position on the Throne.' Disingenuously, he took credit for his newspapers offering nuanced and compassionate support for a morganatic marriage, which was undone by a tide of public feeling, based on an economic crash. As he put it, 'The financial interests, which are very powerful, mobilised against the King, and in favour of a quick settlement.'

The publishing magnate, for all his bluster, was a disappointed man. He had placed his reputation and resources in the service of a bold and innovative plan, albeit one that was without precedent in English history: the creation of a 'King's Party', unaccountable to Parliament or normal scrutiny. He had failed, and knew that the chance would not come again. He complained to Elliott that 'the King's case was not well handled', but blamed Edward himself for being 'often undecided and wavering in his attitude', even as he shrugged and concluded, 'Well, it is all over now.'[26]

Instead, he would have to seek closer integration with the existing government if he wished to obtain greater power. In this regard, he was successful. He held various posts during World War II, including Minister of Aircraft Production and Minister of Supply, before eventually being made Lord Privy Seal. Only his failure to ensure Churchill's re-election in 1945 reminded him of how defeat could feel. He renounced his British citizenship and left the Conservative Party, actions not without petulance, and devoted himself to philanthropic activity. The Canadian city of Fredericton soon contained a Beaverbrook Art Gallery, Beaverbrook Hotel and Beaverbrook Skating Rink. Given his penchant for performing dangerous stunts on thin ice, the latter endowment seems appropriate.

Churchill, meanwhile, had been badly damaged by his ill-fated incursions into the abdication crisis. He might have been better off taking the advice of his wife Clementine; as her daughter Mary later said, 'What my mother saw was that his stand for the King was going to harm his political position . . . By taking up this high-profile position over the abdication, he lost again so much of what he'd gained. She saw this very clearly, which he didn't: a wonderful example of where her judgement was absolutely true and right.'

Yet he remained steadfastly loyal, writing to Edward a few days after his abdication with typical brio. He assured the duke that 'from all accounts the broadcast was successful, and all over the world people were deeply moved; millions wept', and that 'very different was the reception accorded to the Archbishop of Canterbury's performance on Sunday night. There has been a perfect storm of anger raised against him for his unchivalrous reference to the late reign. Even those who were very hostile to your standpoint turned round and salved their feelings by censuring the Archbishop.' He added, 'There is an enormous amount of sympathy and goodwill towards you here, and many people are quite stunned . . . The new reign has started very smoothly. The King looked to me very anxious and strained but is being helped by everyone as you would yourself desire.'[27] He may have expected to stroll off gently into an autumnal retirement at Chartwell, with a seat in the House of Lords and long lunches at the Carlton Club, but events have a strange habit of upending even the most confident of expectations.

And, of course, there were the continued lives of the Duke of Windsor and Wallis Simpson. Tommy Lascelles, in a letter to Dawson on 13 December, spoke for many when he wrote, 'Edward VIII was essentially a changeling, with the three dominant characteristics of changelings – no soul, no moral sense and great personal charm. The chief external cause of his downfall was that the public, all the world over, loved him too well and most unwisely. No man in history has ever been so fulsomely adulated as this modern Stupor Mundi,* and the result was his unshakeable conviction that he could get away with murder.' After warning of the dangers that now faced the young princesses, thrown into the spotlight unexpectedly, Lascelles concluded that 'In all this sad business, the only cause for real rejoicing is the utter defeat of the Powers of Evil.'²⁸

Lascelles was engaging in some entertaining but unfounded hyperbole, as well as ignoring the far greater woes that would befall Europe in less than three years' time. These woes, as related to the complex and unhappy shenanigans that followed Edward's departure from Britain on 11 December, can only now be fully described, given the release of various previously confidential papers and documents. Edward's apparent interest – if not necessarily support – of Hitler and the Nazi regime has attracted a great deal of controversy, as has his time as governor of the Bahamas. They are stories that deserve to be told, and hopefully will be before long.

Until then, it is the conclusion of *Paradise Lost* that encapsulates the unhappy wanderings that he and Wallis faced after the abdication. Like Adam and Eve, they were undone by fate and hubris alike,

---

* An allusion to Frederick II, Holy Roman Emperor and so-called 'astonishment of the world'.

cast out of a new Eden and doomed to walk the earth unhappily. It was an uncertain and difficult existence, but the romantic could take comfort from knowing that they at least had one another.

> Some natural tears they dropped, but wiped them soon;
> The World was all before them, where to choose
> Their place of rest, and Providence their guide:
> They hand in hand with wandering steps and slow,
> Through Eden took their solitary way.

Acknowledgements

Writing a book of this nature requires enormous thanks to the many people who have generously and selflessly contributed to its genesis, often in unexpectedly difficult circumstances thanks to another crisis altogether. To which end, *primus inter pares* must be my publisher Alan Samson, who has been a consistent champion of the book throughout the process. His instinct that a new account of the abdication was not just a good but necessary idea has, I hope, been borne out by *The Crown in Crisis*. My thanks also to everyone else at Weidenfeld & Nicolson, especially my project editor Sarah Fortune, my picture editor Cathy Dunn and my copy-editor Jane Selley, and to its distinguished alumnus Sophie Buchan, who has been an invaluable and witty source of counsel. A glance at this book's bibliography shows how indebted I have been to previous titles published by this house, and I am thrilled to join their number.

I have also been fortunate in my literary agent. Andrew Lownie is both a conscientious advocate of one's interests and a distinguished historian and biographer in his own right, a rare combination that has meant that his advice and guidance carries suitable weight behind it: a weight always leavened with good humour and morale-boosting.

Writing about the events of 1936, one stands on the shoulders of giants. First amongst these must be Philip Ziegler, whose authorised biography of Edward VIII remains the indispensable work about both the man and this period. I was deeply grateful for an audience with Philip during the book's creation, and during our lengthy conversation he offered me the incalculable benefit of his experience and thoughts on the subject, including his own encounters with the Duke of Windsor and Wallis Simpson.

I was also lucky enough to discuss the project with the historians Anne Sebba, Susan Williams and Andrew Roberts. They offered penetrating insights that made me think again about many of the assumptions that I had made, as well as generous hospitality and valuable introductions to other writers and historians. My thanks to them all, and to Michael Bloch, whose disarmingly modest claims to have forgotten the period are belied by the excellence and erudition of his published works dealing with it. I, and all other students of the era, owe him an enormous debt.

Many others have been of great assistance. Marianna Monckton, Walter Monckton's daughter-in-law, kindly invited me to lunch to discuss him and his role within the abdication crisis with me, and from her I gained a sense of Walter's enormous decency and compassion in private as well as public life, which I hope I have conveyed here. Yolanda Green generously provided me with access to the solicitor Robert Egerton's previously unpublished autobiographical account of Wallis's divorce case and its reper-cussions, 'Mr X' offered many revelations about Ernest Simpson, Robin Dalton gave useful first-hand insights into the characters of Edward and Wallis and Paul Elston helpfully clarified details of the Special Branch investigations of 1936.

Any book of this nature needs considerable time spent in the archives. It has been an especial pleasure in this case to unearth new and previously overlooked material, and I hope that I have paved the way for future historians of this period. The staff of the Balliol College Archives, the Bodleian Library, Churchill College Archives, National Archives, the Parliamentary Archive and the Royal Archives have all been extraordinarily helpful, answering my endless queries promptly and thoroughly, and ensuring that my repeated visits to their collections have always been harmoni-ous and easy.

This book has been largely written in the Bodleian and the Oxford Union libraries, and I offer my especial gratitude to the accommodating staff of both splendid institutions. My London base was, as ever, the London Library, meaning that this is now my fourth book to have been written using its resources; my thanks to them for their consistent award of Carlyle membership. A brief but very useful visit to Gladstone's Library was also illuminating. My enormous appreciation also to the Society of Authors, who awarded me an Author's Foundation grant for the book, and gave me a much-needed fillip in the final stages of research and writing.

When I'm not in the depths of an archive or library stack, it is conversations with fellow writers and friends both recent and of long standing that steer my thinking in fresh directions. To this end, I owe deep gratitude to many, including Dan Jones, Gustav Temple, Brice Stratford, Thomas Grant, Nigel Jones, Toby White, Peter Hoskin, Simon 'Boothby' Renshaw, Catherine Bray, James Douglass and Raymond Stephenson, and others besides, not least the Duke and Duchess of Sussex for considerately announcing their own abdication of sorts a few months before this book was published.

My most profound debt, however, remains to my wife Nancy. She has put up with me talking incessantly about my thoughts and ideas on the subject, so much so that I would hardly have blamed her for abdicating herself, and has continued to be the most wonderful, engaging and thrilling companion that anyone could wish to have. She is also mother to our daughter Rose, who has gone, over the course of the book's gestation, from an infant to a self-assured little girl, and I hope that, one day, she reads and enjoys this, and is not embarrassed by the declaration of paternal adoration that I, now and for ever, offer her.

The book is dedicated to my two grandmothers, Barbara Stephenson and Terese Larman, both of whom died while it was being written. It is a source of deep regret to me that neither of them will be able to read it, but some consolation that I was able to talk to them about their own experiences of 'the year of three kings', and I hope that they would have both enjoyed reading the final result.

As ever, any errors of fact, comprehension or taste are my own.

Permissions

The author and publishers gratefully acknowledge the permission granted by the following institutions and individuals to reproduce the copyright material in this book. They would like to thank the Parliamentary Archives for the use of documents pertaining to Lord Beaverbrook and Lloyd George, the National Archives for the reproduction of various documents about internal government and security service matters, including the papers of Sir Horace Wilson, Yolanda Green for the use of Robert Egerton's memoir, the estate of John Julius Norwich for the inclusion of Diana and Duff Cooper's papers, Balliol College Archives for the material pertaining to Walter Monckton and George McMahon, Nicholas Bell for the use of Geoffrey Dawson's papers, the Curtis Brown Group Ltd on behalf of the estate of Harold Nicolson for reproduction of Harold Nicolson's diaries and Charles Simon for the inclusion of Sir John Simon's papers. They would also like to thank Her Majesty Queen Elizabeth II and the Royal Archives in particular for their kind permission to include a significant amount of material pertaining to this period.

Image credits

Page 1

Above – Getty / Hulton Deutsch
Below – Getty / Central Press

Page 2

Above left – Getty / W. and D. Downey
Above right – Alamy / Antiqua Print Gallery
Below left – Getty /Ernest Brooks
Below right – Getty /Bettmann

Page 3

Above left – Alamy / Aclosund Historic
Above right – Getty / Topical Press Agency
Below left – Getty / Popperfoto
Below right – Getty / Imagno

Page 4

Above left – Getty / Popperfoto
Above right – Alamy / World History Archive
Below – Getty / Popperfoto

Page 5

Above – Getty / Universal Images Group
Below – Getty / Keystone-France / Gamma-Rapho

Page 6

Above – Alamy / The Print Collector
Below – Getty Images / Keystone

Page 7

Above – Alamy / Trinity Mirror / Mirrorpix
Below – Alamy / World History Archive

Page 8

Above – Alamy / John Frost Newspapers
Below left – Getty / Hulton Archive
Below right – Alamy / IanDagnall Computing

Select Bibliography

The Baldwin Papers, ed. Philip Williamson and Edward Baldwin, Cambridge, 2004

Beaken, Robert, *Cosmo Lang: Archbishop in War and Crisis*, I. B. Tauris, 2012

Beaverbrook, Lord, *The Abdication of King Edward VIII*, Hamish Hamilton, 1966

Bew, John, *Citizen Clem*, Riverrun, 2016

Birkenhead, Lord, *Walter Monckton*, Weidenfeld & Nicolson, 1969

Blackledge, Catherine, *The Story of V: Opening Pandora's Box*, Weidenfeld & Nicolson, 2003

Bloch, Michael, *The Reign & Abdication of Edward VIII*, Bantam, 1990

Bloch, Michael, *Ribbentrop*, Bantam, 1992

Bloch, Michael, *The Duchess of Windsor*, Weidenfeld & Nicolson, 1996

The Bradford Antiquary, 1986

Bradford, Sarah, *King George VI*, Weidenfeld & Nicolson, 1989

Brown, W. J., *So Far*, George Allen & Unwin, 1943

Channon, Sir Henry, *Chips: The Diaries of Sir Henry Channon*, Weidenfeld & Nicolson, 1967

Cooper, Diana, *Autobiography*, Michael Russell, 1979

Davidson, J. C. C., *Memoirs of a Conservative*, ed. Robert Rhodes James, Weidenfeld & Nicolson, 1969

Donaldson, Frances, *King Edward VIII*, Weidenfeld & Nicolson, 1974

Driberg, Tom, *Ruling Passions*, Jonathan Cape, 1977

The Duff Cooper Diaries: 1915 -1951, ed. John Julius Norwich, Weidenfeld & Nicolson, 2005

Egerton, Robert, *The Woman I Love: Mrs Simpson's Divorce*, private memoir, 1990

Eliot, T. S., *Collected Poems 1909 -1962*, Faber, 2002

Gilbert, Martin, *Prophet of Truth*, Heinemann, 1976

Guedalla, Philip, *The Hundredth Year*, Hodder & Stoughton, 1939

Hardinge, Helen, *Loyal to Three Kings*, William Kimber, 1967

Hesse, Fritz, *Hitler and the English*, Wingate, 1954

Higham, Charles, *Mrs Simpson: Secret Lives of the Duchess of Windsor*, Sidgwick & Jackson, 1998

Hyde, H. Montgomery, *Norman Birkett*, Hamish Hamilton, 1964

Hyde, H. Montgomery, *Baldwin*, Hart-Davis, 1973

Hyde, H. Montgomery, *Walter Monckton*, Sinclair-Stevenson, 1991

Jenkins, Roy, *Baldwin*, Collins, 1987

Jones, Thomas, *A Diary with Letters 1931-1950*, Oxford, 1954

Kinross, Patrick, *Atatürk: The Rebirth of a Nation*, Weidenfeld & Nicolson, 1964

Lascelles, Alan, *King's Counsellor: Abdication and War*, Weidenfeld & Nicolson, 2006

Lees-Milne, James, *Harold Nicolson*, Chatto & Windus, 1981

Lownie, Andrew, *The Mountbattens*, Blink, 2019

MacDonald, Malcolm, *People and Places*, Collins, 1969

Maxwell, Elsa, *I Married the World*, Heinemann, 1955

Middlemas, Keith, and John Barnes, *Baldwin: A Biography*, Weidenfeld & Nicolson, 1969

Nicolson, Harold, *Letters and Diaries 1930-1939*, ed. Nigel Nicolson, William Collins

Ogilvy, Mabell, *Thatched with Gold*, Hutchinson, 1962

Pasternak, Anna, *Untitled: The Real Wallis Simpson, Duchess of Windsor*, William Collins, 2019

Peart-Binns, John, *Blunt*, Mountain Press, 1969

Powell, Ted, *Edward VIII: An American Life*, OUP, 2018

Reith, Lord, *The Reith Diaries*, Collins, 1975

Rhodes James, Robert, *Churchill: A Study in Failure 1900-1939*, World Publishing Company, 1970

Ribbentrop, Joachim von, *The Ribbentrop Memoirs*, Weidenfeld & Nicolson, 1954

Roberts, Andrew, *Eminent Churchillians*, Weidenfeld & Nicolson, 1994

Roberts, Andrew, *Churchill: Walking with Destiny*, Allen Lane, 2018

Sebba, Anne, *That Woman*, Weidenfeld & Nicolson, 2011

Sitwell, Osbert, *Rat Week*, Michael Joseph, 1986

Spoto, Donald, *Dynasty: The Turbulent Saga of the Royal Family from Victoria to Diana*, Simon & Schuster, 1995

Taylor, A. J. P., *Beaverbrook*, Hamish Hamilton, 1972

Templewood, Viscount, *Nine Troubled Years*, Collins, 1954

Vickers, Hugo, *Behind Closed Doors*, Hutchinson, 2011

Wheeler-Bennett, John W., *King George VI: His Life and Reign*, Macmillan, 1958

Williams, Susan, *The People's King*, Allen Lane, 2003

Wallis and Edward: Letters 1931-1937, ed. Michael Bloch, Weidenfeld & Nicolson, 1986

Weitz, John, *Hitler's Diplomat*, Weidenfeld & Nicolson, 1992

Windsor, Duke of, *A King's Story*, Cassell, 1951

Windsor, Wallis, *The Heart Has Its Reasons*, Michael Joseph, 1956

Ziegler, Philip, *Diana Cooper*, Hamish Hamilton, 1981

Ziegler, Philip, *King Edward VIII*, Collins, 1990

Archives consulted

Balliol College Archives
Bodleian Library
Churchill College Archives
National Archives
Parliamentary Archives
Royal Archives

Notes

Prologue: 'Bring Me the English Alliance'

1 Ribbentrop, p.61.

2 Weitz, p.104.

3 Ribbentrop, p.65.

4 Ibid., pp.66-7.

5 Ibid.

6 Beaverbrook, p.16.

7 Eric Phipps to Robert Vansittart, 14 October 1936, MS Simon 84, Bodleian Library.

8 Phipps to Anthony Eden, 21 October 1936, MS Simon 84.

9 Bloch, *Ribbentrop*, p.123.

10 MEPO 10/35, National Archives.

11 Ribbentrop, p.68.

12 Alec Hardinge papers, RA/019/148, Royal Archives.

13 Bloch, *Ribbentrop*, p.75.

14 Ziegler, *King Edward VIII*, p.267.

15 Weitz, op. cit., p.88.

16 Lord Wigram to George V, 14 June 1935, RA/PS/PSO/GVI/PS/C/019/282, Royal Archives.

17 Lord Wigram to George V, 14 June 1935, RA/PS/PSO/GVI/PS/C/019/283, Royal Archives.

18 Cabinet meeting minutes 19 June 1935, RA/PS/PSO/GVI/PS/C/019/284, Royal Archives.

19 Phipps to Eden, 21 October 1936.

20 Bloch, *Ribbentrop*, p.76.

21 Ziegler to author, 10 October 2019.

22 Bloch, p.116.

23 Phipps to Eden, 21 October 1936.

24 CAB 21/540, Churchill College Archives.

25 Ribbentrop, p.69.

26 Duke of Windsor, p.321.

27 Ibid., pp.322-3.

28 Ibid.

29 Ribbentrop, p.69.

30 Bloch, *Ribbentrop*, p.122.

31 Ibid.

32 Weitz, op. cit., p.116.

33 Hesse, pp.31-2.

34 Weitz, op. cit., p.116.

35 Bloch, *Ribbentrop*, p.119.

36 Davidson, p.417.

37 Ibid.

Chapter One: The Royal Concubine

1 Ziegler, *King Edward VIII*, p.233.

2 Lascelles, p.107.

3 Ibid., p.112.

4 Ibid.

5 Ibid., p.105.

6 Maxwell, p.249.

7 Ziegler to author, 10 October 2019.

8 Ibid.

9 Bloch, *Duchess of Windsor*, p.11.

10 Wallis Windsor, p.74.

11 Spoto, p.223.

12 Wallis Windsor, p.83.

13 Vickers, p.310.

14 Pasternak, p.23.

15 Sebba, p.55.

16 Wallis Windsor, p.121.

17 Ibid., p.107.

18 Sebba, p.46.

19 Blackledge, p.182.

20 Higham, p.40.

21 Bloch, *Duchess of Windsor*, p.27.

22 Sebba, p.72.

23 Ziegler to author, 10 October 2019.

24 Ibid.

25 Vickers, p.277.

26 Sebba, p.85.

27 Bloch, *Duchess of Windsor*, p.37.

28 Wallis Windsor, p.175.

29 Cooper, p.397.

30 *Wallis and Edward*, p.56.

31 John Simon, MS Simon 9, Bodleian Library.

32 Wallis Windsor, p.201.

33 Ibid., p.199.

34 *Wallis and Edward*, p.54.

35 Wallis Windsor, p.91.

36 *Wallis and Edward*, p.84.

37 Ibid., p.85.

38 Ibid., p.89.

39 Ibid., p.91.

40 Ziegler, *King Edward VIII*, p.100.

41 Wallis Windsor, p.197.

42 Ibid., p.205.

43 Ziegler, *King Edward VIII*, p.231.

44 Godfrey Thomas to Wigram, 13 February 1935, RA/PS/PSO/GVI/PS/C/019/273, Royal Archives.

45 *Wallis and Edward*, p.112.

46 Ibid., p.117.

47 Lionel Halsey to Wigram, 18 July 1935, RA/PS/PSO/GVI/PS/C/019/287, Royal Archives.

48 *Wallis and Edward*, pp.116-17.

49 Ibid., pp.118-20.

50 MEPO 10/35-1, p.161, National Archives.

51 Ibid.

52 Ibid., p.162.

53 Bloch, *Duchess of Windsor*, p.81.

54 Ziegler to author, 10 October 2019.

55 Bloch, *Duchess of Windsor*, p.63.

56 Hardinge, p.54.

57 *Wallis and Edward*, p.126.

58 Ibid., p.128.

59 Ibid., p.145.

Chapter Two: 'The Most Modernistic Man in England'

1 Duke of Windsor, p.266.

2 Walter Monckton papers, Dep Monckton Trustees 22, Balliol College Archives.

3 Wigram memorandum of conversation on 3 March 1932 between Prince of Wales and George V, RA/PS/PSO/GVI/PS/C/019/269, Royal Archives.

4 Alec Hardinge papers, RA/019/148, Royal Archives.

5 Donaldson, p.174.

6 Ibid.

7 Wigram memorandum, 11 May 1935, RA/PS/PSO/GVI/PS/C/019/279, Royal Archives.

8 Godfrey Thomas to Wigram, 12 May 1935, RA/PS/PSO/GVI/PS/C/019/280, Royal Archives.

9 Wigram memo, 20 January 1936, RA/PS/PSO/GVI/PS/C/019/300, Royal Archives.

10 Walter Monckton papers, p.6.

11 Donaldson, p.178.

12 Ibid.

13 Geoffrey Dawson diary, 20 January 1936, MSS Dawson 38-41, Bodleian Library.

14 Ziegler, *King Edward VIII*, p.242.

15 John Simon, MS Simon 9, Bodleian Library.

16 Ibid.

17 Donaldson, p.181.

18 Ziegler, *King Edward VIII*, p.257.

19 Hardinge, p.76.

20 Alec Hardinge papers.

21 Ibid.

22 Wigram memo, 23 January 1936, RA/PS/PSO/GVI/PS/C/019/301, Royal Archives.

23 John Simon, MS Simon 9.

24 Duke of Windsor, p.278.

25 Walter Monckton papers, p.6.

26 Bloch, *Reign & Abdication*, pp.9-10.

27 Duke of Windsor, p.273.

28 Ziegler, *King Edward VIII*, p.250.

29 Ziegler to author, 10 October 2019.

30 Alec Hardinge papers.

31 Duke of Windsor, p.274.

32 *Wallis and Edward*, p.156.

33 Bloch, *Reign & Abdication*, p.10.

34 Ziegler, *King Edward VIII*, p.248.

35 Lang to Wigram, 26 February 1936, RA/PS/PSO/GVI/PS/C/019/312, Royal Archives.

36 Wigram memo, 4 February 1936, RA/PS/PSO/GVI/PS/C/019/302, Royal Archives.

37 Wigram memo, 20 February 1936, RA/PS/PSO/GVI/PS/C/019/307, Royal Archives.

38 Godfrey Thomas, RA/019/240, Royal Archives.

39 Godfrey Thomas to Edward, RA/019/241, Royal Archives.

40 Ibid.

41 Walter Monckton papers, pp.57-8.

42 Hardinge, p.83.

43 Bloch, *Reign & Abdication*, p.10.

44 Duke of Windsor, p.274.

45 Diana Cooper to Conrad Russell, 20 February 1936, GBR/0014/DIAC, Churchill College Archives.

46 Ibid.

47 Ibid.

48 Alec Hardinge papers.

49 Duke of Windsor, p.285.

50 Bloch, *Reign & Abdication*, p.11.

51 John Simon, MS Simon 9.

52 *Wallis and Edward*, pp.167-8.

53 Duke of Windsor, pp.280-1.

54 Ibid., p.294.

55 Ibid., p.282.

56 Hardinge, p.89.

57 Ibid., p.90.

58 Alec Hardinge papers.

59 Ziegler, *King Edward VIII*, p.262.

60 Ibid.

61 Hardinge, pp.90-3.

62 Alec Hardinge papers.

63 Ziegler, *King Edward VIII*, p.274.

64 Wigram memo, 15 February 1936, RA/PS/PSO/GVI/PS/C/019/305, Royal Archives.

65 Ziegler, *King Edward VIII*, p.274.

66 Reith, p.195.

67 Alec Hardinge papers.

68 Hardinge, p.93.

69 Ziegler, *King Edward VIII*, p.280.

70 Lees-Milne, pp.77–8.

71 Harold Nicolson diary, 2 April 1936, Balliol College Archives.

72 Geoffrey Dawson diary, 24 April 1936, Bodleian Library.

73 Wallis Windsor, p.232.

74 Hardinge, p.97.

75 Walter Monckton papers.

76 Reith, p.188.

77 Alec Hardinge papers.

78 Hardinge, p.98.

79 Ibid., p.99.

80 Ibid., p.102.

81 Ibid.

82 Harold Nicolson diary, 10 June 1936.

83 Hardinge, p.92.

Chapter Three: God Save the King

1 Duke of Windsor, p.298.

2 Ibid.

3 Ibid.

4 Ziegler, *King Edward VIII*, p.264.

5 Geoffrey Dawson diary, 16 July 1936, Bodleian Library.

6 Harold Nicolson diary, 16 July 1936, Balliol College Archives.

7 *The Times*, 17 July 1936.

8 Andrew Cook, 'The plot thickens', *Guardian*, 3 January 2003.

9 *Daily Telegraph*, 15 September 1936.

10 Duke of Windsor, p.298.

11 George McMahon to Colonel Bevis, 1 April 1937, KV 2/1505, National Archives.

12 George McMahon, 'He Was My King', Dep Monckton Trustees 16, Balliol College Archives.

13 Ibid.

14 Ibid.

15 Ibid.

16 Letter to Sir John Simon, 18 October 1935, KV 2/1505, National Archives.

17 McMahon, 'He Was My King'.

18 Ibid.

19 Ibid.

20 Ibid.

21 Ibid.

22 Carew Robinson statement, 21 July 1936, KV 2/1505, National Archives.

23 John Ottaway statement, 27 October 1936, ibid.

24 McMahon, 'He Was My King'.

25 Robinson statement.

26 McMahon, 'He Was My King'.

27 Ibid.

28 Robinson statement.

29 McMahon, 'He Was My King'.

30 John Ottaway statement, undated, KV 2/1505, National Archives.

31 McMahon, 'He Was My King'.

32 John Ottaway additional statement, KV 2/1505, National Archives.

33 McMahon, 'He Was My King'.

34 Harold Nicolson diary, 15 September 1936.

35 Ibid.

36 *Daily Telegraph*, 15 September 1936.

37 McMahon, 'He Was My King'.

38 *Daily Telegraph*, 15 September 1936.

39 McMahon, 'He Was My King'.

40 Ibid.

41 Ibid.

42 *Daily Telegraph*, 15 September 1936.

43 Ibid.

44 Ibid.

45 Ibid.

46 McMahon, 'He Was My King'.

47 Alfred Kerstein to Sir John Simon, 15 October 1936, KV 2/1505, National Archives.

48 Ibid.

49 McMahon, 'He Was My King'.

50 Carew Robinson memorandum, October 1936, KV 2/1505, National Archives.

51 G. Shipley note, 23 October 1943, KV 2/1505, National Archives.

Chapter Four: 'Flatterers, Sycophants and Malice'

1 Ziegler, *Diana Cooper*, p.174.

2 Ibid., p.175.

3 Cooper, p.411.

4 Driberg, p.106.

5 Beaverbrook, p.19.

6 Ibid.

7 Ibid., p.21.

8 Ibid., p.26.

9 Harold Nicolson diary, 8 June 1936, Balliol College Archives.

10 Beaverbrook, p.27.

11 Ziegler to author, 10 October 2019.

12 Beaverbrook, p.28.

13 Ibid., p.27.

14 Diana Cooper to Conrad Russell, June 1936, GBR/0014/DIAC, Churchill College Archives.

15 Ibid.

16 Bloch, *Reign & Abdication*, pp.34.

17 Channon, p.69.

18 *Wallis and Edward*, p.186.

19 Beaverbrook papers, BBK/G/6/19, Parliamentary Archives.

20 Ziegler, *King Edward VIII*, p.282.

21 Ibid.

22 Alec Hardinge papers, RA/019/148, Royal Archives.

23 Kinross, pp.481-2.

24 Ziegler, *King Edward VIII*, p.283.

25 Ibid., p.284.

26 Alec Hardinge papers.

27 Bloch, *Reign & Abdication*, pp.36-7.

28 Wallis Windsor, p.230.

29 Cooper, p.411.

30 Ibid., p.414.

31 Diana Cooper to Conrad Russell, August 1936, GBR/0014/DIAC, Churchill College Archives.

32 Ibid.

33 Ibid.

34 Ibid.

35 Ibid.

36 Ibid.

37 Ziegler, *Diana Cooper*, p.177.

38 Cooper to Russell.

39 Ibid.

40 Ziegler, *Diana Cooper*, pp.177-8.

41 Cooper to Russell.

42 Ibid.

43 Ziegler to author, 10 October 2019.

44 Ziegler, *Diana Cooper*, p.178.

45 *Duff Cooper Diaries*, p.228.

46 Ziegler, *Diana Cooper*, p.178.

47 Sir Sydney Waterlow, HM Minister of Athens, to Alec Hardinge, 1 September 1936, RA/O19/C19/105, Royal Archives.

48 *Wallis and Edward*, p.188.

49 MEPO 10/35, National Archives.

50 *Wallis and Edward*, p.191.

51 Ibid., pp.192-4

52 Ibid., pp.194-6.

53 Hardinge, p.109.

54 Wallis Windsor, p.310.

Chapter Five: 'Power Without Responsibility'

1 Eliot, 'The Love Song of J. Alfred Prufrock', *Collected Poems 1909-1962*, Faber, 2002.

2 Sitwell, p.19.

3 Ibid., p.33.

4 Ibid., p.57.

5 Ibid., pp.33-4.

6 John Simon, MS Simon 8, Bodleian Library.

7 Sitwell, pp.35-6.

8 Ibid., p.57.

9 Ibid., p.62.

10 Ibid., p.64.

11 Ibid., p.59.

12 Ibid.

13 Ziegler, *King Edward VIII*, p.287.

14 Hardinge, p.114.

15 Alec Hardinge papers, RA/019/148, Royal Archives.

16 Duke of Windsor, p.258.

17 Wheeler-Bennett, p.271.

18 Hardinge, p.114.
19 Ibid.
20 Ziegler, *King Edward VIII*, p.262.
21 Bradford, p.172.
22 Ibid.
23 Ibid.
24 Duke of Windsor, p.313.
25 Ziegler, *King Edward VIII*, pp.289-90.
26 Duke of Windsor, p.313.
27 Ibid., p.314.
28 MEPO 10/35, National Archives.
29 *The King and the Lady*, 1937, p.15.
30 MS Dawson 79, Bodleian Library.
31 Harold Nicolson diary, 6 October 1936, Balliol College Archives.
32 Wallis Windsor, p.240.
33 Egerton, *The Woman I Love*, p.25.
34 *Wallis and Edward*, p.200.
35 Ibid.
36 Beaverbrook, p.30.
37 Ziegler to author, 10 October 2019.
38 Duke of Windsor, p.315.
39 Sir Horace Wilson, PREM 1/466, National Archives.
40 Hardinge, pp.116-17.
41 Wilson, PREM 1/466.
42 Alec Hardinge papers.
43 Ziegler to author, 10 October 2019.
44 Duke of Windsor, p.316.
45 Wilson, PREM 1/466.
46 Duke of Windsor, p.317.
47 Ibid.
48 Middlemas and Barnes, p.984.
49 John Simon, MS Simon 8.
50 Middlemas and Barnes, p.985.
51 Bloch, *Reign & Abdication*, p.54.
52 Wilson, PREM 1/466.
53 Ibid., Duke of Windsor, p.317.
54 Duke of Windsor, p.318.
55 Wilson, PREM 1/466.
56 Ibid.

57 Duke of Windsor, p.318.

58 Alec Hardinge papers.

59 Bloch, *Reign & Abdication*, p.54.

Chapter Six: 'The Most Serious Crisis of My Life'

1 Hyde, *Norman Birkett*, p.456.

2 Egerton, p.27.

3 Wallis Windsor, p.240.

4 MEPO 10/35, National Archives.

5 John Simon, MS Simon 8, Bodleian Library.

6 MEPO 10/35, National Archives.

7 Ibid.

8 Walter Monckton papers, Dep Monckton Trustees 14, Balliol College Archives.

9 Egerton, p.21.

10 Ibid., p.22.

11 Ibid., p.39.

12 Ibid., p.22A.

13 Ibid., p.32.

14 Wallis Windsor, p.241.

15 Ibid; Hardinge.

16 Egerton, p.34.

17 Ibid., p.39.

18 Wallis Windsor, p.241.

19 Alec Hardinge papers, RA/019/148, Royal Archives.

20 Hardinge, pp.128-9.

21 Duke of Windsor, p.319.

22 Wallis Windsor, p.242.

23 RA/O19/C19/107, Royal Archives.

24 Harold Nicolson diary, 28 October 1936, Balliol College Archives.

25 Guedalla, pp.241-6.

26 Nicolson, p.277.

27 Harold Nicolson diary, 4 November 1936.

28 Bloch, *Reign & Abdication*, p.60.

29 Sir Horace Wilson, PREM 1/466, National Archives.

30 Duke of Windsor, p.321.

31 Beaverbrook, p.34.

32 Beaverbrook papers, BBK/G/6/19, Parliamentary Archives.

33 Beaverbrook, pp.34-5.

34 Ibid., p.36.

35 *Baldwin Papers*, p.388.

36 Middlemas and Barnes, p.988.

37 Alec Hardinge papers.

38 Middlemas and Barnes, p.988.

39 Ibid.

40 Geoffrey Dawson diary, 26 October 1936, Bodleian Library.

41 Middlemas and Barnes, p.988.

42 Alec Hardinge papers.

43 Dawson diary, 26 October 1936.

44 Ibid., 13 November 1936.

45 Beaverbrook papers.

46 Hardinge, p.133.

47 Ibid.

48 Ibid., p.135.

49 Ibid., p.134.

50 Templewood, pp.218-19.

51 Duke of Windsor, p.326.

52 Ibid.

Chapter Seven: 'Something Must Be Done'

1 Wallis Windsor, pp.243-4.

2 Ibid., p.247.

3 Duke of Windsor, p.327.

4 Walter Monckton papers, Dep Monckton Trustees 22, Balliol College Archives.

5 Birkenhead, p.38.

6 Ibid., p.65.

7 Walter Monckton papers.

8 Ibid.

9 Ibid.

10 Ibid.

11 Ibid.

12 Ibid.

13 Ibid.

14 Birkenhead, p.131.

15 *Baldwin Papers*, p.391.

16 Geoffrey Dawson diary, 16 November 1936, Bodleian Library.

17 Duke of Windsor, pp.330-2.

18 John Simon, MS Simon 8, Bodleian Library.

19 Duke of Windsor, p.332.

20 Middlemas and Barnes, pp.994-5.

21 Ibid., p.995.

22 Dawson diary, 16 November 1936.

23 Middlemas and Barnes, pp.994-5.

24 John Simon, MS Simon 8.

25 H. A. Gwynne to Baldwin, 12 November 1936, National Archives.

26 Louis Mountbatten to Edward, November 1936, RA/EDW/PRIV/ MAIN/A/3032, Royal Archives.

27 Hardinge, p.144.

28 Hyde, *Baldwin*, p.472.

29 Duke of Windsor, p.334.

30 Ogilvy, p.198.

31 Bloch, *Reign & Abdication*, p.88.

32 Duchess of York to Queen Mary, 17 November 1936, RA/PS/PSO/GVI/ PS/C/019/322, Royal Archives.

33 Hardinge, p.141.

34 Duke of Windsor, p.335.

35 Duchess of York to Queen Mary, 20 November 1936, RA/PS/PSO/ GVI/PS/C/019/325, Royal Archives.

36 Alec Hardinge papers, RA/019/148, Royal Archives.

37 Duke of Windsor, p.338.

38 Ibid.

39 Alec Hardinge papers.

40 Bloch, *Reign & Abdication*, p.97.

41 Hardinge, p.146.

42 Ramsay MacDonald diary, 21 November (quoted in Bloch, *Reign & Abdication*, pp.97-8).

43 Hardinge, pp.146-7.

44 Channon, p.91.

45 *Duff Cooper Diaries*, p.230.

Chapter Eight: 'A Clever Means of Escape'

1 Wallis Windsor, p.249.

2 Geoffrey Dawson diary, 26 November 1936, Bodleian Library.

3 Wallis Windsor, p.249.

4 Ibid.

5 Duke of Windsor, p.341.

6 Ibid., p.342.
7 Bloch, *Reign & Abdication*, p.106.
8 Wallis Windsor, p.250.
9 Ibid.
10 Sir Horace Wilson, PREM 1/466, National Archives.
11 Bloch, *Reign & Abdication*, p.107.
12 Alec Hardinge papers, RA/019/148, Royal Archives.
13 *Baldwin Papers*, p.391.
14 Dawson diary, 23 November 1936.
15 Donaldson, p.258.
16 Duke of Windsor, p.342.
17 Hyde, *Baldwin*, p.471.
18 Jones, p.288.
19 Hyde, *Baldwin*, p.471.
20 Jones, p.288.
21 Cosmo Lang to Stanley Baldwin, 25 November 1936, National Archives.
22 *Baldwin Papers*, p.396.
23 Hyde, *Baldwin*, p.474.
24 Duke of Windsor, p.343.
25 Walter Monckton papers, Balliol College Archives.
26 Beaverbrook papers, BBK/G/6/19, Parliamentary Archives.
27 Harold Nicolson diary, 7 October 1936, Balliol College Archives.
28 Ibid.
29 Duke of Windsor, p.345.
30 Beaverbrook, pp.47-8.
31 Ibid., p.42.
32 Ibid., p.41.
33 Harold Nicolson diary, 8 July 1936.
34 Hardinge, p.151.
35 Bloch, *Reign & Abdication*, p.119.
36 Beaverbrook, p.53.
37 Duke of Windsor, p.346.
38 Ibid., p.345.
39 Beaverbrook, p.54.
40 Ibid., p.55.
41 Wallis Windsor, p.251.
42 Harold Nicolson diary, 18 November 1936.
43 *Wallis and Edward*, p.213.
44 Bloch, *Reign & Abdication*, p.123.

45 John Simon, MS Simon 8, Bodleian Library.

46 Bloch, *Reign & Abdication*, p.124.

47 Harold Nicolson diary, 30 November 1936.

48 MacDonald, p.124.

49 Duke of Windsor, p.347.

50 Beaverbrook, p.58.

51 Duke of Windsor, p.347.

52 Ibid.

53 Beaverbrook, p.62.

54 Harold Nicolson diary, 4 December 1936.

55 Hardinge, p.154.

56 Alec Hardinge papers.

57 Bertie to Edward, 22 November 1936, RA/EDW/PRIV/MAIN/A/3035, Royal Archives.

Chapter Nine: 'Make Britain Great Again'

1 *Bradford Antiquary*, pp.54-64.

2 Ibid.

3 Bloch, *Reign & Abdication*, pp.134-5.

4 Peart-Binns, p.154.

5 John Simon, MS Simon 8, Bodleian Library.

6 *Duff Cooper Diaries*, p.235.

7 Bloch, *Reign & Abdication*, pp.131-2.

8 Geoffrey Dawson diary, 1 December 1936, Bodleian Library.

9 Duke of Windsor, p.353.

10 John Simon, MS Simon 8.

11 Alec Hardinge papers, RA/019/148, Royal Archives.

12 Duke of Windsor, pp.353-4.

13 Wallis Windsor, p.253.

14 Hardinge, p.157.

15 Dawson diary, 2 December 1936.

16 Ibid.

17 Bloch, *Reign & Abdication*, p.139.

18 Middlemas and Barnes, p.1005.

19 Wallis Windsor, p.254.

20 Ibid.

21 Sebba, p.166.

22 Hardinge, p.159.

23 Sebba, p.167.

24 Harold Nicolson diary, 3 December 1936, Balliol College Archives.

25 George VI's account of the abdication crisis, RA/019/144-146, Royal Archives.

26 Edward to Queen Mary, 30 November 1936, RA/PS/PSO/GVI/PS/C/019/326, Royal Archives.

27 Mary to Wigram, 15 July 1938, RA/PS/PSO/GVI/PS/C/019/326 (a), Royal Archives.

28 Sitwell, p.55.

29 Harold Nicolson diary, 3 December 1936.

30 Godfrey Thomas to Mary, 30 November 1936, RA/PS/PSO/GVI/PS/C/019/328, Royal Archives.

31 Walter Peacock to Edward, 3 December 1936, RA/EDW/PRIV/MAIN/A/3039, Royal Archives.

32 Lionel Halsey to Edward, 3 December 1936, RA/EDW/PRIV/MAIN/A/3038, Royal Archives.

33 Sir Lionel Halsey to Mary, 4 December 1936, RA/PS/PSO/GVI/PS/C/019/335, Royal Archives.

34 Roberts, *Churchill*, p.408.

35 Gilbert, p.813.

36 Lascelles, p.270.

37 Walter Monckton papers, Balliol College Archives.

38 Middlemas and Barnes, p.1006.

39 Ibid.

40 Gilbert, p.814.

41 Hardinge, p.161.

42 Sitwell, p.53.

43 Duke of Windsor, pp.365-6.

44 Ibid.

45 Walter Monckton papers.

46 Ibid.

47 Duke of Windsor, p.370.

48 Sitwell, pp.55-6.

49 MEPO 10/35, National Archives.

50 Ibid.

51 Beaverbrook, p.70.

52 Ibid., p.72.

53 Ibid., p.73.

54 National Archives.

Chapter Ten: 'The Best Story Since the Resurrection'

1 CAB 301-101, National Archives.

2 Cosmo Lang to Geoffrey Dawson, 6 December 1936, quoted in Beaken, p.116.

3 Louis Mountbatten to Edward, 7 December 1936, RA/EDW/PRIV/MAIN/A/30350, Royal Archives.

4 Geoffrey Dawson diary, 4 December 1936, Bodleian Library.

5 Bloch, *Reign & Abdication*, p.167.

6 Duke of Windsor, p.382.

7 Gilbert, pp.815-16.

8 Ibid., pp.816-17.

9 CAB 301-101, National Archives.

10 *Duff Cooper Diaries*, p.236.

11 Duff Cooper, DUFC 2/16, Churchill Archives.

12 Duke of Windsor, p.384.

13 Ibid., p.385.

14 Ziegler to author, 10 October 2019.

15 Beaverbrook, p.74.

16 Ibid., pp.75-6.

17 Ibid., p.78.

18 Ibid., p.71.

19 Ibid., p.78.

20 Ibid., p.76.

21 Wallis Windsor, p.258.

22 Ibid., pp.259-260.

23 Ibid., p.261.

24 Ibid., p.265.

25 *Wallis and Edward*, p.219.

26 *Baldwin Papers*, p.405.

27 Harold Nicolson diary, 7 December 1936, Balliol College Archives.

28 Duke of Windsor, p.383.

29 Ibid.

30 Ibid., p.387.

31 Ibid.

32 Birkenhead, p.55.

Chapter Eleven: 'This Is a Bugger'

1 Duke of Windsor, pp.387-8.
2 Ibid.
3 Ibid., p.387.
4 Ibid.
5 Sir Horace Wilson, PREM 1/466, National Archives.
6 Walter Monckton papers, Balliol College Archives.
7 Ibid.
8 Sir Horace Wilson, PREM 1/466, National Archives.
9 Beaverbrook, p.78.
10 Beaverbrook papers, BBK/G/6/19, Parliamentary Archives.
11 Ibid.
12 Rhodes James, pp.302-3.
13 Beaverbrook papers.
14 Ibid.
15 Beaverbrook, p.105.
16 Beaverbrook papers.
17 Duke of Windsor, p.391.
18 Ibid., p.392.
19 Hyde, *Baldwin*, p.491.
20 Ibid., p.492.
21 *Baldwin Papers*, p.406.
22 Harold Nicolson diary, 7 December 1936, Balliol College Archives.
23 Universal Service Press, 6 December 1936, MS Sherfield 1027, Bodleian Library.
24 Duke of York to Mary, 5 December 1936, RA/PS/PSO/GVI/PS/C/019/336, Royal Archives.
25 Bloch, *Reign & Abdication*, p.178.
26 Beaverbrook, p.81.
27 Bloch, *Reign & Abdication*, pp.178-9.
28 Walter Monckton papers.
29 Ibid.
30 Duke of Windsor, pp.393-4.
31 Hardinge, p.164.
32 Sebba, p.104.
33 Gilbert, pp.820-1.
34 Ibid., p.821.
35 Ibid.
36 Beaken, p.117.

37 Hyde, *Baldwin*, p.495.
38 Ziegler, *King Edward VIII*, p.321.
39 Ibid.
40 Middlemas and Barnes, p.1012.
41 Hardinge, p.166.
42 Bloch, *Reign & Abdication*, p.183.
43 Harold Nicolson diary, 7 December 1936.
44 Ibid.
45 Gilbert, p.822.
46 Ibid., p.82.
47 Ibid., pp.822-3.
48 Geoffrey Dawson diary, 7 December 1936, Bodleian Library.
49 Duke of Windsor, p.394.

Chapter Twelve: 'Wherever You Go, I Will Follow You'
1 Wallis Windsor, p.271.
2 National Archives.
3 Wallis Windsor, p.272.
4 Ibid., p.273.
5 *Wallis and Edward*, pp.221-2.
6 Wallis Windsor, p.273.
7 Duke of Windsor, p.395.
8 National Archives.
9 Ibid.
10 Duke of Windsor, p.398.
11 Brown, p.220.
12 National Archives.
13 Ibid.
14 Sebba, p.151.
15 Duff Cooper papers, Churchill Archives.
16 Walter Monckton papers, Balliol College Archives.
17 Duke of Windsor, p.399.
18 *Wallis and Edward*, pp.222-3.
19 Sebba, p.172.
20 Sir Horace Wilson, PREM 1/466, National Archives.
21 Ibid.
22 Wallis Windsor, p.275.
23 Sebba, p.172.
24 Wallis Windsor, p.275.

25 Wheeler-Bennett, p.283.

26 Ibid., pp.283-4.

27 Ibid., p.285.

28 Duke of Windsor, p.400.

29 *Baldwin Papers*, p.411.

30 Bloch, *Reign & Abdication*, p.189.

31 Sir Horace Wilson, PREM 1/466, National Archives.

32 Walter Monckton papers.

33 Ibid.

34 Duke of Windsor, p.401.

35 Edward Peacock papers, Balliol Archives.

36 *Baldwin Papers*, p.410.

37 Walter Monckton papers.

38 Wheeler-Bennett, p.286.

39 George VI abdication account, Royal Archives.

40 Bloch, *Reign & Abdication*, pp.190-1.

41 Duke of Windsor, p.402.

42 Ibid.

43 Walter Monckton papers.

Chapter Thirteen: Failing Tragically

1 Sebba, p.174.

2 Ibid.

3 Edward Peacock papers, Balliol College Archives.

4 Sebba, p.175.

5 Wallis Windsor, p.286.

6 J. T. Davies to Lloyd George, 9 December 1936, Beaverbrook papers, BBK/G/6/19, Parliamentary Archives.

7 Stanley Baldwin papers, quoted in Beaken, p.114.

8 Ronald Lindsay to Robert Vansittart, 8 December 1936, National Archives.

9 Winston Churchill to Dawson, 9 December 1936, MS Dawson 79, Bodleian Library.

10 John Wright to Edward, 8 December 1936, RA/O19/C19/110, Royal Archives.

11 Birkenhead, p.150.

12 Duke of Windsor, p.404.

13 Alec Hardinge papers, RA/019/148, Royal Archives.

14 Walter Monckton papers, Balliol College Archives.

15 Birkenhead, p.150.
16 Duke of Windsor, p.404.
17 Beaken, p.118.
18 Queen Mary to Duke of Windsor, 5 July 1938, Churchill Archives.
19 Ziegler, *King Edward VIII*, p.324.
20 Wheeler-Bennett, p.286.
21 Duke of Windsor, p.405.
22 Wallis Windsor, pp.277-8.
23 Harold Nicolson diary, 10 December 1936, Balliol College Archives.
24 Bloch, *Reign & Abdication*, pp.194-5.
25 Duke of Windsor, p.406.
26 Ibid., p.407.
27 Ziegler, *King Edward VIII*, pp.326-7.
28 Edward Peacock papers.
29 Ziegler, *King Edward VIII*, p.328.
30 Egerton, p.38.
31 Ibid, p.39.
32 Ziegler, p.330.
33 Egerton, p.38.
34 *Wallis and Edward*, p.141.
35 Ibid., p.130.
36 Sebba, p.162.
37 Ibid., pp.162-3.
38 Ibid., p.186.
39 Anne Sebba, *Daily Telegraph*, 21 August 2011.
40 Sebba, p.196.
41 Ibid., p.212.
42 Wallis Windsor, p.226.
43 Ibid., p.212.

Chapter Fourteen: 'Pity and Terror'

1 Middlemas and Barnes, p.1014.
2 Duke of Windsor, p.408.
3 Hyde, *Baldwin*, p.503.
4 Ibid.
5 Harold Nicolson diary, 10 December 1936, Balliol College Archives.
6 Hardinge, p.169.
7 Hyde, *Baldwin*, p.505.
8 Harold Nicolson diary.

9 Middlemas and Barnes, p.1014.

10 Geoffrey Dawson diary, 10 December 1936, Bodleian Library.

11 Hardinge, p.169.

12 Jenkins, p.157.

13 Hyde, *Baldwin*, p.506.

14 Harold Nicolson diary.

15 Bew, p.210.

16 Gilbert, pp.827-8.

17 Dawson to Churchill, 11 December 1936, MS Dawson 79, Bodleian Library.

18 Duff Cooper diary, Churchill College Archives.

19 Harold Nicolson diary.

20 Ibid., 28 December 1936.

21 Hardinge, p.172.

22 Ibid.

23 Gilbert, p.828.

24 Beaverbrook, p.106.

25 Lalla Bill to Mary, 10 December 1936, RA/PS/PSO/GVI/PS/C/019/342, Royal Archives.

26 Edward to Lalla Bill, 24 January 1914, RA/PS/PSO/GVI/PS/C/019/343, Royal Archives.

27 Edward Peacock papers, Balliol College Archives.

28 Walter Monckton papers, Balliol College Archives.

29 Sir John Simon to Edward, 10 December 1936, RA/EDW/PRIV/MAIN/A/3066, Royal Archives.

30 Duke of Windsor, p.409.

Chapter Fifteen: 'A Far Better Thing I Go To'

1 *Times*, 10 December 1936.

2 Viscount Snowden to Geoffrey Dawson, 8 December 1936, MS Dawson 79, Bodleian Library.

3 Beaverbrook, p.104.

4 *Times*, 11 December 1936.

5 *News Chronicle*, 11 December 1936.

6 *Daily Mail*, 11 December 1936.

7 *Daily Express*, 11 December 1936.

8 *Evening Standard*, 11 December 1936.

9 *Yorkshire Post*, 11 December 1936.

10 Duke of Windsor, p.413.

11 Walter Monckton papers, Balliol College Archives.

12 Edward Peacock papers, Balliol College Archives.

13 Harold Nicolson diary, 11 December 1936, Balliol College Archives.

14 Hyde, *Baldwin*, p.507.

15 Ibid., p.508.

16 Duff Cooper diary, Churchill College Archives.

17 Edward Peacock papers.

18 Walter Monckton papers.

19 Duke of Windsor, p.409.

20 Hyde, *Baldwin*, p.509.

21 Alice, Duchess of Gloucester, to Edward, 9 December 1936, RA/EDW/PRIV/MAIN/A/30355, Royal Archives.

22 Elizabeth, Duchess of York, to Edward, 11 December 1936, RA/EDW/PRIV/MAIN/A/3068, Royal Archives.

23 Helen Hardinge to Edward, 11 December 1936, RA/EDW/PRIV/MAIN/A/3070, Royal Archives.

24 Violet Rutland to Edward, 11 December 1936, RA/EDW/PRIV/MAIN/A/3074, Royal Archives.

25 Diana Cooper to Edward, 11 December 1936, RA/EDW/PRIV/MAIN/A/3080, Royal Archives.

26 Duff Cooper to Edward, 11 December 1936, RA/EDW/PRIV/MAIN/A/3083, Royal Archives.

27 Gwendolyn Francis to Edward, 11 December 1936, RA/EDW/PRIV/MAIN/A/3090 Royal Archives.

28 Duke of Windsor, p.410.

29 Ziegler, *King Edward VIII*, pp.333-4.

30 Wallis Windsor, p.278.

31 Ibid.

32 Ziegler, *King Edward VIII*, p.343.

33 Duke of Windsor, p.412.

34 Ibid., pp.413-14.

35 Ibid., p.414.

36 Geoffrey Dawson diary, 11 December 1936, Bodleian Library.

37 Hardinge, p.174.

38 Wallis Windsor, p.278.

39 Walter Monckton papers.

40 Duke of Windsor, p.414.

41 Ziegler, *King Edward VIII*, p.333.

42 Walter Monckton papers.

43 Ziegler, *King Edward VIII*, p.334.

44 Duke of Windsor, p.415.

45 Edward to Mary, 12 December 1936, RA/PS/PSO/GVI/PS/C/019/361, Royal Archives.

46 John Simon, MS Eng C 6647, Bodleian Library.

47 Walter Monckton papers.

48 Ziegler, *King Edward VIII*, p.335.

49 Ziegler to author, 10 October 2019.

Epilogue: In the Darkness

1 Gilbert, p.829.

2 Beaken, p.119.

3 Ibid., p.91.

4 Ibid., p.97.

5 Ziegler to author, 10 October 2019.

6 Beaken, p.123.

7 Walter Monckton papers, Balliol College Archives.

8 Beaken, p.123.

9 Ibid., p.124.

10 Cosmo Lang to Clive Wigram, 23 December 1936, RA/O19/C19/120, Royal Archives.

11 John Simon to Lady Hilda Currie, 12 December 1936, MS Simon 84, Bodleian Library.

12 Vansittart to Wigram, 23 December 1936, RA/PS/PSO/GVI/PS/C/019/377, Royal Archives.

13 Wigram to Vansittart, 29 December 1936, RA/PS/PSO/GVI/PS/C/019/379, Royal Archives.

14 Memo from O. G. Sargent, 18 December 1936, RA/PS/PSO/GVI/PS/C/019/378, Royal Archives.

15 Queen Mary to Edward, 16 December 1936, RA/EDW/PRIV/MAIN/A/3101, Royal Archives.

16 Hardinge to Dawson, 13 December 1936, MS Dawson 79, Bodleian Library.

17 Ibid.

18 Hardinge, pp.181-2.

19 Ibid., p.190.

20 Walter Monckton papers.

21 Ibid.

22 Author interview with Marianna Monckton, 13 June 2018.

23 Middlemas and Barnes, p.1018.

24 John Simon to Sir Henry Norman, 13 December 1936, MS Simon 84, Bodleian Library.

25 Margaret Lloyd George, 16 December 1936, in Beaverbrook papers, BBK/G/6/19, Parliamentary Archives.

26 Beaverbrook to R. D. Elliott, 15 December 1936, Beaverbrook papers.

27 Churchill to Edward, 16 December 1936, RA/EDW/PRIV/MAIN/A/3098, Royal Archives.

28 Alan Lascelles to Geoffrey Dawson, 13 December 1936, MS Dawson 79, Bodleian Library.

Index